THE STEP IS THE FOOT

ANTHONY HOWELL

THE STEP IS
THE FOOT

dance and its relationship to poetry

GREY SUIT EDITIONS | 2019

First published in 2019 by
Grey Suit Editions, an affiliate
of Phoenix Publishing House Ltd

British Library Cataloguing in Publication Data
A C.I.P. catalogue record for this book is available from the British Library
Paperback ISBN: 978-1-903006-12-2
E-Book ISBN: 978-1-903006-13-9

Designed and typeset by Kate Hargreaves
Diagrams by Dilys Bidewell

Printed and bound in the United Kingdom
by Hobbs the Printers Ltd.

The frontispiece is a frieze in the Museo Chiaramonti (the Vatican)

Grey Suit Editions
33 Holcombe Road
London N17 9AS
https://greysuiteditions.org/

CONTENTS

ॐ

Now let's look below the surface, to something I find far more mysterious, the unconscious or subliminal effects of reading and writing in traditional form... We are hypnotized or spellbound by form because the traditional aural techniques of verse, the mnemonics of rhyme, metre, and rhetorical schemes, are designed to fix the poem in the memory, to burn it in deeper than prose. And because it stays in the memory a split-second longer, because it 'sounds right', it seems to be right. Advertising copywriters and political speech writers know this, and take advantage of those venerable schemes of classical rhetoric to convince us below the level of reason, to sell us fags or governments.

Take chiasmus, for example: at John F. Kennedy's inauguration Robert Frost was scheduled to read his poem 'The Gift Outright' which began with the lines 'The land was ours before we were the land's . . . Possessing what we still were unpossessed by, / Possessed by what we now no more possessed'. Shortly afterwards, Kennedy's own speech contained the calculatedly memorable line 'Ask not what your country can do for you. Ask what you can do for your country.' The content of Kennedy's sentence is political propaganda, Frost's 'a momentary stay against confusion', but both share the familiar shape of 'Beauty is truth, truth beauty' like a dance step in which two couples change partners -never mind that beauty and truth can only be identical from a viewpoint shared by God, Grecian urns, and mathematicians...

—Michael Donaghy, *The Shape of the Dance*,
Picador 2009, p. 13-14

PREAMBLE

❧

THE GAIT OF THE LIZARD
The gaits of animals / the units of orthometry

I NEVER HAD A PRAM. From the earliest age, I was put on a horse. Perhaps this is why rhythm has played such an important role in my life. I have spent many years dancing and as many years writing. Rhythm is common to both pursuits. Increasingly I have come to feel that dance is a language and that language is a dance. In this book, I explore the relationship between dance and poetry.

All mammalian locomotion has a rhythm, and many beasts have an ability to walk with a variety of gaits. A horse can walk, trot, canter and gallop. The horse's walk can be analyzed as having four beats, its trot two, its canter three. The gallop is the fastest of all its gaits and it's a four-beat pace with each of the horse's legs striking the ground in quick succession with a moment of suspension between each stride. Besides these basic gaits, horses trained to perform dressage may also move with a lateral slow gait, a lifted gait and a running walk as well as an "extended" trot. Some gaits are genetic traits in specific breeds known collectively as gaited horses.

A rider often "rises" to the trot, elevating the seat out of the saddle on the "trit" and lowering it on the "trot". Musically it is equivalent to rising on the downbeat and sinking on the upbeat in order to rise on the next downbeat. This co-ordination of the movement of horse and rider makes the trot a smoother ride for the horse's passenger—and for the horse! The

I

push into the stirrups on the downbeat places the emphasis on the rise, so the sitting movement that follows is minimalised—instead of crashing down on the horse's spine.

The springbok gets its name from its ability to use a springing sort of jump as a means of locomotion. Thus it is that this beast is famed for its *pronking*—that is, its ability to travel by leaping into the air in this eccentric spring, also known as a *stot*. It is behaviour that you might see a sheep perform but it is particularly characteristic of gazelles. When springboks pronk they spring into the air, lifting all four feet off the ground at the same time. Usually, the legs are held in a relatively stiff position and the back may be arched concavely to the ground, with the head pointing downward. Many explanations of pronking have been proposed; there is evidence that at least in some cases it signals to predators that the pronker is not worth pursuing. The rhythm of a pronk would have to be an iambic of considerable quantity—"The moon! The moon!"

Most other gaits involve the diagonal forwards co-ordination of left forefoot with right hindfoot—even in pronking I detect the wraith of such diagonal co-ordination in the landing.

Perhaps this goes back to our snaky origins before legs were invented, let alone hands and arms! Mind you, what is being suggested here is an entirely mythic notion of evolution, since rather than their limbs emerging from some limbless ancestor snakes seem to have mislaid their limbs. Still, the spine is so fundamental to movement that it's worth considering how the spine copes with locomotion when there are no limbs to help it along.

Snakes have several ways of moving around. They are basically a spine. This they undulate in order to progress. Since they don't have legs they use their torso and their scales to do this. Of course, a snake can coil, and strike, but neither is a means of locomotion.

For locomotion, there's the *Serpentine method:* imagine a snake slithering forward across flat sand, pushing off from any bump or verticality—a rock or root—in order to get going. It is that wavy motion which we think of as serpentine. This movement is also known as lateral undulation. Speaking figuratively, it's as if the snake were swinging its hips one way and its dorsals the other on a rough horizontal surface that allows for points of purchase. On a slick surface like glass it would not be able to get very far.

Then there's the *Concertina method*: This is harder for the snake but effective in tight spaces. The snake braces the back portion of its body while pushing and extending the front portion. There is a hint of the caterpillar in this as it contracts some of itself together and stretches out the rest. Then the snake contracts its front portion and drags the back portion along. It thus projects itself forward.

Then there is *Sidewinding*: here the snake uses a sideways movement to move forward at a diagonal. This works well in sand. The snake curls its tail to achieve gravitational purchase, then appears to throw its head forward, contract its "dorsals" and thereby bring its lower half with it while the head is thrown forward again. Only two locations on the snake's body are in contact with the ground at any one time, so there is a subtle vertical ripple as well—which works well with the ripples on a dune.

Finally, there's the *Rectilinear Method*: this is similar to the concertina but less visible, just a slow, creeping, forward movement. The snake uses some of the wide scales on its belly to grip the ground while pushing forward, sliding on the others.

Sidewinding looks as if it might be fun. We may imagine that the sidewinder enjoys doing it, just as we enjoy walking. I think all animals enjoy their gaits. If it's good for a human to run, then it's good for a horse to gallop. But we should be clear about one crucial difference between humans and animals here. A snake may appear to dance when it raises its head and sways, and cranes may appear to perform a pas-de-deux as a preliminary to their mating while the canter of a horse has a rhythm. However, when a horse canters in a show to the accompaniment of a band, the band is playing to the rhythm of the horse. A horse cannot alter its pace to canter in time to a band. A chimpanzee may drum on a log, but it cannot do this in time to an external source – this point is well made in *The Dancing Chimpanzee* by Leonard Williams. A flock of birds may sing in unison, or one bird may respond to another. But animals cannot alter their rhythms so as to be in time with an external beat. Only human beings can do that. In this sense, the beasts are rhythm blind.

IN THE LATE SIXTIES, the American dance pioneer Simone Forti developed *Sleep Walkers*. These dance pieces were inspired by Forti's observations of animals at the Rome Zoo, now known as the Bioparco di Roma. Forti specifically refers to developing the movement of swinging her head back and forth from watching polar bears and elephants move at the zoo, writing "Yes, I felt a kinship with those encapsulated beings." In the essay *Animate Matter: Simone Forti in Rome*, Julia Bryan-Wilson writes, "In *Sleep Walkers*, Forti takes cues from animals that develop (and continually replicate) patterns of movement in response to environments of confinement. By segmenting and then repeating small passages of movement, for instance by isolating a few steps out of the flow of the elephant's many other motions, she creates an almost musical sense of pause, interval and tempo."

I witnessed Forti perform several of these pieces back in the sixties, and I must say the implication of incarceration was less apparent to me than the extraordinary accuracy of Forti's analysis of animal gaits. The hopping of a bird or the weight shifting of an elephant got translated into human movement. I was particularly struck by her rendition of a lizard. Horizontal, her knees and elbows splayed, Forti very precisely simulated the movement of the reptile; and what was interesting was the ("snake-like") counter swing of hips and torso. As the right elbow swung forward in conjunction with the forward movement of the left knee, a diagonal could be drawn between that knee and that elbow. This diagonal co-ordination accompanied each swing of the spine, and it's already been observed that such cross co-ordination can be seen in the majority of gaits. It is there in the human walk, for as our left foot goes forward, it is accompanied by the forward swing of our right arm.

This relationship can be seen in the walking of all mammals—from the lion to the dog, and we inherit it from our days as a creature that required the forelimbs as integral to its means of locomotion. It's put to use in the run as well. Running and walking are particularly good forms of exercise because by practising these gaits we encourage our innate diagonal crossover. Bear in mind that a large part of human thinking is done by the left side of the brain, while for many of us the right is the side of our body we control best. The body is a construct of crossings-over. The predominating left side of the brain is significant for our species and gives us a useful bias we will return to later. For now, let's simply focus on the walk.

This basic ambulatory gait of ours shares its diagonal swing with the serpentine progression of the snake. Tango dancers know how to take advantage of the oblique connection between left hip and right shoulder, and they call making use of it "dissociation"—in that what we don't do is to move forward "associating" our right shoulder with our right hip when we walk! We do the opposite. The tanguero uses dissociation to generate pivots and wavings of the leg sometimes generated by counter-momentum. It is what gives the tango its serpentine enchantment.

The walk also reinforces alternation—after all, we don't hop along on one foot—or not for long. But we do do the same thing with the left as we just did with the right. So that is a basic binary underpin to our movement, and in all probability to our minds. Walking may well have generated fundamental oppositions – yes and no, off and on, zero and one, left and right. And while the hands swing in opposition, the hands are now nevertheless freed from the business of necessarily contributing to our locomotion—and this has significance for our evolution into becoming "the language animal".

There's plenty of people who find walking an aid to thinking. Famously, Ben Jonson walked to Scotland, in order to gossip with William Drummond of Hawthornden, who had just returned from the grand tour. Wordsworth walked for inspiration, and Charles Dickens knew that the "black dog" could be sent back to its kennel by a brisk twenty-mile walk. Virginia Wolf loved to walk and think, and Peter Porter used to compose his poems on walks through Hyde Park. Henry David Thoreau was an inveterate walker, while Constantin Brancusi, the sculptor, walked much of the way between his home village in Romania and his destination, Paris. The list of walkers includes George Orwell, Thomas De Quincey, Friedrich Nietzsche, Vladimir Nabokov and Bruce Chatwin. All of them thought at the same time. And Nietzsche wrote, "All truly great thoughts are conceived by walking."

In a paper entitled *Give Your Ideas Some Legs: The Positive Effect of Walking on Creative Thinking* Marily Oppezzo and Daniel L. Schwartz of Stanford University showed how experiments demonstrated that walking boosts creative ideation:

Whether one is outdoors or on a treadmill, walking improves the generation of novel yet appropriate ideas, and the effect even extends to when people sit down to do their creative work shortly after.

Walking, thinking, speaking. They seem to feed off each other. And we talk about babies "learning to walk", and then, later, "learning to speak", but its questionable whether "learning" is the appropriate word. It might be more appropriate to define learning as something we do *after* we master the ability to speak. Thus we may "learn" a second language, but not our first, not our mother tongue.

That mother tongue we *acquire*, as, earlier, we acquire walking. For sure, parents can help—by making expressive sounds at us—so that we can respond, and by not carrying us everywhere, by not suspending us in some contraption, and by not strapping us into buggies while they occupy themselves with their mobiles. But we get the first words sorted out by expressively trying out all possible sounds, gradually homing in on the ones that elicit a response, and we get the motor organisation sorted by trying out all possible movements and then by crawling – by moving our left knee with our right hand to master the diagonal co-ordination of this skill; and of course our crawling may be encouraged by a parent smiling and calling us with open, welcoming arms but it is not tuition. We seem to have an imitative tendency that helps us get the hang of it. But you don't have language when you get the hang of walking.

You do have walking when you get the hang of talking, but—and this is important—you don't have language when you acquire speech. That is obvious, though you may have the imitative skill, used by the little language animal you become, to "pick up" more and more. Both skills are acquired pre-linguistically. And when you lose these skills owing to some disability, such as Parkinson's, then you have to try to get the hang of them again as you might learn a second language. That is, you *learn* them now, through language, through being told how to do them. This may open up alternative neural channels.

Everything about the acquisition of these two skills suggests an affinity between them. Perhaps there is more than an affinity, perhaps there is a primordial connection. It's this notion of a connection, even a fusion, of step and expression that intrigues me. And in order to explore the relationship between them it will be necessary to overlay two specialised fields—that of poetry and that of dance. Perhaps this will generate a new arena, but as we shall see, it is also a very old one, that of the *aloni*—the threshing floor—where the chorus first stepped in time to the words they recited—or vice versa. But how did I get into this line of enquiry? Where did it begin?

Allow me to take you on a journey. For now, it's a journey through my adolescence, and here it may provide an illustration of what the relationship between the dance step and the metrical foot has meant to me. We may pick up this autobiographical thread again in later chapters, as I show how the two disciplines have been interwoven in my life.

∂₹

AS A BOY I COULD GET LOST IN READING AND WRITING, but I also enjoyed modelling with clay or plasticine. I was a keen gymnast and a good rider. At the age of fifteen, I wanted to choose a career that might bring about a fusion of my enthusiasm for bodily agility and my love of art. I saw John Gilpin dance and decided to become a ballet dancer. I was starting late, but because of my gymnastic skill I got into the Royal Ballet School. I was also writing overblown poetry. I was immersed in Swinburne, my father's favourite poet. Swinburne's two-volume collected poems, now mine, had belonged to him. One could as easily be transported by the rhythm of Swinburne's poems as by their meaning, but being in the throes of adolescence I was also appreciative of the passion they invoked:

> Alas, Lord, surely thou art great and fair.
> But lo her wonderfully woven hair!
>> And didst thou heal us with thy piteous kiss;
>> But see now, Lord; her mouth is lovelier.

Laus Veneris

The verse quoted is written in *Iambic Pentameter*. I was learning how to scan, since I wanted to write sonnets and sestinas. I had picked up on these forms through reading my grandmother's copy of Rossetti's translations of *Dante and his Circle*. It was later that I realised that the sonnet of fourteen lines can be extended to the sixteen-line sonnet-form Meredith uses so brilliantly in his sequence *Modern Love*; later still, that I realised there were quatrains and dizains, four and ten-line verses with various rhyme schemes, and then there were troilets and villanelles—these with specific and quite rigid rules of repetition for entire lines—and rondels, rondeaus and roundels. Such forms with set recipes were formerly considered poetic trifles.

Until recently, it has been common, though not universal, to sneer at these supposedly hackneyed forms. But now, a new generation has found them worth returning to. The twentieth century tended to pitch all too easily into loose free-verse—in order that modernism might liberate itself from the rule-bound raptures of Rossetti and Swinburne. Back in the sixties, in my adolescence, I initially struck out *against* the modern grain. I fell into an enthusiastic study of how verses were constructed in the Elizabethan age and before, among the Greeks and Romans and among the troubadours. I was dancing every day, and rhythm seemed integral to everything. I could sense its power in Pound, Eliot and Stevens, not just in the poets of earlier centuries. I became aware that the skill of sonnet making was as much to do with how one handled pentameter as with obeying a set rhyme scheme. I soon realised the dynamic latent in pentameter; since its five stresses continually sway its caesura one way or another.

Here I am aware that before going any further I should apologise to the poets among my readers, who may feel I am teaching their grandmothers to suck eggs. Dancers may feel the same, when I go into technical details about our movements. It's a problem that confronts any author trying to write a book that bridges two disciplines. Bear with me, please. To achieve my goal of showing the connection between the step and the foot, I will sometimes need to reiterate the basics that govern these arts. You are of course welcome to skip those passages that you feel you know inside-out.

Iambic Pentameter means that it's in Iambic metre (de Dum) with five feet per line:

Name of Foot	Accents	Name of Metre
Iambus	∪ —	Iambic
Trochee	— ∪	Trochaic
Anapest	∪ ∪ —	Anapestic
Dactyl	— ∪ ∪	Dactylic

Below is a list of the metres possible in English:

Monometer—verse of one foot
Dimeter—verse of two feet
Trimeter—verse of three feet
Tetrameter—verse of four feet
Pentameter—verse of five feet
Hexameter—verse of six feet
Heptameter—verse of seven feet
Octameter—verse of eight feet

These *feet* can be Dissyllabic (two syllables long) or Trisyllabic (three syllables long). There are other kinds of metre in fairly frequent use which may be mixed with these fundamental units – the Spondee (two strong syllables) and the Pyrrhic (two unstressed syllables). There is a line in Milton's *Lycidas* that is of interest in this regard:

For Lycidas is dead, dead ere his prime,

Now this can be scanned conventionally as iambic pentameter. I'll underline the stresses:

For <u>Ly</u> cid <u>das</u> is <u>dead</u>, dead <u>ere</u> his <u>prime</u>,

Here, the regular iambics gives us a *dead* which carries and another *dead* that does not carry the *ictus*, or stress (and that shift of stress on a word used twice was also a device enjoyed by Donne). The stress shift from *on* to *off* a specific repeated word in the standard iambic interpretation of this line should not be confused with secondary stress. It is simply that the first *dead* is stressed and the second unstressed. However, it could have been that Milton intended to introduce a Spondee into the line:

For <u>Ly</u> cid <u>das</u> is <u>dead</u>, <u>dead</u> ere his <u>prime</u>,

following his Spondee with an Anapest. This is perhaps a far-fetched interpretation, but it would give the line a dynamic impulse, and more anguish!

Milton is also good at introducing preliminary trochees into his pentameter. Three lines above, he has:

Shatter your leaves before the mellowing year.
Bitter constraint, and sad occasion dear
Compels me to disturb your season due;

Shatter and *Bitter* both turn the standard iambic beginnings of their lines around, giving a syncopating force to the verse. I will return to the opening passage of *Lycidas* later, when discussing madrigals.

It's the four rhythms shown in the box above which are the most commonly employed feet in English verse. And in English the iambic is by far the most common, and often inadvertently slipped into in supposedly free verse. Since so many of our sentences begin either with an article or a pronoun, it is obvious that an upbeat will usually precede the first word with content in the sentence. *The* Foot, *I* ran, *she* saw, *the* gently moved desire…

And just as a change in angle can change the momentum or the nature of a gait (as leaning forwards, almost tipping over, and taking smaller steps can change a walk into a trot) a change in the metre of a line can change "the pace" of a verse. I do wonder, though, whether Milton meant to put "drear" instead of "dear".

It has been suggested that the Ancient Greek: ἴαμβος iambos, has a pre-Greek origin. An old hypothesis is that the word is borrowed from Phrygian or Pelasgian, and literally means "a step" (compare dithyramb and thriambus). H. S. Versnel rejects this etymology and suggests instead a derivation from some cultic exclamation. The word may be related to Iambe, a Greek minor goddess of scurrilous verse. In ancient Greece iambic metre was mainly used for satirical poetry, lampoons: these did not automatically imply a particular metrical type. Iambic metre took its name from being characteristic of iambi, not vice versa. Still, one supposes that *une jambe* (a foot in French) is derived from iambos, and so it has been taken to mean "foot" for a very long time, though a strong possibility is that it derives from a Greek word meaning "to thrust" or "to dart" – as with the footwork for lunging and riposting in fencing.

A trochee means a "running foot" and comes from the Greek trokhaios, 'running (foot)', from trekhein 'to run'—*tripping, tripping on*. When we run we send body weight ahead so again this may explain the quickening movement it gives when contrasted with another type of foot – as in *Shatter your leaves* and *Bitter constraint* (a trochee followed by an iambus in both cases). However, the truth is that in English verse a regular set of trochees often feels more like marching than running. When iambs are compared to trochaic rhythms we can feel how it's the difference between *Today, today, today, today* and *Left right, left right, left right, left right*.

A dactyl is a "finger" in Greek, and its strong stress followed by two shorter ones suggests the progressively shortening bones of a finger. An anapest is a galloping rhythm and it means "struck back", i.e. reversed, since it is the dactylic rhythm reversed or turned around.

The study of poetic metre is called Orthometry, and though, as I have suggested, it went somewhat out of fashion with the advent of "free verse" in the twentieth century, it appears to be returning to the spotlight with the popularity of creative writing and a renewed interest in poetic forms. Deriving from ancient rules of scansion, orthometry is a method of analysis of the syllables that make up a poetic line which has continued to fascinate me ever since those days of adolescence when I fell for a girl at the ballet school and my love of poetry became entangled with the love of a person. I felt then that a love poem could spark a reciprocal flame if it were sufficiently well-written. It may not be the case, but I am not the only adolescent to have felt this.

Classical ballet has a formidable technique, and so does the tango (though it's a very different technique) but so, obviously, does poetry. In English verse, the principle of arrangement is the regular recurrence of accented and unaccented syllables—this is what sets up the rhythm.

Walking too has an accented step and an unstressed "collect"—as one ankle passes the other.

Dancing, song and poetry have rhythm in common. The accented and unaccented syllables are traditionally notated by a horizontal concave bracket for an unaccented syllable and a dash for an accented syllable (the *ictus*). A syllable is a word or part of one, which may be an elementary sound, or a combination or fusion of several. Made up of consonants and vowels, like these elements themselves, it can be rough, smooth, harsh, easy or difficult to say. As well as being accented or unaccented, syllables may be differentiated by their quantity, but more of quantity in a later chapter.

Regarding the nature of accent, here is what R. F. Brewer has to say in his handbook of *Orthometry: The Art of Versification and the Technicalities of Poetry*, from the revised edition published in 1918 (unfortunately with erroneous metrical symbols):

> *Accent is* a certain *stress* of the voice upon a syllable in pronouncing it. Every word of more than one syllable has an accent invariably attached to one of its syllables which is called the *tonic accent,* and no word, however long, has more than one accent, e.g. deplóre, térrible, eleméntary. Monosyllables are accented or not according to their grammatical importance; thus all nouns, verbs, adjectives, and adverbs are accented, while the articles, prepositions pronouns (when not emphatic), and particles are unaccented. We shall see as we proceed that the exigencies of metre require that *metrical accents* be attached to syllables in verse in addition to the tonic accent, and that the stress occasionally varies in degree, e.g.:
>
> *Swéét are the úses of advérsity.*
>
> The precise nature of accent has given rise to diversity of opinion; some maintaining that it is an alteration in the pitch of the voice, others an increase in loudness of tone; we will content ourselves, however with regarding it as *stress* merely, as is now generally accepted.

If we do a "step ball change" in jazz dance, we also seem to deal with accentuation—the accents falling on "step" and "change". In dancing this is thought of as stepping on downbeat or the upbeat—down, up/down in this case. This last notion brings us back to the "The Foot". The Foot is the unit of measurement in verse—not the syllable.

> A *foot* is a group of two or three syllables, hence the division into *Dissyllabic* and *Trisyllabic* verse. The names given to the different kinds of feet in English poetry are usually those of the classic metres, and the method of marking the accented and unaccented syllables is from the same source... Thus the usual marks for long and short (– U or I +) must be taken to indicate accented and unaccented syllables.

(ibid)

Again, we can find equivalents in dance. Take Dactylic Hexameter:

/ + + / + + / + + / + + / + + / + +.

"Dum de de, dum de de, dum de de, dum de de, dum de de, dum de de." As Thomas Hood has it in *The Bridge of Sighs*:

> Make no deep/ scrutiny/ into her/ mutiny/ rash and un/dutiful

Pretty clear how this could be a waltz! So what will be explored in this investigation is why we call such a unit of poetic metre a "foot".

꣠

IF WE DELVE DEEPER INTO THE RELATIONSHIP between metrical feet and dance steps some surprises come to light.

Trochaic metre turns out to be common in the tango. A dancer will step and then the foot which has just pushed into the floor (and now has no weight left in it) will pass by the ankle on its way to becoming the next step. We call this passage past the ankle "collecting", so the rhythm of the walk is commonly: step, collect, step, collect...or down, up, down, up—with the stress on the step or the "down" beat. This makes the trochaic rhythm a march—as in *left and right and left and right*. It may quicken to *left right left right*—very regular and alternating the feet with each step.

While widely used in a dance such as the tango, it is actually not so common in poetry. It can feel a bit obvious.

> Should you ask me, whence these stories?
> Whence these legends and traditions,
> With the odours of the forest
> With the dew and damp of meadows,
> With the curling smoke of wigwams,
> With the rushing of great rivers,
> With their frequent repetitions,
> And their wild reverberations
> As of thunder in the mountains?

The Song of Hiawatha, Henry Wadsworth Longfellow

If instead we dance the rhythm of iambic metre, we must actually start with a ball change. A simple way to envisage this is to stand with the left foot in front of the other, with the weight on that front foot. Now bring the ball of the back foot in to the heel of the left foot and put weight into that ball on the "and", stepping forward *again* onto the left. This creates what might be thought of as that "limping" movement, in contrast to the left/right of the trochees (though remember the sense of iambics darting: the ball-change confers impetus). And left, and left, and left, and left—chi dum, chi dum, chi dum, chi dum. This is the dance equivalent of *anacrusis*, a term poetry shares with music, meaning that the melody or poem takes off before the first strong beat—*and one*, or *and a one*, for example. Iambic metre is, as already mentioned, far more common in English verse than trochaic metre. The limp actually becomes a dynamic thrust—as is suggested by that alternative etymology of its name—*to dart or to thrust*. When done with the right foot forward, it becomes the preparation for a lunge with the épée. It has less monotony than the regular left, right, left, of trochees. And in English it has never lost its ancient association with satire.

> Come keen *Iambicks* with your Badgers' feet
> And Badger-like, bite till your teeth do meet.
> From *The Rebell Scot*, John Cleveland, *Poems*, 1647

Note the (ironic) use of dactyls in the second line.

While a whole passage of trochaic metre overwhelms the ear with its regularity (as with *Hiawatha),* very often in English verse, the trochee is butted up against an iambus to provide syncopation, as in Milton's *Shatter your leaves before the mellowing year/Bitter constraint, and sad occasion dear....*

But perhaps I am being too dismissive of trochees. Here, their martial sense of certainty is handled with aplomb by Lady Mary Wroth:

Love peruse me, seeke, and finde
How each corner of my minde
    Is a' twine
     Woven to shine.
Not a Webb ill made, foule fram'd,
Bastard not by Father nam'd,
     Such in me
     Cannot bee.
Deare behold me, you shall see
Faith the Hive, and love the Bee,
     Which doe bring.
     Gaine and sting.
Pray dissect me, sinewes, vaines,
Hold, and loves life in those gaines;
     Lying bare
     To despaire,
When you thus anatomise
All my body, my heart prise;
     Being true
     Just to you.
Close the Truncke, embalme the Chest,
Where your power still shall rest,
     Joy entombe,
     Loves just doome.

The Countesse of Montgomery's Urania, (1621)

So, although trochaic metre can be managed well, nevertheless, in general it is neglected, and iambic metre proves the standard rhythmic tool of our verse. But, within this iambic context, we invert a foot here, or add in an extra unstressed syllable there, to vary the overall rhythm—such variety as we can see realised by the second line quoted from Cleveland (and Badger-like, bite—de dum de <u>dah</u> <u>dum)</u>—the secondarily stressed *like* a stepping stone to the strong ictus of *bite.*

⁊₺

SECONDARY STRESS HAS BEEN MUCH DEBATED among grammarians who have deemed the term *secondary accent* obsolete. Secondary stress is the weaker of two degrees of stress in the pronunciation of a word; the stronger degree of stress being called *primary.* The International Phonetic Alphabet symbol for secondary stress is a short vertical line preceding and at the foot of the secondarily stressed syllable: as before the *nun* **in** *pro͵ nunci ͈ation* (the higher vertical line denotes primary stress). Another tradition in English is to assign acute and grave accents for primary and secondary stress: *pronùnciátion.* My gut feeling is not to let oneself get bogged down here. It grows out of the dogma of there being only one primary stress to a word. Clear enough in *revolutionary,* or even *balaclava.* But theatre shows us how fluid it is, this sense of a pecking order among the stresses. I can perfectly see how Frankie Howard might say, *But darling, it's your pronúnciàtion!*

This customary attribution of primary and secondary stress to the vowels that make up a word differs from the situation in *For Lycidas is dead, dead ere his prime,* if we agree to scan this as regular iambic pentameter: *For Ly cid das is dead, dead ere his prime.* In my view, the ictus has simply shifted off the repetition of *dead,* so that it becomes unstressed, to allow *ere* to carry the ictus.

With any regular metrical form, the possibilities of "secondary stress" may be explored—that is, we may utilize the accent on a syllable of a word or breath group that is weaker than the primary stress but still stronger than a syllable with no stress at all. Remember, marking stress is not the same as marking metre. A perfectly regular line of iambic pentameter may have anywhere from 2 to 9 stresses, but it is still felt to exhibit 5 major pulses or beats. Free verse can often take advantage of the principle of relative stress.

16

This states that an unstressed syllable between two even slightly weaker syllables may be perceived as a beat (*promotion*); and the reverse is true of a stressed syllable between two even slightly stronger syllables (*demotion*). Thus a syllable, regardless of its level of stress, that definitely realizes a beat is *ictic*; and a syllable, regardless of its level of stress, that does not is *nonictic*.

Then again, one ictus can impact against another. Here is an example from Shakespeare in pentameter.

```
 /    x  x  /    x  x  /  /   x   /
When to the sess | ions of sweet si | lent thought
```

(Sonnet 30)

Two pulses come together here with no *nonictic* syllable between them, though the stress on *sweet* is slightly less strong than that on *silent*.

Utilising a degree of stress weaker than primary stress but stronger than lack of stress can lead to a single word being scanned as if it had two ictic stresses when in ordinary speech it might not. The effect of this is to slow the verse down:

> Tis most true
> That musing meditation most affects
> The pensive secrecy of desert cell,
> Far from the cheerful haunt of men and herds,
> And sits as safe as in a Senat House:
> For who would rob a Hermit of his Weeds,
> His few Books, or his Beads, or Maple Dish,
> Or do his gray hairs any violence?

These lines are from Milton's *Comus*. They show what a master he was at controlling the pace of his verse. For instance, the last line quoted requires two stresses on *violence*, so the dipthong must be properly and slowly enunciated, so as to bring out a final ictus on the last syllable which would in ordinary speech be the very softest of secondary stresses. Later in *Comus*, we get:

No goblin, or swart faery of the mine,
Hath hurtful power o're true virginity.
Do you believe me yet, or shall I call
Antiquity from the old Schools of Greece
To testifie the arms of Chastity?

To make this scan, every syllable in it has to be discovered (even *o're* will be pronounced oh-er, so that it resonates with pow-er). *Schools of Greece* brings quantity (the length of syllables) into play, another strategy for deceleration, and two stresses each must be found in *testify* and in *Chastity*—which so effectively slows the verse that we must pause (as if for an answer to the question) before continuing with a stressed trochee butted up against the next iamb:

Hence had the huntress Dian her dred bow…

It is not so easy for free verse to make use of secondary stress in this way, since only a passage of regularly scanning feet can suggest to the reader the pattern that requires that some secondary stress must be given the emphasis conferred by having the ictus. However, as Ezra Pound put it, 'No vers is libre for the man who wants to do a good job,' and there is no reason why free verse should not be free to employ passages of a specific metre in which such complexities of scansion can come into play.

T. S. Eliot's comments on vers libre are entertaining. People never seem to mention his wry sense of humour. His article published by the *New Statesman* in 1913 is included in the Appendix. As Eliot points out, it might be that pentameter has just been "tweaked" a little; it might be that the number of stresses in a line has been varied—"played by ear"—while a general sense of scansion may still apply. One can also attempt to create a line where the same syllable in a repeated word is stressed and then unstressed in a single line; a gambit dear to John Donne.

+ / + / + / + / + + /
Our storm is passed, and that storm's tyrannous rage.

(The Calm)

William Empson provides us with a valuable insight regarding the nature of the rhythm in poetry:

> ...it is the meaning which must show at what pace the verse is to be read. And, of course, it is not one rhythmical beat, like a bell tolling, which is apprehended; or if it is (since the ear insists on imposing rhythms, and cocaine can make one stroke into a series), then the word should be used in the plural; the foot, the grammatical clause, the line, the sentence, the stanza or paragraph, and the whole canto or subject heading, are all rhythmical units; the total rhythmical line which results from them must be regarded as of an immense complexity entirely defined by the meaning; and even then it is the meaning which must imply how it is to be interpreted.

William Empson, *Seven Types of Ambiguity* (p.30), Penguin 1961.

❧

AS AN ASPIRING POET, I worked hard at the metrical technicalities demanded by verse, inspired by poetry such as the rousing chorus (in Anapestic Tetrameter) from Swinburne's *Atalanta in Calydon:*

When the hounds of spring are on winter's traces,
    The mother of months in meadow or plain
Fills the shadows and windy places
    With lisp of leaves and ripple of rain;
And the brown bright nightingale amorous
Is half assuaged for Itylus,
For the Thracian ships and the foreign faces,
    The tongueless vigil and all the pain.

I read Ezra Pound's *ABC of Reading* (which I would still recommend to any poet starting out), and, as well as experiencing the thrill of dancing onstage at Covent Garden in the school matinee at the opera house, I read everything I could find on the philosophy of courtly love—since my passionate attachment was still inextricably bound up with poetics, and my interest in well-wrought verse had been fanned by Pound's translations of the troubadours and the poems of Guido Cavalcante. My poetry was technically quite proficient, but it was also undeniably "soppy".

Frustrated by the fussy but inadequate teaching for the boys at the ballet school, I decided to leave for a while and went to study further at the Centre pour la Danse Classique, which was run by a ballerina called Rosella Hightower (of native American stock), in Cannes. I studied there for two years. This was a form of self-exile that only enhanced my courtly crush on the young lady—who had by now joined the Royal Ballet Company. But while in the Midi, I studied the Italian of Dante, and read Petrarch, and continued to hone my orthometric skills—though writing as soppily as ever. Then I returned to the Royal Ballet School, much improved as a dancer, and soon after I joined the company myself.

A while before this, I had heard Christopher Logue read *Red Bird* with a jazz ensemble. After the performance I had introduced myself to Christopher and asked for his advice as to how to become a poet. He invited me to visit him at his mews flat off the Portobello Road, and in essence, his advice was that I read. In fact, he confirmed my own inclinations, since he was himself an admirer of Pound. I was to read Chapman's Homer, Golding's *Metamorphoses*, and all the poets suggested in the *ABC*. It was in this way that I was introduced to the longer line, for both *The Iliad*, in George Chapman's version, published in 1611, and Ovid's *Metamorphoses*—as rendered into English by Arthur Golding in 1567—are written in what are known as "fourteeners". It's a line with fourteen syllables and seven iambic feet *(Iambic Heptameter)*. It rolls along, as a rhythm, and seems particularly suited to epic narrative verse. I was intrigued by this metrical warhorse, and subsequently I have experimented with it myself. But here is Hector, taking up his son, in the Sixth book of *The Iliad:*

This said, he reach'd to take his son; who, of his arms afraid,
And then the horse-hair plume, with which he was so overlaid,
Nodded so horribly, he cling'd back to his nurse, and cried.
Laughter affected his great sire, who doff'd, and laid aside
His fearful helm, that on the earth cast round about it light;
Then took and kiss'd his loving son, and (balancing his weight
In dancing him) those loving vows to living Jove he us'd,

And all the other bench of Gods: "O you that have infus'd
Soul to this infant, now set down this blessing on his star:
Let his renown be clear as mine; equal his strength in war;
And make his reign so strong in Troy, that years to come may yield
His facts this fame, when, rich in spoils, he leaves the conquer'd field
Sown with his slaughters....

(Chapman)

And here is the start of the Second book of *Metamorphoses:*

The Princely Pallace of the Sunne stood gorgeous to beholde
On stately Pillars builded high of yellow burnisht golde,
Beset with sparckling Carbuncles that like to fire did shine.
The roofe was framéd curiously of Ivorie pure and fine.
The two doore leaves of silver cleare a radiant light did cast:
But yet the cunning workemanship of things therein farre past
The stuffe wherof the doores were made. For there a perfect plat
Had Vulcane drawne of all the worlde: Both of the sourges that
Embrace the earth with winding waves, and of the stedfast ground,
And of the heaven it selfe also that both encloseth round.

(Golding)

Although written later, Chapman's fourteeners seem more rough-hewn than Golding's. There's a willingness to step outside the confines of the metre, giving a freer "spilling out" of the narrative, compared to Golding's polished feet. This gives the sense of a natural speaking voice with the rhythm sometimes surging up through the sense, sometimes allowed to fall into the background. Poets tend to locate themselves in a specific relationship with rhythm and metre, some keeping it more in the foreground than others. Christopher Logue chose to translate *The Iliad* into free verse, seeking a twentieth century equivalent—a tough account of a war narrated by fighting men that followed the pauses of natural speech:

I thank the Lord that king Odysseus has found the words
To bring Greece to its senses, and hope it manages to keep
   them.
     Similar silliness
Made me begin the quarrel with Achilles
About some foreign she.
     Well, well. God's ways are strange.
     So no regrets.
This is the morning of the day
Whose dusk will see Troy won.
     The lords will join me for the battle sacrifice.
The less will eat and arm.
     Never forget that we are born to kill.
We keep the bloodshed to the maximum.

War Music, (The Noonday Press, NY 1997) – p. 78-79

This demonstrated to me that "Making it new"—as Ezra Pound's battle-cry demands—might exchange a set scansion used in the past for a sense of the contemporary "speaking voice"—bringing an old tale to life. Logue also insisted that I read Francois Villon (who I already knew from Swinburne's and Rossetti's translations). These are all writers Pound advocates in his *ABC*. And read them I did, voraciously. The list set out in this book by Pound is in some ways an alternative canon to the authors to be found on standard Eng. Lit. courses. But I had a friend who was reading English at Cambridge, and, magpie fashion, I read the books on his list too, and at last, after I was rather finally dumped by my ballerina, I managed to let go of the soppiness, as well as a decidedly precious versification. At the same time, I grew disaffected with the ballet, feeling that I was more of a creative artist than an interpretive performer.

This was the Sixties. I smoked my first marijuana, was completely bowled over by John Berryman's *Dream Songs* and dropped out of the ballet as I began to write a tougher sort of poetry just as I entered my twenties. Dancing and verse-making had completely dominated my adolescence. But while these two interests ran parallel to each other, they were still separate preoccupations, or that was how I imagined them to be. In the chapters that follow, I want to show how these two strands of interest, which have structured my life, have sometimes converged for me, sometimes diverged into distinct entities. I know that both activities demand my engagement, and today I feel that the step and the foot are intimately connected, as they have always been.

BEFORE HISTORY

1. WHICH CAME FIRST?
The prehistory of walking/the transition to song and ultimately to language

Once we evolved into an upright animal our forelimbs became redundant as far as helping us transport ourselves was concerned. Before that, we moved on all fours on the ground or swung from branch to branch through the trees. We retain much of the wiring of that earlier time. As has already been noted, like all mammals and all four-legged reptiles, we dissociate arms from legs. Animals do not move by sending their left foreleg forward at the same time as their left hind leg moves forward. The opposite is the case. There is diagonal co-ordination, and we remain haunted by this mechanism. When we walk, our right arm swings forward as the left leg takes its step. Not only that, the body and the brain have a diagonal relationship, the left side of the brain controlling the right side of the body. These crossover connections have importance for coordination, as well as a bearing on just about everything to do with movement—from military drill to dancing the tango.

Not enough attention has been given to the differences in gait in later hominins. It is true that such research is hampered by the paucity of feet in the fossil record. But we do know that first we needed to develop nails instead of claws and to lose our tails, and that bi-pedalism began with the Toumai 6-7 million years ago (MYA), while Ramidas who flourished 4.4 MYA is the earliest diagnosed hominin. But this is not to say that our feet had already evolved into mechanisms specifically designed for walking. "Lucy"—the remarkably intact Australopithecus Afarensis (3.9-2.9 MYA)—had a gait that was extended. The lower limbs lacked stabilization and had great freedom of movement—indicative of arboreal behaviour still—and her hallux, that is her big toe, remained opposable, so it could still grip branches, even if she could walk when she so desired. What makes her a walker is that her toes were capable of dorsiflexion, which is crucial for a good stroll.

Habitual bipeds emerged some two million years ago with Paranthropos Robustus and Ergaster, though hominin trails have been found at Laetoi in Tanzania 3.7 MYA. Robustus had a well-developed arch and the big toe aligned with the others, not abducted as in apes. However, he moved with a long striding lope and a different weight transfer system to ours. Ergaster had short toes (bad for completing the forward push) and we think he had an arch that was still more flexible and thus less stable than ours—so although he was capable of long range bi-pedalism he may not have been quite out of the trees. Then Erectus had a stabilised arch, and Heidelbergensis and the Neanderthals seem to have a foot fairly similar to that of Sapiens—but not quite, though it's difficult to say for Heidelbergensis as he does seem to have been a long-range walker but none of his foot bones have been found.

Researchers exhibit an ambivalence when it comes to the Neanderthals. Were they a different species or were their differences merely racial? Genetics shows that we interbred. Unlike Sapiens, they left no art (but see note on page 42), though they were adept at surviving in harsh ice-age conditions, so perhaps they did have clothing. Their gene type can be isolated and, as far as I can discover, it isn't found in us all. What is clear is that they were a type. The Neanderthal has been described as the utility truck of the hominins, as opposed to the sportier Sapiens.

More robust, with a larger heel bone and a wider spread to the foot, there is a potentially heavier "loading pattern" to the Neanderthal gait. And, from what I can deduce from their skeleton, their femurs (thigh bones) were set wider apart than ours. Could they carry more than we could? Did they bring their meat home in one piece? Carrying might have been done on a pole shared between two individuals, which might have meant that there was less scope for gesture and the development of dialogue. They were stocky, and the distance between their thighs suggests a side-lurching gait—what tango dancers would call a "cowboy" walk—whereas our inner thighs can brush together, giving tactile punctuation to the swish of one leg as it passes the other on its way to the next step, just at the midpoint of the stride. So our rhythm is crisper, clearer than their lumbering steps would have been. And here is a chicken-before-egg question. Did this straight kneed, elegant, narrow walk encourage us to dance (the dancing generating a syntax that could be pinned to our song), or did the dancing encourage our elegant walk?

⅌

IT IS LANGUAGE THAT DISTINGUISHES US FROM OTHER ANIMALS. But why did we acquire this gift and when did it evolve? A new theory suggests that language may have developed in tandem with tool making.

The very first tool is the human hand itself, with its opposable or pre-hensile thumb which greatly improves the ability to grip objects. The hand itself can be used as a cup, as a hook, as a back scratcher, a nose-picker or a masturbatory implement, and it has many other functions besides these. The evolution of our thumb is usually associated with Homo Habilis, the forerunner of Homo Sapiens, but it may go back to Homo Erectus and have happened well over a million years ago. This links our standing up with the evolution of our unusual and useful thumb. According to Steven Mithen, in his illuminating book, *The Singing Neanderthals* (Weidenfeld & Nicholson 2005), gorillas can stand on two feet but they find it hard to do. Possibly we developed the ability in order to pick fruit from trees. It is possible that our *habile* hand, specialised and precision gripping, actually preceded walking, with the dedicated adaptation of the spine, pelvis and lower extremities developing after this more advanced part. It seems logical that a highly functional adaptation that conserves hereditary traits (like inhabiting trees) could be followed by a series of more complex ones that complement it—perhaps then enabling a change in environment. So it has been suggested that walking may have been a bi-product of busy hands and not vice versa. But then, possibly, there were further evolutionary adjustments to the hand to make it as habile as it is today after we began to walk.

The debate is pretty hypothetical, since until it is written down, or engraved in stone, speech leaves no trace on the archaeological record. Researchers base their notions on proxy indicators such as early art or the developments in tool-making, but none of these indicators are conclusive.

The origin of our ability to speak is even more up in the air than the dating of our prehensile thumb's evolution. It provokes an enquiry that resembles metaphysics—in the realm of probability or possibility rather than proof. Perhaps all scientific discovery is a matter of turning some metaphysical question into physics. One interesting theory is that the ability to communicate (with more than animal calls) began with hands rather than the vocal cords. Phonetic production requires a particular configuration of the vocal tract that evolved in man and facilitated the ability; a "lowering" of the larynx that enables us to create the wide variety of sounds we utilize in speech. But that this instigated speech has been called into question. Red Deer are also able to lower the larynx, and, when stags confront rivals, the deeper roar that results suggests that they are larger than they are. Similarly, when a boy's voice "breaks"—it signifies that he has passed through puberty, so the larynx lowering may have more to do with sexual advertisement than with speech ability. Still, it is worth bearing in mind that sexual selection may have as much bearing on evolution as natural selection, and the lowered larynx gave us an ability to produce a wider range of audio frequencies known as formants—the most important cues in human speech, accounting for our ability to form a variety of vowel sounds. Mithen points out that standing changed the anatomy of the throat and the neck, that emanates from the back of the head of a non-walking creature, while in humans, the neck is below the head and supports it, allowing more room for the larynx.

Some recent research suggests that speech might have made it easier for our ancestors to teach each other how to fashion flints into axes and arrow heads—a "handy" skill that gave us a crucial advantage over other species and enabled us to take control of our environment. This would give the hands a role in the development of speech and indicate that they were also tools that encouraged language. *Science Magazine* reports on an interesting experiment:

A team led by Thomas Morgan, a psychologist at the University of California, Berkeley, has attacked the problem in a very different way. Rather than considering toolmaking as a proxy for language ability, he and his colleagues explored the way that language may help modern humans learn to make such tools. The researchers recruited 184 students from the University of St. Andrews in the United Kingdom, where some members of the team were based, and organized them into five groups. The first person in each group was taught by archaeologists how to make artefacts called Oldowan tools, which include fairly simple stone flakes that were manufactured by early humans beginning about 2.5 million years ago. This technology, named after the famous Olduvai Gorge in Tanzania where archaeologists Louis and Mary Leakey discovered the implements in the 1930s, consists of hitting a stone "core" with a stone "hammer" in such a way that a flake sharp enough to butcher an animal is struck off. Producing a useful flake requires hitting the core at just the right place and angle.

The students in each of the five groups learned to produce Oldowan flakes in different ways. Subjects in the first group were presented with a core, hammer, and some examples of finished flakes and told to just get on with it by themselves. In the next group, a second student learned how to make the tools by simply watching the first subject and trying to duplicate what he or she did with no interaction at all between them; in the third group, subjects actively showed each other what they were doing but without gesturing; in the fourth group, gesturing and pointing were allowed but no talking; and in the fifth group, the "teacher" was permitted to talk to the "learner" and say whatever was necessary.

In each group, the learner became the teacher in the next round. In this fashion, the research team created five different "chains of transmission" of Oldowan toolmakers, which produced a total of more than 6000 flakes. The results of the experiment, reported online today in *Nature Communications*, were striking. As might be expected, subjects sitting alone and attempting to "reverse engineer" Oldowan flakes simply by looking at cores, hammers, and examples of the flakes had only limited success. But performance improved very little among students who just watched others make the tools. Only the groups in which gestural or verbal teaching was allowed performed significantly above the reverse engineering baseline on several indicators of toolmaking skill, such as the total number of flakes produced that were long enough and sharp enough to be viable and the proportion of hits that resulted in a viable flake. For example, gestural teaching doubled and verbal teaching quadrupled the likelihood that a single strike would result in a viable flake, the team found.

Michael Balter

http://www.sciencemag.org/news/2015/01/human-language-may-have-evolved-help-our-ancestors-make-tools

It is interesting that gestural teaching doubled the effectiveness of the striking, though in its entirety this experiment has been criticised on the grounds that the contemporary learners have all grown up with spoken language, so they already have a propensity to learn via linguistic communication. There is also a problem with tools as early as the Oldowan ones, since the process was then so primitive that what looks like a deliberately shaped flake may have been as much a matter of luck as design—others are simply bits of stone smashed off a larger rock.

Another theory puts forward the notion that we learnt to sign before we spoke. As hypotheses go, I like the idea that at least some aspect of language may have evolved out of gesturing and pointing and that before speech there may have been a language of signing with the hands. We know that the mirror neurons enable early learning to take place simply by creating an urge to copy what is seen. Gestures can be easily copied, and they are silent—which would have been pertinent when early humans were stalking an easily alerted prey (African click-languages may have come about from a similar requirement not to alert what one was stalking). Signage can also be more universal than aural language. We know that in remote parts of the world, such as the Amazon, there can be many small tribes, each with different languages—which help to signify whether they are fisher people or jungle people; so aural language may be an indicator of identity. In such languages the signifier may not be directly mimetic of that which is signified, any more than it is in a developed language (even languages used by the deaf can have a syntax that includes words with a merely grammatical function). However, in general, signage and gesture tend to be far more mimetic in their essential nature: to point "over there" is actually to create an action that represents what is meant—thus signage among hunters might have been a simplistic *lingua franca* that enabled different families to hunt together. After all, it would have taken quite a number of hunters to bring down a mammoth. A hunting signage may have enabled us to utilise some form of indicative communication 1.4 to .5 million years ago, but it may have been manipulative only, that is, strictly concerned with supper. Animals can be trained to use language, but they use it in order to 'manipulate' matters, that is, to get a reward. Humans also use language to 'reflect'.

Before our fully developed language with its representational and communicative properties emerged, there may have been a simpler, primarily representational "proto-language". Here again, Mithen is worth reading, since he suggests there was a largely emotive singing proto-language he calls Hmmmm—that was Holistic, multi-modal, manipulative, and musical.

Might there have been a sexual component—a Flintstones theory of language acquisition?—with rhythm and moan becoming sounds and actions associated via mimesis with mating in a dance? Was language always originally associated with an action? The thrust provokes an expressive grunt, and then the expression of the grunt implies the thrust—becoming a sign that refers to it, albeit an aural sign, though possibly linked to mimetic action. Most thinking is accompanied by movement, and most movement is accompanied by thought.

If some aspect of aural language developed out of signing, then talking is very much connected to our initially having acquired the ability to walk, because the redundancy of the hands *à propos* movement through space is what enables them to be free to engage in tool-making and to develop the signage which may have constituted an internal representation system related to the world outside the mind. Indeed, too much "gossipy" signing may have impeded the development of tool-making—since after the initial ability to make a fairly rough implement there is a long period where no development occurred, so perhaps it was only when language became aural (much later) that we made the transition from a merely representative proto-language to a syntactically viable means of communication.

The mimetic tendency of signage reveals a problem with merely using the hands. Its purpose in the main might be to represent events in the natural world, but while good at denoting things spatially, our signage system may have been weak when it came to the expression of time and the relation of the sequence of events. Indeed, it may not have been capable of generating the very notion of time itself. Even among extant languages, time can be a factor that is not taken into account. In the Amazon, among the Pirahá, a language has been come across that has no indication for tense—that is for past, present or future—(see Daniel Everett, *Don't Sleep there are Snakes*, Profile Books, 2008). Since arm and hand movement occurs in space, gesture is good at "painting a picture", whereas the nature of language as we know it shows it to be more of a *communication* system than a *representation* system. As James Hurford explains, while

> a communication system properly includes a representation system, there are elements in a communication system that are not part of the inherent representation system. Analogously, there are elements in a computer system which relate only to keyboard and screen functions and not to the core business of computation. Any aspects of a communication system which pertain only to the mapping between external forms (i.e. sounds or signs) and the internal cognitive representation system are not part of the representation system *per se.*

(from an essay contributed to *The Transition to Language*, edited by Alison Wray, Oxford University Press 2002—p 314.)

While a representation system provides mental structures which relate to, or denote, external situations, it lacks the charting from external forms onto meanings. An effective communication system, according to Hurford,

> maps external forms (such as speech sounds or manual signs), via mental structures, to meanings (where many, if not all, meanings relate to external objects, events or situations). Such a communication system is typically public, shared by many individuals.

(*Ibid*)

I am not sure I agree with the use of the word *map* here, since mapping traces in space the nature of a far larger space, and as such it remains representational. I prefer to consider *notation*.

Music which is audible can be notated on a stave which is spatial. The temporal sounds can be "translated" into the lucid code that is provided in space. For a communicative system to develop, there needs to be a shift from the medium which is occupied with the raw information into a medium which is unoccupied by the phenomena one is dealing with. The sign for a semi-breve does not in any way sound like a semi-breve—it is not a mini-version of a semi-breve. The sign does not have a sound, though of course we can give it a name, precisely because it is a symbol for that sound in a dimension other than that of sound.

Music is fortunate in that it does not have a spatial dimension, *pace* modern experiments and observations. A problem arises with dance 'notation' (and this is true for both Laban and Benesh 'notations'), because dance does have spatial dimension. Laban notation views the body from above. Benesh notation equates the musical stave with the height of the body. Clearly, these so-called notations do not exist in a form external to the phenomena they purport to notate, and thus they are more like mapping, in fact, than genuine notation—Laban in "plan" and Benesh in "cross section". Where a notation occupies a dimension removed from the phenomena it "translates", it becomes in effect that "world" in another dimension, and then it can be used very effectively to compose new pieces which can then become realised as events in the original dimension.

If we accept that notation requires translation into another sphere or dimension (if music requires translation from the sphere of sound onto the page and thus into the dimension of space), it becomes interesting to consider turning this process around. True language, where what is signified gets pinned to "meanings"—as Hurford puts it—may have evolved from the reverse of the process of musical notation. Essentially, we perceive space, and objects which incorporate space, moving through spaces. Since sound has no spatial dimension, it can be the dimension onto which space and what happens in space can be notated. So just as space is where sound gets notated, sound can be where space gets notated. And once we had cracked the essential metaphor behind this process, we would have been able to use a language that was both communicative and representational.

But this notating of space and visible action onto sound involves a sophisticated ability to avow "a similarity between dissimilar things." Perhaps registering our stepping—"first this one, now that one"—as we walked (stringing steps together) stimulated the notion of stringing words together, and as we walked a long way, youngsters and pregnant mums and elders might have grown tired, so just as marching is encouraged by martial music, walking may have been encouraged by chanting "left, right, left, right," and this might eventually have become predicative, the order of the words affecting their meaning. Sequence is essential to speech. And sound, of necessity, incorporates sequence in a way that is not so obviously available to signage.

W. Tecumseh Fitch considers a musical aspect to the mystery of the transition to language while examining Darwin's theory of language evolution:

> Darwin's model of the phylogenesis of the language faculty, like most models today, posits that different aspects of language were acquired sequentially, in a particular order, and under the influence of distinguishable selection pressures. The hypothetical systems characterized by each addition can be termed "proto-languages". Darwin's first hypothetical stage in the procession from an ape-like ancestor to modern humans was a greater development of proto-human cognition: "The mental powers in some early progenitor of man must have been more highly developed than in any existing ape, before even the most imperfect form of speech could have come into use." He elsewhere suggests that both social and technological factors may have driven this increase in cognitive power.
>
> Next, Darwin outlines the crucial second step: what I have dubbed "musical protolanguage". Having noted multiple similarities with birdsong, he argues that the evolution of a key aspect of spoken language, vocal imitation, was driven by sexual selection, and used largely "in producing true musical cadences, that is in singing". He suggests that this musical proto-language would have been used in both courtship and territoriality (as a "challenge to rivals"), as well as in the expression of emotions like love, jealousy, and triumph. Darwin concludes "from a widely-spread analogy" (amply documented with comparative data later in the book) that sexual selection played a crucial role driving this stage of language evolution, in particular suggesting that the capacity to imitate vocally evolved analogously in humans and songbirds.

http://homepage.univie.ac.at/tecumseh.fitch/2010/08/05/musical-protolanguage-darwins-theory-of-language-evolution-revisited/

This idea, though subject to critical modification, has not been entirely discredited, and it is interesting to note that again there is the inference that language may have developed through the pressures of sexual selection as much as through natural selection.

There is a very wide range of hypotheses concerning "the transition to language"—many of them introduced and discussed in the book of that title. From the standpoint I aim to develop here, I found Kazuo Okanoya's research into the song of the Bengalese finch particularly pertinent.

The male finch has a song that employs a remarkably sophisticated "syntax"—which appeals to potential mates. Syntax therefore may have developed as a form empty of any meaning except that of showing off—though virtuoso singers focus so much on their song that they are more likely to attract and be gobbled up by predators. Here sexual selection finds itself at loggerheads with natural selection, and, in fact, this particular finch has been bred in captivity, so that he has been protected from predation while developing his elaborate song.

The song is perceived as having a complex syntax because the bird can put together its notes in an amazing variety of orders or patterns. Its virtuosity concerns sequencing. But what is intriguing here is the notion that syntax may have developed independently from a representative pro-to-language. After all a word is a sequence of consonants and vowels, as a movement has a beginning, middle and end. There is an indication that the Finch's song is associated with the basal ganglia which also controls sequencing in our actions, and this is an area of the brain distinct from where we store our imagery or proto-nouns, in other words our spatial representations. Okanoya concludes:

> Sexual selection has shaped complex syntactical behaviour in Bengalese finches. If human language syntax also evolved by sexual selection, we can devise the following scenario. The self-domestication that occurred after ancestral humans adapted to a savannah environment freed humans from some of the risks of predation. This permitted the elaboration of sexual

displays, including dancing and singing. Since the ability to dance and sing is an honest indicator of the performer's sexual proficiency, and singing is more effective than dancing for broadcasting, singing evolved through sexual selection until it obtained a finite-state syntax.

In parallel with the evolution of syntax, some of the state-dependent gestures were gradually replaced by calls through natural selection, because calls could be simultaneously addressed to multiple colony members. After syntactical singing and semantic calls were independently established, the acoustic tokens used in singing were sometimes replaced with calls that had a particular semantic content. Initially, the semantic content of the calls was erased in the context of singing, because the performance was not message-carrying—it was syntactically, not semantically, grounded. Gradually, however, a string of semantic tokens sometimes assumed the role of a public address in addition to its sexual display role. This could have been the beginning of syntactical language. Such vocalizations would be rather fictional or poetic, because syntactical grounding would dilute the semantic content. Or, to put it another way, the semantics of a display message would be ritualistic and not tied into the immediate temporal environment and, hence, more honest than the news-bearing communication that dominates language today.

The Transition to Language, edited by Alison Wray, Oxford 2002, p. 60.

The basal ganglia are located in the mid-brain, and the relation of the basal ganglia to syntax shown by Okanoya's finches is very exciting for me as I have developed a therapy I call *Tango for Balance*—which is designed around helping people with gait problems such as Parkinson's disease to walk safely and strongly. In the lower brain, a deficiency of dopaminergic neurons in stuff connected with the basal ganglia, stuff called the *substantia nigra,* causes this debilitating condition that affects the sequence that walking incorporates. *Substantia nigra* is Latin for "black substance", reflecting the fact that parts of this substantia nigra appear darker than neighbouring areas. What is clear is that this area of the brain is concerned with sequence rather than representation. Walking requires memory. You can forget how to do it. And memory may be prompted by a motor sensation or by an image, but it is just as essential to be able to place sensations and/or images in order of occurrence as it is to place the components of an action in their order.

What other inputs might there have been to the acquisition of speech? The notion that girls learn to speak quicker than boys, as is documented, prompts thoughts of an original dual happening—an emotive female "expression" concerned with the upbringing of infants and a male "signage" devoted to hunting. Neither of them would have been language as we know it.

So would the masculine signage have been more gestural, silent, to facilitate stalking the prey? It might have been largely representative, spatial. Yes, there is a sequence, a temporal mechanics, even to using your hands in a gesture—but its purpose might have been mimetic, to generate an image in the mind of the watcher and indicate a location, thus it took up its domain on the spatial side of the brain.

On the sequential side, sound making for its own sake may have ultimately evolved into an ability to control the order of sounds, and such ordering may have led to word order and the temporal sequencing essential to sentence construction.

Were women the first to use the voice? I think of nursing mothers and the change that must have been wrought when our brains expanded, as they did with Erectus and Ergaster about 2 MYA, and the increased nurture that was required for the lengthy, helpless infancy which now transpired. Standing on two feet and walking caused anatomical changes to the pelvis that meant that, in a sense, all human babies have to be born "prematurely"—the birth canal being just too narrow to deliver a fully developed infant—unlike the birth canal of a mare. It's at this point that women might have become more physically differentiated from men, and segregated, because of the new, home-bound role entailed in nurturing the baby as it develops further. Babies coo and mothers coo back. Some simple version of a lullaby may be humanity's earliest form of song. If this woman's "language" was a largely emotional response—its initial message was in the feeling rather in the signification. It is nevertheless as crucial to human development to acquire emotional empathy as it is to designate meanings. This emotional auditory response could have been how music originated. There was no need, in this context, for the sounds to signify anything beyond their emotional charge.

In *The Singing Neanderthals* Steven Mithen presents the case of Vissarion Shebalin, a Russian composer who retained his ability to compose symphonies even when his linguistic capabilities were completely knocked out by strokes. Russian neurologists concluded that "the brain has quite separate systems for music and language." So have music and speech developed in different areas of the brain? There is evidence that this is the case, though some aspects of both are shared and occupy common areas. My contention is that music's non-representative syntax of notes may have eventually become linked to steps in ritual dance.

Women encourage their offspring to walk. This is basically empathetic encouragement, with a meaning which may be vague but is essentially friendly. Rather than a representation of meaning, the message is in the emotion. Equally, women have a vested interest in retaining male attention during the extended period of pregnancy, nursing and protection of their not yet self-sufficient offspring, and they may seek to ensure fidelity to themselves and disguise freshly menstruating adolescents from philandering male attentions by creating some ritual that blurs the focus of the oestrus by ritual dances where all the women are painted up to look bloody and off-limits. Such ceremonies continue in parts of Africa, or did until very recently. As Chris Knight points out:

> Associated with the earliest appearance of anatomically modern *Homo Sapiens* in sub-Saharan Africa—dating to between 100,000 and 130,000 years ago— archaeologists report evidence for the deliberate mining, selection, treatment, and artistic application of red ochre pigments. Arguably this is evidence of the world's first art.

Ibid. p. 153

This suggests that women had a specific, manipulative interest in evolving such a ritual. Music would have been a great help to them in this regard. As is the case with wolves, singing generates singing, and people love to do it together. It is a pleasure to sing in unison—and, unlike conversation, it makes sense to sing in chorus. Conversation is more effective as a one-to-one statement/response ping-pong. The women's singing would have drawn the women together and generated the steps of the dance which accompanied that ritual.

So there may have been a ritualistic singing or chanting syntax—a music— concerned either with sexual display or with hiding nubile young girls in dances that camouflaged their fertility—wrong animal, wrong sex, wrong time; the freshly menstruating "game" got up as male antelope in a universally blood-stained community of women. This syntax would have been communicative only in the sense that it was expressive (for manipulative purposes admittedly).

Meanwhile there may have been a hunting and a gathering signage that preceded the singing, maybe by thousands of years; a representational proto-language concerned with tool-making and indicating manipulative events such as where supper might be found. The singing (or chanting) might well have been non-semantic, except in respect to the steps of the dance. These, and other, parts of speech—isolated from each other but all necessary to a fully-fledged language—may eventually have grown together out of a bricolage of their disparate elements.

Just as the embryo develops through all stages of our evolution, in infancy the voice explores all possible sounds that can be made before homing in on the sounds utilised by a particular "mother tongue". A baby will also play with the natural sounds of laughter, gurgling, clicking, coughing and sneezing. Dr Catherine Hobaiter studies how apes communicate with each other, and she spends a lot of her time in the forests of Uganda. From observing troglodyte chimps, bonobos, and gorillas, she has discovered that human children between the ages of one and two may share up to forty gestures with our ape ancestors (shooing, begging, pointing and appeals to be picked up). It seems that we explore the evolution of gesture as well as the evolution of the sounds that we can make. Children also play with natural foot movements: slips and trips, slides and hops, spins and jumps, thus becoming familiar with the gamut of their possibilities.

The step itself shares several parameters with the verbal utterance. Speed, strength, repetition and size are sliding scales that apply to both. And just as the formants of articulation may glide in a variety of ways between one consonant and another, bi-pedal movement glides in a variety of ways between the axis being on one foot and then being transferred to the other. Language, like dance, is always on the move.

Note:

Latest research now suggests that the Neanderthals did leave us art in the caves—thanks to new discoveries and improved dating techniques. According to comparatively recent theories, the development of cave art coincided with the displacement of Neanderthal man by anatomically modern man, starting around 40,000 BCE. However, traces or caches of pigment have now been found in Zambia—at the Two Rivers cave—that may date back 400,000 years. That puts the Neanderthals "in the picture", so far as art-making goes. New discoveries are likely to be made between submission of this manuscript and publication, so let us abandon science and simply speculate. For instance, since the Neanderthals had larger skulls at the back, rather than become extinct, did they become an elite? Few in number, but highly privileged, please entertain the notion that they may have become the pharaohs. These rulers had Neanderthal-style heads, as we can see from Egyptian sculpture. A friend of mine who is a descendent of Charles 11 and Nell Gwyn tells me that she has two-thirds more Neanderthal DNA in her than the average human. Perhaps the Stuarts inherited the gene from these ancient demigods of Egypt.

2. WALKING AND TALKING
Points about walking/Sequence in song and dance

WHILE LINGUISTS AND ARCHAEOLOGISTS ACKNOWLEDGE the importance of bi-pedalism so far as freeing up the hands is concerned (which, one way or another, may have enabled the emergence of a proto-language), few seem to have considered whether the very act of walking may have stimulated language acquisition, especially as regards the linking-up of sequence to meaning. Intrigued by this thought, I want to explore my own perceptions about how the gift of walking might have prompted the development of speech. To this end I have written down some points about walking—several of which tempt me to hypothetical speculation, while others remain simply observations, from which others may draw conclusions not envisaged by me.

How might walking have stimulated the emergence of a symbolic structured communication system using the voice?

Walking can take a long time—especially on a trek from one continent to another. Not much else you can do but look around you, observe and *reflect*.

Walking is repetitive. Therefore, walking has a rhythm—the commonest rhythm we know. Here we should bear in mind that like many animals we have a variety of gaits: a slowed-down walk, the normal walk, the trot, the run, the hop, the skip (a hop and a step), a lope, jumping from one foot to another, from two to two, from two to one, from one to two. Each generates a different rhythm in multiples.

We can walk in unison, just as we can sing in unison. Many primitive dances involve a line of performers stepping in unison. We can follow a walking sequence, as we can follow a musical sequence or stagger it, as in a fugue.

In the preamble, I mentioned that animals cannot alter their rhythms so as to be in time with an external beat, but that this is something we can do. Why is this? I think the answer lies in play. The specific sort of play I am considering here is that which synchronises parts of us that are capable of operating independently. We can walk while gesturing with our hands, for instance. If I step on the down beat and the ankle of one foot passes the other on the upbeat just before I take the next step, I can clap on that upbeat then step on the downbeat: step, clap, step, clap, step, clap, step. In doing this, I am inventing a game for myself: I am clapping in time to the rhythm of my own walk. Only a bi-pedal animal capable of an independency of arms and legs can perform this feat. Therefore, I maintain, we can dance in time to an external source, and sing in time to an external source, because we can synchronise our own independent parts.

I am not a scientist, but for what it is worth, my gut-feeling is that the brain has an arms part to it and a legs part to it. The arms part concerns *space*, since it is connected to the eyes, and indeed the scope of the eyes corresponds to the "range" of the arms. If I hold my arms wide apart, that more or less corresponds to the breadth of my vision. The arms part of the brain is linked to our notion of space, and we often use our arms at the same time to describe a shape, to gesture and so on—which is why I think that cave drawings may have been executed by an artist using both hands at once. The legs brain concerns *sequence*, and since we often use one leg and then the other (well of course we are using both but moving by making alternating pushes from one heel and then from the other), it is this part that has invented *time*, since we use the legs to travel, to get from place to place.

Walking can be expressive—which is important for language development if language has more to do with output than representative input, that is, more to do with communication than picturing the world. After all, the world can only be perceived as a multi-dimensional mental representation—the actual perception happens within us: this is what most animals do, and it does not necessarily generate language.

However, like utterances, there can be surges and declines of pressure when we walk. I can walk with purpose, or I can amble. I can walk noisily or silently. I can walk towards you, away from you, with you, behind you and in front of you. We can have walking exchanges—common in ritual dance: I walk x steps towards you, you walk y steps away from me. There are similarities to various courtship dances among birds here.

We perceive symmetry in space, when we look at each other or at an animal. Out of tool-making may also have emerged an increased awareness of what symmetry was—of course, our bodies appear symmetrical—but the symmetry of an object we fashion is a symmetry we have become conscious of and have externalised—the axe or arrowhead having symmetrical sides, as well as a front and a back. This produces a sense of completion, as a sentence may seem complete. The process of making an arrowhead out of a stone has a beginning, a middle and an end. In his book, *The Singing Neanderthals,* Steven Mithen argues that the fine artistry of creating a symmetrical handaxe may have had courtship implications for our ancestors: the ability to knap a well-tempered flint might have shown off how adept one was and intelligent. Certainly, a comprehension of symmetry was crucial for the development of flint knapping. It is also fundamental to grammatical construction. We talk of parts of a sentence agreeing, and this is an acknowledgement of symmetry. Symmetry is a fundamental aesthetic value—affecting everything from arrowheads to scansion. It therefore has an ethical dimension (see Wittgenstein "ethics is aesthetics"—*Tractatus*). In fact, symmetry in time is as important as spatial symmetry. I believe that walking would have stimulated this perception because walking is symmetrical. And it's specifically symmetrical in time.

Walking is binary, as are many concepts—yes/no, black/white, 1/0, night/day, left/right, right/wrong, subject/object and so on. Many of these oppositions shape our being. Perhaps it's because we are 'conditioned' by our primary binary gait. An octopus may embrace an altogether different philosophy! We also have a "disassociated" brain, that is, the left hemisphere controls the right side and vice versa. Walking has a dissociated swing, an anatomical and motor movement inherited from earlier four-footedness. Might this have stimulated the development of torque in the right front and back left brain? Having identified this bias in our anatomy, researchers are exploring how this may have stimulated language acquisition.

At some point, the lateralization of brain function came about—which means that most of us are right-handed. Lateralization refers to how some neural functions, or cognitive processes tend to be more dominant in one hemisphere than the other. Maybe we once lived on a diet of oysters and used one hand to hold the shell while we delved into it with the other. Usually, however, our feet are more equally attuned—because of our ongoing habit of walking—though most do have a dominant step, usually the right; but this is far less marked than handedness. Commonly the left is considered the "weak" foot (as is shown in the reasons for marching by the left in military drill)—is this the result or cause of torque in the brain?

Long walks are challenging—which might suggest that walkers evolved more than stay-at-homes in secure environments. However, it is likely that walking evolved into dancing when the environment was more secure—and that this stimulated sexual selection, with evolutionary consequences.

You can talk while walking. You can't do very much else. You can't chip away at a flint. So could the referential, non-manipulative "talking for its own sake" aspect of the transition to speech have been stimulated by our lengthy hikes? Here we are back to reflection. You can discuss things, gossip and tell stories while you walk. Think of Chaucer regaling us with the stories that flourished on the pilgrimage to Canterbury. In his wonderful book *The Songlines,* Bruce Chatwin describes the pathways that criss-cross Australia, ancient tracks connecting communities and following primeval boundaries. Along these lines, Aboriginals passed the songs that revealed the creation of the land and the secrets of its past. Here I will quote from a poem I have written, since the passage was inspired by Chatwin's book:

Melodies

That accompany the Odysseys of Aboriginal hikes
Illustrate the actions of the feet: a slurred phrase
For a salt-pan slog, a cadence for the threading
Of a creek. 'Spinifex', 'Ant-hill', 'Mulga-scrub'.

Music can serve as a memory map. To find our way about,
We will pluck notations from the wheeling constellations
And weather-lore from some old ballad line:
'I saw the new moon late yestreen with the old moon in her arm...'

From *Epping,* unpublished.

Walking can often have words assigned to it. Consider this instance of just such an assignation:

> You remember that the young men of the American Revolution who came to Concord and Lexington to join the Army were many of them so unschooled that they did not know the right foot from the left, and so could not obey the drill-master's "Right-left". The disgusted officers said, "Send these green-horns home, for if they cannot keep step they will be of no use as soldiers." But there was one officer there who used his head for something besides a hat rack. [...] "These farmer boys do not know right from left, but they do know hay from straw. Tie a little hay on every right foot, and a little straw on every left foot, and send them to the awkward squad to be drilled." "Hay-foot—straw-foot, hay-foot—straw-foot." They drilled, very awkwardly at first, and then more firmly, and at last they marched to victory at Yorktown.

From Wilbur Fiske Crafts, 1922

Walking may get us from A to B, stimulating awareness of a past we left and a future at which we will arrive (part of *Deixis* awareness), reinforcing the notion of time. Walking may also take us in a circle, delineating a territory, reinforcing a sense of home, but also delineating space, prior to any ownership.

You can walk in a straight line. A sentence is a straight line—I put one word after another, as I put one foot after another. Here it would be worth bearing in mind what Bernd Heine and Tania Kuteva say in their essay on *The Evolution of Grammatical Forms:*

> The human body provides an outstanding structural template for describing spatial concepts, and in many languages terms for body-parts such as 'back',

'face', 'head', or 'belly' have been used to develop expressions for the deictic spatial notions 'behind', 'in front', 'above', and 'inside', respectively. In addition, there is a pool of environmental landmarks (e.g. rivers, mountains, terms for earth/ground or sky) that tend to be grammaticalized to terms for locative concepts, and finally there are two natural phenomena, the sun and regular wind directions, that provide templates for expressing absolute references, essentially for cardinal directions.

The Transition to Language, p.386.

A *deictic* expression (or *deixis*) is a word or phrase (such as this, that, here, there, these, those, now, then) that points to the time, place, or situation in which a speaker is speaking. *Deixis* is expressed in English by way of personal pronouns, demonstratives, and tense.

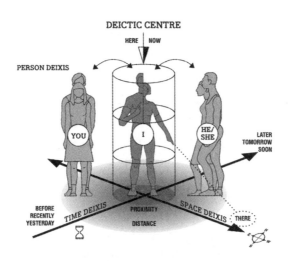

You may walk keeping the sun or the moon behind you, or in front or to the side of you. The migratory sequences utilised by other species could have a bearing on language here. Birds may make use of a point-to-point method when flying from one continent to another, that is, they may fly to a particular church steeple, for example, and this may prompt them to fly from there to tall hill on the horizon and from there to another landmark.

I have often wondered whether early man was migratory. Caves with paintings in them sometimes have bear-claw marks. Did the humans use the cave in summer and the bears hibernate within it during the winter? Walking would have become associated with the seasons, if so, stimulating annual deixis.

You can step forwards. You can step backwards. You can also take a side step; useful for avoidance of missiles, but also useful for games of throw and catch—which encourage expression, registration and response in an ABBAAB sequence. This is the basic sequence for conversation. The tango teaches us that walking actually has four simple variants—forward, backward, sideways and a change of weight on the spot. This produces a highly complex syntax of variations. Think of line dancing.

Consider also the "Clock Ray Method" which is used by the military to indicate less obvious targets that may be hard to locate. Rather than using the location of the target on its own, an obvious reference point is decided upon, such as a signpost, a bridge, a gate, or some other clearly identifiable object. Then, by agreeing that the object chosen is located at "twelve o'clock", we can take aim at the target which may be located at 5.30 (for example) in relation to the chosen twelve o'clock object. In terms of walking, this can establish a common direction to move in—whether you are a platoon or a corps de ballet.

⁂

WALKING SEQUENCES CAN BE MEMORISED OR IMPROVISED—which is also true for speech. Sequences of walking variants can be memorised and rehearsed—very similar to the syntax patterns of the Burmese Finch. In ritual, such sequences may be repeated.

Thus a ritualised song with no more meaning than the song of the Burmese Finch might have become attached to a ritualised dance. This would mean that notes in the song would become associated with steps which would equate with referential meanings. Such assignation would create the link-up between syntax and semantics. One can then improvise with the linked-up system. Surely this bears out one linguist's observation that—"referential language can only take place at all if restricted to fiction, ritual and play?"—where there is no incentive to lie.

Properly speaking, a single step is not the walk. It takes two steps to walk. Even the simplest walking thus constitutes a sequence:

> 1 Put weight on one foot—*R*—(A)
> 2 Push off from base leg *R* with the weight in it (B)
> 3 Land on free leg—*L*—(C)
> 4 Push off from new base leg *L* (D)
> 5 Land on free leg—*R*—(E)
> Continue: BCDEBCDEBCDE

From the sequence above, we can see that the left step is the predicate of the right step, the right step the predicate of the left step (which is not nearly so clear for any four-footed creature). The linguist, Derek Bickerton, highlights the significance of predication—*dogs bark, Mary left, rain fell*. Predication is "Possible in no other animal communication systems."

So walking has a syntax. And Bickerton maintains that syntax is "the core distinguishing feature of human language". Our vocal chords limit the range of our utterances and there is a similarity to the structure of our meanings, so the *order* of sounds has to do a lot of the work. This is why sequence—syntax—is crucial. A proto-language has no functional words, no tenses, no moods and no recursion (one phrase bracketed inside another). Most of these tasks are eventually facilitated by word order. Recursion is an essential feature of syntax. It is also very possible, and often utilised, in dance. In tango, a woman experiencing a "block" may add in extra steps before being invited to step over the block, this is known as "ornamentation".

The sequence shown above is a mechanistic model of walking. Studies in syncopation have shown that if four "ticks" are repeated we "naturally" begin to hear "tick, tock, tick, tock,"—that is, we divide the quatrain of beats into downbeats and upbeats—one to eight will be heard as "one and two and three and four." Now let's start off on a brisk walk. We are moving too fast, when moving at a normal brisk pace, to break down each step into "push" and "land". Now each step is a beat. 12341234 is left right left right left right left right. Here each left step is a downbeat—a tick—while each right step is an upbeat—a tock or an "and".

Slowing down again, we get left *and* right *and* left *and* right. This corresponds to trochees in poetic metre. We collect (as one ankle passes the other) on the upbeat, step on the downbeat. Thus the step has a stressed and an unstressed aspect corresponding to metrical units rather than syllabic units. Even so, a step has a beginning, a middle and an end—in tango this may be thought of as a push (or projection), a transfer of weight, and a collection of weight on the other foot. But just as a solitary beat does not exist in metre, a solitary step does not constitute walking.

I'm aware that some Eastern languages do not utilise stress, at least, not in the way we do, that is words may not have an accepted stress pattern. But two points need to be made here:

1) accepted stress patterns of English words can be altered—if the poet is so minded:

> Short summer-time and then, my heart's desire,
>> The winter and the darkness: one by one
> The roses fall, the pale roses expire
>> Beneath the slow decadence of the sun.

In this, the last verse of a poem by Ernest Dowson, aptly titled *Transition,* the rhythm of the last line dictates that decadence be pronounced "decay-dence"—with the strong stress on the second syllable.

2) Listening to Chinese poetry being recited—four short words or syllables followed by a long syllable—it is clear that while the four words are of equal value, the tick-tock effect causes a stress to fall on the first and the third short word. I feel that the innate walking rhythm of verse can still be felt.

Even Indo-European languages that do have stressed and unstressed syllables have been derived from quantitative syllables rather than qualitative ones (length was once used, rather than stress, in ancient Greek—and I'll talk more about this in the next chapter). But this may be because of the evolved artifice of the dance that was parallel to the poetic recital. I don't say *accompanied* because it may have been the words that accompanied or illustrated the dance. By evolved artifice, I mean that the steps may have been executed at a slower pace than normal walking. The tango step today is twice as slow as that used to scurry down a shopping mall. Length of syllable may have been more appropriate to the ritual steps of prehistory, danced perhaps by a chorus of women. In tango, unless we step in "double time" or dance the milonga (which is a brisker dance) we move at the slower pace of the first sequence cited above—with a push and a land. This is half the speed of our heart's beat.

When we walk at a brisk pace we move into the 12341234 sequence which takes up eight steps. As the rhythm takes over and energy begins to be required, we may find ourselves breathing in for two steps, breathing out for two steps, so now the syntax of the walk has become more complex—it takes eight steps to complete the cycle. This is not an absolute ratio. You could breathe out for three steps, breathe in for three steps, walking in waltz time. Runners may breathe out hard on every fourth step taken. For our ancestors, all this would have contributed to sound control—to expressing noise loudly or softly.

It has been said that a line or two of iambic pentameter will match the inhalation then exhalation of your lungs. If you listen to your breath without disturbing your rhythm as you walk, it becomes a song, or so it seems to me. And perhaps it seemed so for early Sapiens too. This walking "song without words" may very well have stimulated what is sometimes referred to as *Mentalese*—or non-linguistic mental representation (morphemes unattached to phonemes?). But you cannot have a song without there being a sequence. Trotting and running give us other rhythms, as does swimming. Consider that the heart beat is calibrated to fit in with each of these rhythms and we have a complex overlap of steps, pushes, exhalations and beats. If we are looking for the origin of sequencing, surely it is here—in the ordering required for action?

All this suggests a major linguistic difference between images and sequences—sequence being related to the basal ganglia, noted for its importance for action selection which must always involve sequencing. It's a distinction between time-based and space-based brain-work. I like to entertain the notion that words as things appear in the space area, while order (syntax) is controlled by the time area.

It's obvious that this sense of the walk as a sequence is also Sapiens specific

᷍

LANGUAGE IS DYADIC—it develops between speaking and listening—so its evolution fits with a feedback theory. Mothers make noises at babies' faces, so children learn to mirror the sound, the emotion and the visual expression of the noise, and the mother may then repeat the noise, emphasising her approval. One major division in the debate about how language came into being is between those who like Bickerton believe that it came about through discrete words (perhaps naming things) to which an order ultimately accrued—i.e. they acquired a syntax—and the holistic view, promoted by Alison Wray, and shared by Steven Mithen, that a vocal outburst was originally more than just a single signifier—i.e. the sound made when a menace such as a large eagle was seen meant, "this is the sound I make when a dangerous thing in the sky comes hovering over our children"—rather than a simple, specific identification of an object. In Alison Wray's terminology, input of large lumps of wiswiwyt *(what I say when I want you to)*—do this or that may have generated an emotive, musical communication based on empathy before we actually learnt to speak (rather as children learn to babble in a hugely varied way, sometimes imitating the way their parents "babble" into the phone).

There may also have been an output of choric mantras: pure time-based syntax (repetitive chants or simple songs) for sexual purposes or for wishful thinking. This Bengalese Finch-type syntax may then have generated dancing. My view is that a holistic mantra (what we all say when we wish the rain to fall down, for instance), may have generated, through repetition, an equally holistic dance sequence—what we all *do* when we wish the rain to fall down. Repetitive dance input would ultimately have attached step-meanings to syntactically ordered notes hitherto lacking in any segmented meaning for each note. Repetition would then have associated step-meanings (which now have an aural dimension) with lumps of wiswiwyt do this or that, breaking down these lumps into parts.

Within the chorused mantra, an ooing and aahing of formant sounds—basically vowel-noise, may have become increasingly sophisticated as we mastered the use of consonants—which would have made the vocalisation more distinct, naturally sectioning or segmenting it into syllables. Formants equate to weight transference in movement terms, while the consonants beginning and ending syllables may be equated to the push that instigates a transference and the landing that ends it. Transference concerns forwards-ness, back-ness, side-ness or transition on the spot. The nature of the actual push and the actual landing—heel to toe, heel to heel, toe to heel, toe to toe—may have been aided by consonant usage, making the dance movements more separate, and thus segmenting the dance-mantra into precise steps. Dance would then have been an externalisation of the sound feedback loop, sound in the mind an internalisation of the dance. Dance would therefore have been an externalisation that clarified the syntax.

※

WALKING AND STANDING STIMULATE DEIXIS. I am standing here now. You are there. I can walk to you and you can walk to me and now we share a new here and now. I am walking behind you. You are walking in front of me. You are walking beside me. Ritual dance would have strongly reinforced this sort of awareness—while deixis seems to constitute the model for the principle requirements of grammar.

The very notion of direction can very easily acquire a temporal dimension: forward step equating with the future; standing, sidestep or weight change equating with the present, while the back step may symbolize the past. Therefore, these can serve as a model for the time-line in deixis.

Standing in itself is interesting—note the supported stand of the Nuer, on one foot, the other foot at the knee, supporting the joint. A Nuer tribesman can stand like this for hours—like a crane. Simply to stand is an act of linguistic consciousness. It creates the ego, or the focal point of deixis. Humans can feel stillness. Motionlessness can become an action, an expression. The power of stillness is utilised by ceremonial sentries and by performance artists.

If we take our cue from Michael Corballis's research (*The Transition to Language,* pages 161-179) and entertain the notion that language may have evolved from manual gestures, should we not ask whether the phrase "manual gesture" is not constraining our perception? Gesture, even in ASL (American Sign Language) goes further than the hands, and involves the face, the chest, and so…actually, should we not be considering that any action, out of the whole range of bodily performance, may be considered as gesture? Such gesture might incorporate semaphore over distances, jumping up and down, mimesis and what might be termed performance art—any action invested with significance—of which dance is probably a sophistication, possibly coming much later, but finally linking up the sequence of tactile performance with an articulated sound.

So performance art may not be just a recent innovation. Perhaps it was one of the very earliest forms of art, practised possibly by the Neanderthals, who were supposed to have left us no art in their caves! Such an art might have evolved out of or in tandem with gesture. I'm suggesting that there could have been a total body gesture system, which, when linked to singing, became dancing, and that enabled syntactically organised sounds to became attached to a sequence of movements in the dance of gestures— and thus sounds turned into meanings.

❧

WE THINK OF VISUAL ART AS BEING DONE for the purpose of being seen. This has not always been the case. In the early days of the Christian church, religious images were often hidden away in the depths of crypts, and brought out only once a year to be carried in a procession on some particularly sacred day. In the Jewish tradition, a screen hid "the holy of holies"—and within it a golden altar of incense was attended only by the high priest. Art and artefact can be created in order to be hidden, and it is possible that this accounts for why very early drawings may be found in the deepest recesses of caves. For certain aboriginal people, the heart of mountains (where bears may hibernate) contain the archetypes of all the animal species, and caves are ideal places to get in touch with the spirits of the beasts upon which you depend for your survival.

Because there is an absence of any trace of soot on the rock ceiling above the cave paintings, might they have been executed in darkness, without the aid of torches? Were these images which were intended to be hidden, which were never seen, even by the artist who created them! When, I look at such cave paintings and drawings, I often wonder whether they were done with simultaneous movements of both hands. There's a certain sense of a space enveloped by movement, a space that has grown into the body of the bison or the tiger there on the wall. Please suspend your disbelief and humour my imagination here. My hypothesis is that the line is grown in both directions at once. And this tells us something about hands, and about manual gesture. There is a retinal aspect to our hands. They describe what we have seen. They can move in unison to create a space in front of them. This space can duplicate what has been in front of the eyes. A bow is drawn back and fired by the hands working together, not mirroring each other's movement (as the feet tend to do in sequence), but collaborating with each other to create one action. In this sense the hands are spatial.

Doubtless, as we evolved, cross-over connections occurred—hands learnt to behave like feet and drumming was born, feet learnt to behave like hands, and dance disovered how to mimic the birds.

It is said that the dinosaurs had such large tails and hind legs that they required a posterior brain to control these areas, located at the back of the pelvis. Certainly, the hind legs have a job to do that is radically different to that of the hands. For us, the job of the legs is to ensure that one foot is placed in front of the other. Gravity plays a part in this. We push forward from where we were, which is where the heel impacts with gravity. Our foot lands where we will be, and we transfer the weight onto it. In this process, time is of the essence. While some birds hop forward on both feet, this is not the way our natural gait is designed to work. For us, we move one foot at a time, and the foot from which we pushed passes the foot on which we land, and we use that landed foot to push into the next step. In this sense, the feet are wired to be sequential in their movement.

Let us go back to my aforementioned intuition and imagine a much-simplified model of the brain: say it has a retinal side, concerned with space, connected to the hands, and a rhythmic side, concerned with time, connected to the feet. The spatial side can use both eyes working in unison to see the visible world, which can be described by the hands. When it engages in dialogue, one image is delineated, and after that a reply is generated by the responder delineating a fresh image. The passage of time is hard to get across. The sequential side can travel through space, but it is unnatural for the feet to move in unison, however, unison is achieved by several humans taking their steps at the same time. Sound helps the humans to achieve this, say by the beat of a drum, done by the hands.

In order for language to come about, some cross wiring had to be put in place that connected the spatial to the sequential and thus the hands to the feet. It was the mouth and its sounds, and the ear that registered those sounds, which eventually succeeded in creating the bridge that was needed: a bridge that could not in itself be of the hands or of the feet—remember what was said about notation (pages 38-39).

⚹

MORE ABOUT SONG AND DANCE

"*This* sound means *that* move." A ritual dance related to a non-verbal song is a self-contained system of denotation without reference to external meanings—unless the steps are mimicry. Whether they are or are not mimetic, if the sequence of sounds is a regularly repeated one this sets up a syntax pinned to a specific set of actions.

Some dances have commonly used sequences which behave very like sentences.

Take the 'basic eight' in the Argentine tango. It comprises eight specific steps for the man which physically indicate eight steps for his partner. In the basic eight, the fifth step led by the man is the lady's right foot *crossed* in front of her left. If singers had an eight-note song, the fifth note of which was always a *soh,* and the ritual dance always comprised those eight steps, the *soh* would signify *the cross.* With a sentence, the fifth *stressed* syllable would signify the cross.

> A ***mog*** *who* ***mewed*** *intensely* ***got***
> *some* **<u>milk</u>** *to* **slake** *his* **urgent thirst**.

Taking account of the upbeat (in italics) the cross would be on the word "milk".

The ictus (stress) is on the syllables printed in bold. It's simple to see now how *milk* is the cross, on the fifth beat of the eight. There's what amounts to a subject clause and a concluding predicate. When danced to a melody, there is a sequence of sounds attached to a sequence of moves in an agreed order that has a beginning, a middle and an end. At an early stage in our transition to language, a dance "sentence" (such as the basic eight) specifically linked to a sung phrase that was merely a sequence of notes would be an example of a linear order of vocal-coupled-with-physical elements playing their own communicative role in a strictly self-referential context.

The tango is of interest here as it is basically a walking dance and walking is our fundamental gait. Languages with stressed and unstressed syllables mirror the walk, which has a stressed tread and an unstressed transition. We have seen how appropriate 4/4 time is to walking.

Auxiliary verbs like w*ill* and *have* are of interest to linguists. How did they come about? They can indicate past and future, taking us beyond an atemporal proto-language. Ancient usage associates *will* with *want* and *have* with *hold*. It is easy to see how *I hold a stick* can turn into *I have a stick,* and how the possessive and the past are related. Meanwhile the future relates to aspiration, and *I want (to) build a house* can become *I want/will build a house. Want* and *hold* are action/signs which very common in dance. Many dances—in remote societies as well as in the here and now—begin with an expression of *wanting to dance.* In the middle ages, this might be expressed via a flourish of one's hat and a bow, acknowledged by a curtsey. In the tango, it may be expressed by the *cabaceo*—an exchange of glances. And then? Then one takes the other's hand—*holds* it. *I hold a walk* suggests a walk that I have done, as a mountaineer might claim to *hold* three mountains—to have climbed three summits. The complexity of mountaineering holds is interesting in this regard—mountaineering, indeed all climbing, is very sequential—so was the sequential side something that not only developed out of walking and dancing, but was also prompted by our "grasp" of a sequence of holds—inherited from our climbing days in the trees?

ঽ

HOWEVER, IF WE PURSUE THE NOTION THAT DANCING as we chanted or sang in chorus encouraged us to acquire language, doesn't this raise an issue hidden in the shade of that notion? Why do we sing? Why do we dance? How did we acquire these skills, especially if they came to us *before* we were able to speak, as Steven Mithen maintains? I believe that dance (and song) came about through our innate gift for imitation. To some degree, imitation is fairly widespread among animals: cats may knead their human, in memory of kneading the breast of the mother, while bitches may nip their puppies instead of biting them in play fights. Our own particular flair for imitation can be observed in infants, who may pick up the phone and babble into it before being able to speak or they may stroke flat rectangular objects in imitation of adults stroking their interactive screens. Children cough and sneeze, but they also imitate coughs and sneezes—as Bob Stuckey observes in *Appendix 7: An Infant Speaks*.

Chimpanzees may be our nearest genetic relatives, and they appear to have imitative abilities, but early man may not have had much to do with apes. Homo Sapiens might not have shared environments with his relatives, and anyway, we are much more likely to have identified with upright beings walking, as we do, on two legs: beings such as the birds. The first pipes ever made were made out of the bones of birds. When the Red-Crowned cranes of Hokkaido dance, they leap in the air, open their wings, float to the ground. They bow to one another. One may stab at a stick, toss it into the air, as if it were a frog he had caught, showing off his prowess with a physical metaphor. They mate for life, and in Japan they have, since time immemorial been a symbol of fidelity and longevity. One of the oldest dances done by men and women together is the *Geranos*—or "Crane Dance" of ancient Greece. My view is that, even before we spoke, it is very likely that we imitated the birds, copied their dances and learnt to sing their songs.

An essay by Tom Zentall and Chana Akins on imitation in animals—included in *Avian Visual Cognition*, 2001—Robert G. Cook (editor)—points out that mimicry may often be used as camouflage (an evolutionary strategy) while imitative learning can be found in a variety of species. "A special case of mimicry involving behaviour is the broken-wing display of the ground-nesting killdeer and avocet (Sordahl, 1981). When the female bird is near the nest and a predator approaches, the bird flies away from the nest while mimicking the erratic flight pattern that might be shown by a bird with a broken wing."

Fear of snakes may be acquired by laboratory-reared monkeys exposed to a wild-born monkey in the presence of a snake. Parrots have a tongue-structure that allows them to mimic human words and Australian lyre-birds show off to potential mates by demonstrating how many sounds they can imitate; from the call of the kookaburra to the whirr and click of an electric camera, the sound of a chain-saw or the firing of a child's toy gun. Many species of birds sing in a regional dialect and young song birds learn their dialect by imitating the song of more mature conspecific locals.

One can then ask if an animal can learn to match any behaviour of another "on cue". (i.e., can an animal learn the general concept of imitation and then apply it when asked to do so in a "do-as-I-do" test). Hayes and Hayes (1952) found that a chimpanzee (Viki) learned to respond correctly to the command "Do this!" over a broad class of behaviour. More recently, Custance, Whiten, and Bard (1995) have replicated this result under more highly controlled conditions. Furthermore, Custance and Bard (1994) using the "do as I do" procedure, have found that actions on parts of the body that cannot be seen by the performer were just as readily copied as those that could be seen. The importance of behaviour that cannot be seen by the performer (e.g., touching the back of one's head) is that it rules out the possibility that some form of visual stimulus matching might account for the behavioural match. The establishment of a "do as I do" concept not only verifies that chimpanzees can imitate, but it also demonstrates that they are capable of forming a generalized behavioural-matching concept (i.e., the chimpanzees have acquired an imitation concept).

Zentall and Akins on imitation in animals—*Avian Visual Cognition*, 2001

In one observational study, interactions were documented between chimpanzees and zoo visitors and it was found that the two species imitated each other at a very similar rate. Imitation appeared to accomplish a social–communicative function, as cross-species interactions that contained imitative actions lasted significantly longer than interactions without imitation. Was there an intention behind these imitations, other than the intention to get the other species to respond? It's not clear from the report whether the chimps actually made gestures for which a response was expected or whether they were mainly the respondees.

It may be assumed that true imitation involves some degree of intentionality, such as when a human dancer repeats the movements of a teacher.

> Unfortunately, intentionality, because of its indirect nature, can only be inferred, and evidence for it appears most often in the form of anecdote rather than experiment. Ball (1938), for example, noted the case of a young rhesus monkey that, while kept with a kitten, was observed to lap its water in the same way as a cat. Ball noted further that lapping is extremely rare in rhesus monkeys. Similarly, Mitchell (1987), in an analysis of various levels of imitation, provides a number of examples of imitation at these higher levels. For example, he discusses the young female rhesus monkey who seeing her mother carrying a sibling, walks around carrying a coconut shell at a same location on her own body
>
> (ibid)

Imitation involves trial-and-error. A hunter may imitate a moose call in order to lure the prey into range, but the canny beast may be wary of such subterfuge and choose not to respond. Zentall and Akins point out that the benefit of species typical behaviour is its certainty.

> Birds do not have to rely on trial-and-error learning to build a nest. They are genetically predisposed or programmed to build them. On the other hand, there is a cost to such inflexible behaviour. Should the environment change in a way that is inconsistent with an animal's predispositions, there may not be enough flexibility in the system to allow for survival. The giant panda lives almost entirely on bamboo shoots. There has been little competition for this resource and thus, there has been little need for the panda to develop a varied diet. When bamboo is plentiful the panda can thrive. But with the

encroachment of human populations the bamboo forests have shrunk in size and the panda has become an endangered species.

(ibid)

Trial-and-error learning allows an animal to adjust to a changing environment.

> For example, many animals (including humans) are predisposed to follow the rule, "If one encounters a novel taste, one should eat only a small amount; if one then gets sick, one should stay away from that taste; if one doesn't get sick one should eat more". Thus, animals can learn which foods are good to eat and which are not.

(ibid)

As well as the apes, dolphins and a number of avian species including parrots, pigeons, and Japanese quail show evidence of imitative learning. But my hunch is that most of these imitations are done for manipulative reasons—i.e. to get a reward or procure a mate. However, in *Imitation in children*—(University of Chicago, 1971) Paul Guillaume suggests that imitation in human infants is linked to the child's notion of self and he proposes that "imitation enables the child to see himself in the person of another."

Poor, featherless birds, the first humans could only fly in the dance of their imagination. In this way, though, a female could see herself as an eagle protecting her young, a male could see himself as an eagle soaring in search of prey. Then the women could link hands and form a snake, in a chorus of vertebrae, chanting to bring the rain down to the earth the snake so loved to slide across. But just as we use language to reflect, not solely for manipulative purposes, imitation seems to have become something to do for its own sake. It became a pleasure to do, and to do well. It became play. And here, it seems appropriate to remind ourselves of the notion of simile and metaphor, since these are clearly imitative devices. If imitation provided us with the incentive to sing like the birds, and to dance like the birds, then it was our innate sense of metaphor, our awareness of the similarity between dissimilar things, that led us towards language: a poetry that created us before the first poem was said.

3. THE THRESHING FLOOR DANCE
The heel in Egypt/Theran fresco/The harvest circle/The birth of dance attributed to Crete.

Our inquiry concerns the walk itself, as well as its expression in poetic metre, and I wish to trace the history of its depiction in art, since the evolution of poetic rhythm seems to parallel the increase of fluidity in art and sculpture.

Among art historians, the traditional view (epitomised by E. H. Gombrich in *The Story of Art*) is to trace the development of sculpture from the flat-footed Gods of the Egyptians to the actively strolling *Kuroi*—the upright youths of the Greeks—suggesting that art "progressed" from symbols to epitomes. I am not so sure about this notion of a "development". A painted limestone relief from a Fifth Dynasty tomb in Saqqara (2465-2323 BC)—in the Cairo museum—shows men in boats spearing fish. They are actively plunging in their spears, punting their slender boats, and threatening rival boats. They spring forward onto the balls of their feet, pushing off from their heels, twisting in their spines to attack if necessary, every bit as tactilely alive as Greek sculpture became centuries later. The relief is typical of the fluid art of the 'old kingdom', which relied more on observation than on the aesthetic protocol that characterises the bureaucratic art of later dynasties. It is hard to believe that the decision to ground the soles of the feet was due to some primitive lack of perception about movement.

The record of art is also the record of its destruction. Noses are particularly vulnerable. They may be knocked off with a mallet or they may get damaged when a sculpture is toppled over. To knock a nose off is a form of facial castration, an attempt to drain power from the god whose presence is still felt in the stone, even though the despoiler of the tomb may have no idea who the god is. When the material art is made of is imbued with a transparency that shows us some aspect of life, in other words, when art is representational, a fiction inevitably emerges. Time seems to be suspended.

This is a crucial aspect of visual art, and an aspect that must affect its presence, from the cave paintings to the still lives of Giorgio Morandi. The sensation of time arrested is clear in the paintings of back yards by Pieter de Hoogh, for even the immobile things depicted are stilled in time. The cobbles are stilled, and the walls. It is not just the people who are stilled as they go about their business. For the Egyptians, the God is "there" in the stone's stillness, long after his worship has been forgotten, and the raider may feel the need to destroy a perfection which seems to keep the god present. Toppling the statue or knocking off its nose may not help though, since the god is everywhere in that stillness and may yet be experienced through the fragment.

This time-suspending attribute of representation may be felt particularly strongly in orthodox Egyptian sculpture of a later period. Take the block statue of Hor from the Twenty-Fifth Dynasty (770-712 BC). The young man is seated on the base of the sculpture which is carved out of a single block of schist. This is a dark stone which very much makes its presence felt—formed by the metamorphosis of mudstone, shale or igneous rock, and compacted to a higher degree than slate; its darkness speckled with crystals.

Hor's knees are bent upwards towards his chest and he rests his folded arms on them. His body thus forms a cube, with his head above it. His hair (in fact a double wig), which spreads downwards, connects neck and face with broad shoulders. Between his knees, a text is incised, telling us that his family has been associated with priestly functions for five generations. The block statue type was already old when Hor was carved and is indicative of a tendency towards archaism—even the double wig is an ancient style. We are looking at a large block of schist but we look through this to see a young man. However, from this transparency a deeper opacity emerges. We look through the young man to experience the stone.

Critics have noted that the sculpture is "vibrant and full of tension"—one feels how his knees are brought up against his chest. *And* (I use the connective deliberately) he is stone. He is seated firmly on both the "sit bones" within his buttocks, and the soles of his feet are one with the plinth. His presence projects lastingness. He embodies timeless stability. Since his plinth is cut from the same mighty stone as his body is, his statue, in its entirety, rests securely on the ground, projecting a unity with eternity itself.

In two-dimensional depiction or relief, the Egyptian ground is a customarily a horizontal line. This horizontality also generates a stability in itself. The flat connection of the soles to the ground in Egyptian art is not born of some failure to grasp anatomy. Depiction projects the same message always: the essential message that time has been stilled. Artists and cultures may seek to emphasise this aspect, as the Nubian kings of 770 BC Thebes chose to do by embracing archaism in dress along with an ancient form, or as the Dutch masters did by depicting a woman from the back, removing the liveliness of an expression but emphasising the presence, the sheer presence of the person, occupying space, there on that day which, because of this artwork, will last forever. Shakespeare understood that this sense of the everlasting could be done in words:

> Shall I compare thee to a summer's day?
> Thou art more lovely and more temperate:
> Rough winds do shake the darling buds of May,
> And summer's lease hath all too short a date:
> Sometime too hot the eye of heaven shines,
> And often is his gold complexion dimm'd;
> And every fair from fair sometime declines,
> By chance, or nature's changing course, untrimm'd:
> But thy eternal summer shall not fade,
> Nor lose possession of that fair thou ow'st;
> Nor shall Death brag thou wander'st in his shade,
> When in eternal lines to time thou grow'st:
> So long as men can breathe, or eyes can see,
> So long lives this, and this gives life to thee.

The soles adhering to the earth concern stability. But artists may choose to de-emphasise this aspect instead of reinforcing it. Gombrich sees Egyptian art as adhering to a set of rigid rules—and he points out that the feet are shown in profile only from the inside, from the "big toe" side that is. When facing right, this would mean two left feet! Clearly life-like depiction was not the aim.

However, it is worth remembering that the Egyptian royal cubit *(meh niswt)* is the earliest attested standard measure. The cubit is derived from the length of the forearm. It approximates the length of a man's arm from the elbow (we get an "ell" from this too) to the tip of the middle finger, or about 18 inches. Fields were measured in cubits and their areas could be calculated—which greatly aided the taxman. The Egyptians also used the palm as a measure, which was divided into four fingers, and the fingers were further subdivided. Two feet, one in front of the other, bear witness to a measurement. The inner view of the feet is standard because the measurement is a standard.

Similarly, the torso may be turned in a painting or a relief towards the viewer, thus associating the shoulder with the forward foot below it—which, as we have seen earlier, is *not* how we walk. We walk by dissociating—left arm, right foot. However, the Egyptian torso now becomes a geometrical entity, a trapezoid. Is it walking that is being depicted? I doubt it. It is more like a simple version of the figure as the measure of things that permits a view of all its measurable parts.

"Man is the measure of all things" is a remark attributed to Protagoras according to Plato in the *Theaetetus*. As well as the foot, and the yard which is a stride, there is the onyx (the nail, equating with width of finger), and in Old English we get *ynche*—which is a thumb-joint width. So another perception conferring stability to Egyptian art was their grasp of measurement, as derived from our human proportions. And these measurements can be fitted into each other as the thumb's inch goes twelve times into the foot, while the cubit provides a convenient middle unit between the foot and the yard.

Now, if we reconsider the foot, we realise that it has a fourfold meaning. It is at the same time an anatomical part, a unit of poetic metre, a step in a dance *and* a unit of measurement. Dance steps are often associated with spatial terms. In the tango a *baldosa* is a step that can be danced on a single tile (the baldosa) of a black and white tiled floor.

The stillness that evokes eternity which is so ably projected by Egyptian sculpture is a power that has been re-discovered by contemporary performance art. Stillness has been explored by many performance practitioners. Perhaps there was a similar use of corporeal stillness in ritual performances presided over by the Pharaoh and his priests: stillness and the exegesis in a physical way of their notion of measure. It is said that the Egyptians moved into battle very slowly, projecting a massive display of power and weaponry while banking on the enemy capitulating before actual onslaught took place. Their army was a slowly rumbling forward phalanx of eternity and stability. This strategy was successful until finally bested by the Scythians, whose custom was to ride very fast as close as they could to the enemy and then reverse the gallop of their mounts and fire backwards at their foe with their bows.

Soldiers executing a funeral march will move at a pace that is half the speed of a standard regimental march. Modern performance artists have experimented with moving "so slowly no one can see them moving." The image takes time out of reality, and it also, *ergo,* takes time out of words. Hieroglyphs engraved in stone may represent a song or a poem stilled, just as Shakespeare's sonnet is stilled by it being written down. Ian Hamilton Finlay has engraved his brief poems in stone, and laid these stones out at Little Sparta, his garden in Scotland. Stillness is the stone out of which the statue is carved, stillness is the unity which allows the poem to rest within its own equilibrium and stillness is the ground on which the performer's fundamental primaries, repetition and difference, are based.

A poem, such as a sonnet, is 'stilled' by the sense that, because of its structure, because of the inevitability of its rhythm and the "rightness" of its rhymes, it can never be altered. This is what Shakespeare's sonnet is suggesting.

Measure is a crucial contribution to civilization that we owe to the Pharaohs. The Egyptian system was an analogue system, based, as I say, on lengths generated by our own proportions. In the sixties, Situationist thinkers decried the introduction of decimalisation and the European metre. If you see culture as a process of enlightenment, evolving towards some Platonic notion of perfection, then the introduction of the metric system may seem ideal. To other minds, it is a disaster. A comparatively recent notion concocted during the dictatorship of Napoleon Buonaparte, it replaces measures analogous with the body's proportions with a mathematically appropriate system which makes no reference to us. It makes for more convenient maths and poorer management. The notion that management is a self-referential "science", that one trained to "manage" can run any business, and that no knowledge of the nature of the business is required, puts a similar emphasis on a notional, self-referential completeness. It amounts to a shibbolethic dogma that equates management with an abstract ideal of financial economy. It demands that all institutions make a profit, and it may well destroy our art schools, hospitals and repositories of historical culture. However, to Napoleon, it was integral to his code, and represented an improvement in efficiency.

The rivers of the Tigris, the Euphrates, the Jordon and the Nile formed a crescent of fertility in a vast expanse of desert. The Egyptian ground is the mainland, near rivers which flood at regular, manageable intervals. The pyramids are built on firm, mainland ground. Only Akhenaton and Tutankhamen posited any release from the overwhelming stability of this "mainland" sense of the horizontal floor by looking upwards, towards the sun. Sculpted on the back of his throne, Tutankhamen relaxes—as can be seen in the soft creases of his stomach. The sun shines. He is there with his lady. The garden grows. He bathes in the light. But this heretical "enlightenment" was put aside even before the reign of Tutankhamen ended. "The old beliefs were restored, and the window to the outside world was shut again," as Gombrich puts it. Egyptian art returned to its sense of measure, timeless stability and the notion of dynasty.

⁂

BUT DID THE NEW BELIEFS DIE, or did they continue to flourish underground? Is this relaxed image of Tutankhamen one of the first instances of an impulse in art and society to embrace pastoral, as an aesthetic theme? Is Tutankhamen abandoning his bureaucratic god duties, and here reclining in loosened stays like Marie Antoinette on her illusory farm? Is this art as escapism? Here, first, I would refer the reader to William Empson's, *Versions of Pastoral:*

> The essential trick of the old pastoral, which was felt to imply a beautiful rela-
> tion between rich and poor, was to make simple people express strong feel-
> ings (felt as the most universal subject, something fundamentally true about
> everybody) in learned and fashionable language (so that you wrote about the
> best subject in the best way). From seeing the two sorts of people combined
> like this you thought the better of both; the best parts of both were used.

In art, perhaps in art alone, the court can mingle with the proletariat. A thread of this pastoral reaction to officialdom runs on through history via Sappho and the lyricists of Greece to the Arcadias of the Elizabethans and beyond. With the pharaoh, the reaction to being seen as a god was to go camouflaged as a man; for the Renaissance, it was the court min- gled with the countryside or with some courtly notion of it. However, an art of pastoral retreat enables the artist to focus on the dynamics of the medium, rather than the urgent issues pressing in from society. As the pastoral enthusiasm deepens, the instigating realism fades and instead an idealism becomes abstracted from it. Music flourishes, and so does paint- ing, and scansion gets discussed by courtier poets among the yew's broad hedges that create private gardens and intimate nooks—as at Sir Philip Sidney's residence at Penshurst.

Outdated forms are abandoned or modified, new techniques are explored in a realm removed from the manipulative corridors of the court. A drive for the completion of all projects, for security ensured by power and perfection as pomp and ceremony is exchanged for a tolerance of imperfec- tion, an urge to explore the remotest of realms, and a wish to understand truths that apply to us all. Many of our innovations have emerged out of this idyllic sector of Platonic research.

What is for sure though, is that Tutankhamen's vision of realising the idyllically carefree on earth was swiftly eradicated. Egyptian society returned to its symbolic sense of man as a measurable unit, stilling the walk and replacing it with an associated stance, feet planted firmly on the ground.

~

MEANWHILE, ON THE ISLAND OF CRETE, young men and women were dancing with bulls. The Minoan bull was associated with Poseidon, lord of the
sea. Many of the men of Crete would have been fishermen or merchant sea-
men or maritime adventurers. In 1627 BC a tsunami may have destroyed
the powerful fleet the Minoans used to extract tribute from Greece, and later
they may have become part of the marauding "Sea Peoples" who opposed
the might of Egypt and launched raids on that corner of the Middle East.
However, for many generations before that, the Cretans preserved a certain
independence from Egypt while paying them a degree of homage.

The culture of the Cyclades was a sea culture, and women played a key
role in its heyday. Residence after marriage was matrilocal, the husband
making his home with the relatives of the wife's mother. With the men so
often away at sea, matriarchal administration was necessary; the queens
either acting as powerful regents in the absence of their spouses or embody-
ing sovereignty itself. A seafaring warrior might come from elsewhere and
ally himself with the culture discovered at his landfall. The Odyssey bears
testimony to this, its hero taking up with several women who are clearly
in charge of their islands, while the suitors proposing to Penelope, in the
absence of Odysseus, do so because she embodies the property, and she is
in effect the sovereign of Ithaca. It's her island.

Thus it is the sea which dictates the nature of island society, and this
may fashion the roles of the sexes.

On the flat ground of a floor, still depicted as a horizontal line, the
Cretans in the frescoes are rooted to that floor-line in the Egyptian manner. When serving in a palace, bringing gifts of fish or vases full of saffron, the feet of the figures remain grounded on a horizontal floor, as in
Egyptian art. One can imagine them offering tribute to that empire to
the south. Elsewhere, though, the Cretans inhabit the air—as if it were
the sea. Insteps can be detected, allowing light to show between heel and
ball, and when performing acrobatics with a bull, the dancers can be seen
to be entirely off the ground. It is almost as if they were swimming, as if
the the bull was the spirit of the sea. In artistic terms, it's an iconoclastic
liberation. Then there's a fresco from the palace at Knossos, dated around

1400 BC, that shows a Minoan officer with two spears leading a group of black soldiers, probably mercenaries from Nubia. It's a fragment. The feet have been lost, but from the angle of the hips, reconstruction has hypothesised that the officer is running—the back foot off the ground, heel and ball activated. This running is happening in a space where the ground is not depicted as a line beneath the figures. They are simply running against a sea-blue background.

Henriette Groenwegen-Frankfort observes that Minoan art differs from Egyptian (and ancient Near Eastern) art in its 'absolute mobility in organic forms'. Minoan society was not—as the Egyptian one—dominated by writing, listing, and measurement, and therefore Minoan art was not subjected to hieroglyphic clichés and a rigid canonical order.

Minoan culture is credited with the invention of fresco, letting the paint soak into the still damp plaster. The Minoans were renowned for their skills as artists and inventors. Daedalus invented the maze, and he is celebrated as an ingenious architect and designer. The Minoans delighted in puzzles and in the fashioning of mysterious articles. It has been discovered that connecting similar signs arranged in concentric circles on an enigmatic artefact known as the "Disk of Phaistos" enables a hidden geometry to emerge. This curious baked clay disk, dating to about 1700 BC, was discovered in the basement of the Minoan palace of Phaistos, on the south coast of Crete. It is about 15 cm in diameter. It seems to show signs amounting to a language but if it is a language no one has found a way to decipher it. However, Claire Grace Watson has argued very cogently that these signs are ideograms not hieroglyphs—so perhaps this disk is in itself the maze. Her practice of connecting similar signs on the disk with each other, as in a drawing puzzle where you join the dots, has generated startling results. Geometrical shapes are readily generated. The disk employs a geometry of alignment that goes beyond number and a set-square. Hers is an ingenious solution to a long-standing enigma, and it reinforces the notion that the ingenuity of the Cretans was valued in Egypt and throughout that fertile zone of the ancient world.

Akrotiri is a Minoan Bronze Age settlement on the island of Santorini which is 127 miles due north of Crete. The island's ancient name was Thera. The settlement was destroyed in that Theran eruption that brought about the 1627 BC tsunami. Entire buildings got buried in volcanic ash, which preserved the remains of fine frescoes and many objects and artworks. The blue monkeys visible on the walls here leap through the air in an almost waviform manner. It is as if they are the waves of the sea in epitome.

In a Theran fresco dating from 1650 BC, Saffron gatherers can be seen, and one of them is climbing a mound or small hillock to harvest the saffron crocus. Both feet are on the ground but the ground is rugged and steep, so the balls of her feet and her heels follow the contour of this uneven land, this heaving ground, which seems to billow, just like the sea. While still married to the ground, the legs and feet take on a new dynamic, a climbing dynamic, with the heels and the balls of the feet activated.

Saffron has medicinal benefits. It's useful in many ways, and in the bronze age it was a precious ingredient in dyeing and perfumery. It was traded throughout the Mediterranean. When dried, the spice emits a pleasant aroma described by Aristophanes as a "sensuous smell". It might be mixed with myrrh. Saffron and crocus iconography abounds in ritual and symbolic contexts. Only the women wore fabrics dyed with saffron. Yellow was a sacred colour, a woman's colour.

So saffron can be seen as a distinct symbol of Minoan women and the zone of the female. And these women had influence. They wore corsets and proudly displayed their breasts. There was nothing abject about this. They "wore" their breasts with as much confident hutzpah as their men wore their helmets. Cretan midwives used saffron—and they were the most powerful midwives in the Eastern Mediterranean. They were snake charmers. They understood the properties of venom. They ran hospitals. Their sacred ingredients could induce abortion or ease menstrual pain.

Until very recently Crete abounded in *alonia,* or threshing circles. Cora Greenhill describes the making of one of these:

> The first major task was making the floor of the aloni smooth enough for the grain to be threshed and collected as a clean product. This meant remaking the floor each year before the harvest, using mud and straw beaten down and smoothed, along similar principles to making mud bricks.
>
> Making the floor of the circle smooth was big job, utilising all available resources of donkeys... plenty water, hay, sheep to make mud, and

children—presumably to help stir it all up with the straw and get dirty. They must have loved it. If I understood correctly, a great deal of mud is created with hay mixed in, then a big stone or cement wheel is dragged around to smooth it all down before it's left to dry in the scorching July sun. The word used for the process of preparing and smoothing the floor is *patoma*, the same word as is used for the marriage bed...

Undoubtedly, there was a lot of work involved in that too: the making of the mattress and the fine linen, ironing and smoothing it all down. And there would also be the hoped-for harvest of the marriage bed to symbolically connect the two activities!

Cora Greenhill, *Alonia, The Threshing Circles Of Crete*

Alonia go back to times as ancient as threshing itself, the clouds of chaff being dedicated to Aeolus, the God of Winds. Sometimes the circle has a perimeter of upright stones, sometimes the flat surface is made of stone. A donkey tethered to a central pole walks the circle drawing the heavy sledge that crushes the grain, while gradually being obliged to come to the centre as the rope wound around the pole gets shorter. Here perhaps, in this natural spiral, is the origin of the compass and circular geometry. Cora Greenhill goes on to say:

We are told that in ancient times, circle dances originated in the threshing circles: the criss-crossing steps that still characterise Greek dance were originally the kicking of the grain to separate it from the straw. We also read theories that say that the alonia were at the birth of Greek theatre: the celebrations following the harvest would evolve into theatrical performances, and the circles themselves become stages. I have certainly seen some circles set into hillsides in such a way that people could sit on the slope and look down on the action within it.

(ibid)

So here we have a culture that, while offering tribute to Egypt, also sought liberation from Egypt's horizontality by activating the heel and the ball of the foot and showing people running, leaping and dancing! There is a fresco from Cnossus which shows a group of finely dressed people, watching a dance by girls in an olive grove; another shows a woman dancing freely and alone, her hair flying.

Most significantly for our investigation, the Mycenaean Greeks, who came later, considered that the Cretans had invented dancing. In the 18th book of the *Iliad*, Homer describes how when Vulcan forges the arms of Achilles and sets about creating his shield he embosses it with warring cities and pastoral scenes, and then:

>   Next to these he cut a dancing place
> All full of turnings, that was like the admirable maze
> For fair-hair'd Ariadne made by cunning Daedalus;
> And in it youths and virgins danc't, all yong and beauteous,
> And glewed in another's palmes. Weeds that the wind did tosse
> The virgins wore, the youths, woven cotes that cast a faint dimme glosse
> Like that of oyle. Fresh garlands too the virgines' temples crownd;
> The youths gilt swords wore at their thighs, with silver bawdricks bound.
> Sometimes all wound close in a ring, to which as fast they spunne
> As any wheel a turner makes, being tried how it will runne
> While he is set; and out againe, as full of speed, they wound
> Not one left fast or breaking hands. A multitude stood round,
> Delighted with their nimble sport: to end which, two begun
> (Mids all) a song, and turning, sung the sport's conclusion.
> All this he circl'd in the shield, with pouring round about
> (In all his rage) the Ocean, that it might never out.

Chapman

It is likely that the dancing place attributed to this mythical inventor was originally an Aloni, though it is worth considering that, long before these threshing floors provided a dance-space, there were flat spaces cleared by the Neanderthals in their caves, where singing and dancing may have gone on, away from where the butchery of game occurred, from stone anvils where flints were knapped and where mothers sat dandling their young. Dance and song go back far further than Crete, further even than our species, according to Steven Mithen in *The Singing Neanderthals*. The dance that Homer describes, perhaps the earliest of all recorded dances, might have been similar to the Tsakonikos of today - the only Greek dance with ancient origins that is done by men and women together. The rhythm is in 5/4 and the count is 1-2-3-4-pause. It is thought by many to be the Crane Dance, which Theseus learned from Ariadne just before he abandoned her on the island of Delos.

This Crane Dance—from which the Tsakonikos may be derived—has the name Geranos. We mentioned the mating dance of the birds themselves in the previous chapter. During their dance the cranes sometimes revolve. Could this "Geranos" be at the root of our word—"to gyrate"? It is thought to have originally been "a chthonic maze dance around a horned altar in honour of a female divinity" according to Lillian Brady Lawler. Though scholars have associated the dance with the flight in formation of cranes, Brady Lawler argues convincingly for it being a snake dance—the line of dancers originally carrying a python between them—the sacred python that inhabited a nearby cave. Also, the donkey's tethered itinerary around the threshing floor might have suggested the way a coiled snake may embody a spiral, while the weaving and unravelling of the dance could be imitative of the sinuous coiling of a serpent. This ties in with the figures of divinities and priestesses discovered in Crete.

Here I can't resist mentioning the Anasazi—who were troglodyte North Americans—cliff dwellers who built sophisticated palaces within the cliffs. Although their dates are far later, the Anasazi engaged in art and customs that are similar to the Minoans, and their existence on a far-away continent suggests isolation from any European influence. I find it intriguing that their cliff palaces were decorated with spirals and with similar maze patterns to those of the Cretans—patterns which can also be found on their pottery. They inhabited the Four Corners country of southern Utah, south-western Colorado, north-western New Mexico, and northern Arizona from about A.D. 200 to A.D. 1300, leaving a heavy accumulation of house remains and debris.

The Anasazi ("Ancient Ones"), are thought to be the ancestors of the modern Pueblo Indians, of whom the Hopi are the westernmost group. Traditional Hopi culture emphasized monogamy and matrilineal descent. Hopi people also practiced matrilocal residence, in which a new husband becomes part of his mother-in-law's household. For the Hopi, the most widely publicized of Hopi rituals is the Snake Dance, held annually in late August, during which the performers dance with live snakes in their mouths. For these people, the snake is close to the ground, and only the snake can bring the rain down to the earth. They also have corn dances in which the dancers line up face-to-face in two or four long files. They cross over, circle, and interweave in elaborate formations.

The well-known Minoan figurine holding a snake in each hand is now thought to be an acolyte, not the Goddess herself; but there is a second Minoan figurine which is slightly larger: a female who wears a tall purple hat with a white border and stands with her arms extended out and down before her with the palms up. Her right hand offers the head of a long greenish snake spotted with purple, the body of which winds up the upturned underside of her forearm, over her right shoulder, down one side of her back, over her buttocks, up the other side, over her left shoulder, and down her right arm. It is thought that a second snake also winds around her and around her breast and up to the summit of her hat, and it would appear that a third snake entwines her waist, its body forming a formidable knot in the front. However, of the original figurine, only her torso, right arm, head, and part of her hat were found. Perhaps it is one exceptionally long snake which has its head in her right hand and its tail in her left. The way the snaky coils follow the contour of the breast and the reptilian knot at the waist suggests the midwifery of the Cretan women and their power to control lactation and plumb the mysteries of the female pelvis.

It was Ariadne who gave the clue of thread to Theseus so that, when he entered the Labyrinth in search of the Minotaur, he could find his way out again. This clue (or ball) of thread could also be associated with the coiled knot of a snake. It should also be noted that the name of the palace on Crete was the Labyrinth, a name which refers not to a maze but to the double headed axe (The Labrys) which is supposed to have been used in seasonal cults—such as are described in Fraser's *Golden Bow*—to behead the Sacred King at the end of his time of rule. Crete was always associated with snakes as well as bulls and double axes. Apollo fled to Crete for purification, after he had slain the python at Delphi. The bull is of the sea, and the men of Crete are seafarers. The women preside on land. They weave cloth and are famed for their powers with potions and poisons. Do we have here the ship's bull prow defeated by the cunning of the land's loom? Penelope demonstrated that cunning later when beset by over-eager males. In the story of Theseus, are there overtones of a conflict between patriarchy and matriarchy? It was patriarchal tribes from the north who eventually overran Greece and its islands, including Crete and Thera, after that devastating tsunami.

Could that early circle dance on the threshing floor, the epitome of a ritual fusion of phrases and steps, be considered a work rather than a product? Henri Lefebvre elucidates this distinction he makes in *The Production of Space:*

> It may be pointed out right away that, whereas a *work* has something irreplaceable and unique about it, a *product* can be reproduced exactly, and is in fact the result of repetitive acts and gestures. Nature creates and does not produce; it provides resources for a creative and productive activity on the part of social humanity; but it supplies only *use value,* and every use value—that is to say, any product inasmuch as it is not exchangeable—either returns to nature or serves as a natural good. The earth and nature cannot, of course, be divorced from each other.

The Production of Space, p 70

And earth we know through the soles of our feet. The *work* of dance is to celebrate this primordial relationship perceived through the touch of the earth, the sense of its gravitational pull, how we lie on it, kneel on it, stand on it. Dancing is a work of balance, our shifts of balance set to a rhythm. The floor is the dancer's white page, just as the page is the floor on which the words of the poet dance. In ancient times, dances were repeated, along with their gestures each year, accompanied by their sacred words; words sung or intoned as the dance was done, in those early days on Crete or Santorini. Dance could not in itself be separated from its ritual verses any more than it could be divorced from the earth. It had a purpose, in its ceremonial significance: it epitomised the cycle of seed planting and harvest. It was not yet a production. It was a work that grew out of the earth, flourished with the harvest, as did the corn itself. In a real way, the dance was nature.

After the eruption on Santorini and the decline of Mycenaean culture, Dorian invaders from the north took over. This was a mainland tribe, which allied itself to other tribes such as the Heraclidae in order to dominate Greece and the Peloponese. Many Minoan cultural customs were adopted by these invaders, and the chorus evolved into the chorus of the plays, but now with male actors. I detect in this the takeover of isolated island matriarchies, such as we encounter in the *Odyssey*, where the men were off marauding at sea, so that home and hearth were presided over by women; a takeover effected by a people travelling as a horde across the mainland, a horde dominated by a warrior patriarchy. It is interesting to think how, centuries later, isolated Cathar castles high up in the Pyranees maintained the right of the firstborn to inherit, whether male or female, allowing for powerful female rulers and fostering the earliest tradition of courtly love celebrated by male and female poets. Compare this to the emphasis on masculine ferocity we meet in warrior hordes of invaders from the plains—such as the Mongols.

The Tsakonikos danced these days is the most intricate Greek "labyrinth" dance in that slow 5/4 metre. Its variety comes from the many snake-like patterns which the line of dancers may trace. As the name implies, the dance is associated, not with Crete, but with the isolated Tsakonia region of the Peloponnese and it is significant as one of the few local Peloponnesian dances which is still actively danced; otherwise, later Pan-Hellenic dances dominate this part of the mainland. The hold is unusual, with one dancer's right arm hooked in another's crooked left elbow. Did Theseus bring this dance with him to this region, after he had abandoned Ariadne?

4. THE MOLPÊ

The heel in Greece/The chorus/ Molpê—"dance-and-song/What is scansion?

In non-literate cultures, of course, the only way to preserve knowledge is to make it memorizable, and the most efficient way to do this is to render that knowledge into a mental pattern—an invisible dance which only comes alive with the participation of an audience. This even holds true for classical oratory. From antiquity to the Renaissance, the rhetorical art of memory entailed the committing to memory of real or imaginary buildings such as temples, law courts, or cathedrals. A speaker could commit to memory, for example, the four virtues, the seven deadly sins, or a list of Roman emperors, by associating each in succession with the fixed parts of the building. To facilitate this feat of memorization, each part of the building would be equipped with a highly symbolic figure or striking image, to help fix the point for both the speaker and the audience. The individual alcoves or columns were known as the rooms or places, and this comes down to us today in expressions like 'topics' of conversation (from *topoi*, place); a 'commonplace' meaning a cliché; or in the *stanza*—Italian, room—of a poem. *Strophe*, another kind of stanza, described a dance in the Greek choral ode, the chorus pacing in one direction chanting the strophe and back again chanting the antistrophe, arranging the parts of the song in theatrical space.

Michael Donaghy, *The Shape of the Dance*, Picador 2009, p. 8-9

The Northerners who overran Minoan mainland holdings and finally Crete itself may have been patriarchal barbarians, but just as English and Norman society eventually integrated, so the Mycenaean Greeks took on many of the attributes of Minoan civilization. Nothing alters the fact that this is a region of islands and peninsulas, so many aspects of the sea's culture persisted into Mycenaean times. Naturally, harvesting the wheat and threshing its grain continued, and the threshing circles provided a focus for village life. Greece was not controlled by a single dynastic power such as presided over Babylon or the Nile delta. Each village had its *demos*—its people—and the threshing floor became the meeting ground where political decisions might be discussed. Sometimes, a bench or a seat of stone would be provided on the slope above for elders to sit on. The Greeks seem to have understood difference and the fusion of differences. Perhaps this is partly due to an accommodation arrived at between Minoan and Mycenaean customs. It's an unusual and at the same time vital aspect of a society's sensibility. Where a single creed prevails in a society, stasis is its hallmark—or repression.

With the emergence of the maze dances on the threshing-floor came the establishment of the chorus. Initially there may have been one lead singer, and the dancers linked to each other were the chorus, perhaps stepping in unison to the refrain voiced by the community. It's here that we arrive at the fusion of the dance step with the foot of poetic metre. Linking hands, the chorus stepped out the rhythm of the *strophe* in one direction and the *antistrophe* in the other, mapping the trajectory of a plough in a field, and it is worth noting that in the early versions of the alphabet, the Greeks adopted the Phoenician practice of writing from right to left with the letters having a left-facing orientation unlike their own archaic script. This was followed by a period of bidirectional writing, which means that the direction of the writing was in one direction on one line but in the opposite direction on the next, a practice known as *boustrophedon*—which means "the turning of the ox"—as when the ox-drawn plough reaches the end of a furrow. Such writing matches the left to right, right to left progress of the chorus line. Below is an example from the ruins of Gortyn, in central Crete, where some of the ancient laws of Crete are preserved in stone:

Boustrophedon writing can be found on inscriptions in the Agora in Athens, as well as on archaic vases. In boustrophedon inscriptions, non-symmetrical letters change their orientation in accordance to the direction of the line that they are part of, as do the movements of the chorus when the line switches direction on the dance floor. It was only during the latter part of the 5th century BCE that the direction of Greek writing was standardized as left to right, and all the letters adopted a fixed right-facing orientation (perhaps marking a transition from an agriculturally organised society to a more militant one).

Accompanying the narrative of dance and song discovering the subsequent complexities of dramatic theatre, there is the evolution of Greek sculpture from a rigid canon of rules to the liveliness of forthright observation.

Initially those working in stone located the soles of the feet firmly on the ground in a manner that is similar to the Egyptian sense of two footed groundedness on a horizontal plane with one foot in front of the other. The airborne freedom of the Minoans seems to have vanished. Also, there is no clear line from the 6th century BC sculptures of upright *kuroi*—young men with a foot projected forward—to the bas-relief known as Gradiva, who trips confidently along, and which is thought to be a copy of some 4th century BC original. With the *kuroi*, there is no lifting of the back heel from the floor, to demonstrate forward movement, as we see almost exaggerated in Gradiva. It's not that gradually the back heel lifted and the walk became more life-like and dynamic. Rather, the quest for anatomically accurate observation bore fruit when sculptors tackled the body at rest rather than when it was (seemingly) progressing in a forward direction.

I think there has always been a quandary concerning profile. It has always had a somewhat rigid, "official" aspect. Ancient sculptors (whether they worked in a bureaucratic Egyptian milieu or in an archaic Greek one) projected one foot in front of another to show, from angles other than the obvious full-frontal view, that there *were* two feet; or they aligned one foot exactly in front of the other as an expression of measure. It is doubtful whether they were trying to emulate the stride. If it ever did concern progress through space, by the time of the Kritios Boy (480 BC), the dilemma of bodily fluidity was actually being solved by a change in the pose. Later in history, profile portraits in Rennaissance Italy were very concerned with establishing identity, and even today, "mug shots" scrupulously include a profile as well as a full-face view.

On vases, however, Greek draughtsmanship had already begun to master perspective, as Gombrich points out, citing one foot shown with its toes directly facing the viewer while the other foot is in profile: a triumph for observation—as opposed to the rule-bound demonstration of measure that had preceded it on the horizontal floor of early freizes. It's hard to show how sculpture evolved in any smooth transition from the early kuroi to a fluency of movement. The trouble is that on most free-standing sculpture marking the transition from the archaic period (600-500 BC) to the classical period (500-323 BC) the statuary is truncated at the knee, so we can only hypothesise what the pose might have been. However, we do get upright charioteers standing with their feet as grounded as ever, but now these feet are parallel. Then, with the Kritios Boy, we get the sense of the weight being mainly on one foot; not in a walk, but in an easy stance, which is not in forward movement at all: the body is resting more on one foot than the other. It's a stance that will eventually affect the hip and swing the pelvis into what came to be known in the Renaissance as the *cuirasse esthetique*.

Slightly camp, to our eyes maybe, but this manner of showing the standing body persists from Polykleitus to Donatello. Now there is a base leg, sustaining the bulk of the torso, and a leg free of weight with a three-dimensional heel that has been liberated from the horizontal: the ankle of the free leg leads to a foot at ease. Only its big toe rests on the ground. From here, drawing inspiration from sport rather than dancing, observational sculpture develops rapidly. Dying warriors recline along the horizontal, held up for a last breath by the hip and by the elbow, and all parts of the anatomy are fully sculpted, while the invention of the pillar or plinth allows sculptors to rest an elbow of a standing figure on a support, which might be a club in the case of Herakles. This allows for still more of a dynamic shift of weight from two feet to one. But it doesn't concern motion. It concerns repose.

Nevertheless, the freize had also evolved. As the Egyptians had already discovered, bas-relief could provide the support for action more easily than free-standing sculpture: it allowed an easier depiction of movement since the backing wall could work as that support while perspective could enable the expression of troops marching in ranks, or chariots drawn by teams of horses, and then, as the sculptors became more adept, centaurs engaged in mortal combat with Lapiths. Finally, it enabled Gradiva to emerge, who, as the novelist Wilhelm Jenson imagines her, shows her lovely ankle as she moves from stepping stone to stepping stone so as to cross a sunken street in Pompeii.

⁊⪽

THE GREEK WORD MOLPÊ means "dance-and-song."

Apollo was accompanied by the nine muses when he sang to his lyre on Mount Olympus. This "lyre" may have been more like a cithara, or a harp— but it's clear that it was a stringed instrument, and so, in accordance with traditional usage, I will call it a lyre. The reed instruments—pipes—were sacred to Dionysus, so initially these instruments pertained to discrete cults.

The old chorus, or the chorus proper, was always accompanied by the cithara or other kinds of stringed instruments; but when the musical accompaniment was the flute, it was not a chorus, but a *Comus*—a riotous Bacchic procession after a hymeneal banquet in which there was often no lead singer or bard, but every one joined into the song or cry of joy at his pleasure.

The terms "Apollonian" and "Dionysian" are terms used by Nietzsche in *The Birth of Tragedy* to identify two central principles in Greek culture. The Apollonian is seen as the domain of all types of form or structure, since composition emphasises skill and the adherence to a form. Rational thought is also Apollonian: it builds perception and establishes distinctions. The Dionysian impetus is directly opposed to the Apollonian. Drunkenness and madness are Dionysian because they break down the ability to control oneself; so all forms of enthusiasm and ecstasy are Dionysian. One is carried along by the crowd in the revelry, being driven by instinct. Dionysian expression is chaotic. In contemporary poetics this can be a division reduced to the notion of artifice versus sincerity or "being true to oneself." Allen Ginsberg and the "beat" poets are sometimes labled Dionysian (compared to, say, Allen Tate and the fugitives)—though, to my mind, there is plenty of artifice and skill in Ginsberg's supposed ranting— an astute sense of cadence, derived possibly from Hebrew poetics. And the work of his fellow beats shows them to be equally adept at balancing skill with a sense of "letting it all hang out." In dance, a formal discipline such as ballet or "ballroom" might be contrasted with getting high and just "letting go" in a nightclub.

It's worth reminding oneself that the Apollonian paean (or praise-song) is connected to the circle, and to hard work and to the nurturing work of the sun itself, via the *alonia,* while the Dionysian outburst is a spillage, a ramble that was initially associated with the dithyramb: a song to the god of wine that was rough and ecstatic—though pretty soon it became formalised as a competitive chorus for a mass of voices—rather like the *Haka* of the Maoris.

I have said that the Greeks seem to have understood difference and the fusion of differences. One of the most significant of such fusions was when pipes and lyres got to be used together. This suggests the possibility of a dialogue between the measured paean of Apollo and the wild dithyramb of the God of wine. Once the possibility of such a dialogue is established we can see a shared path can lead to the invention of drama, to dramatic dialogue and the representation of voices which may be opposed, even violently, on the democratic ground that is also the dramatic stage which concentrates the attention of an amphitheatre around what was once a threshing floor.

The two gods get together in several ways. In the ancient tradition, it was the *Poietes*, the maker, who composed the Molpê, which was then sung with ecstatic feeling by an *Aoidos* or bard. We see this tradition revived in the Middle Ages. The Occitan troubadours of Southern France and the trouvères of the North were aristocrats, or poets favoured by the aristocracy. They would compose the albas, sestinas and pastorelas that the less privileged jongleurs and minstrels would take from court to court, from castle to castle and from town to town, singing them for the lords and ladies who had written them. This is how Bertran de Born set the hostile castles surrounding his own against each other.

> Anyone who has read anything of the troubadours knows well the tale of Bertran of Born and My Lady Maent of Montaignac, and knows also the song he made when she would have none of him, the song wherein he, seeking to find or make her equal, begs of each pre-eminent lady of Langue d'Oc some trait or some fair semblance: thus of Cembelins' her 'esgart amoros' to wit, her love-lit glance, of Aelis her speech free-running, of the Vicomtess of Chalais her throat and her two hands, at Roacoart of Anhes her hair golden as Iseult's; and even in this fashion of Lady Audiart 'although she would that ill come unto him' he sought and praised the lineaments of the torse. And all this to make 'Una dompna soiseubuda' a borrowed lady or as the Italians translate it 'Una donna ideale'.

Ezra Pound—Note to *'Na Audiart,* Selected Poems, 1959

Then de Born sent out his jongleur to sing this song at the neighbouring castles, and of course all the great ladies grew envious of each other's attributes, and thus became averse to their husbands joining forces and obliging them to ally themselves with their own rivals in beauty, and ganging up against the author of this divisive song. You get an evocation of this story in Pound's *Near Périgord*.

In the *Récits d'un Ménestrel de Reims* it is suggested that the crusading King Richard Coeur de Lion was arrested in 1192, while attempting to return to England via Europe. He was taken prisoner by Duke Leopold of Austria who he had offended at the Siege of Acre (by removing the Duke's raised colours from the walls of that captured town). The legend has it that a minstrel named Blondel went in search of him, going from castle to castle, singing Richard's songs and seeking the whereabouts of his master. At last one day, while singing one of Richard's songs near the walls of Dürnstein castle, he sang a particular song that only he and Richard knew, and from a window high in a tower the imprisoned Richard replied with the second verse—thus identifying where he was imprisoned. Subsequent pressure from the English on Leopold got Richard released. It's a good story, if apocryphal, since Leopold made no secret of the King's whereabouts while negotiating his very hefty ransom. It does demonstrate that a minstrel could be singing a song composed by a king.

Well before that, in the ideal age that inspired the ancient Greeks, there was one bard, the teller of the whole story, who was accompanied by dancers; such a bard as King Alcinous commands should sing for Ulysses in the eighth book of *The Odyssey* as described by Homer, in pentameter—in Chapman's version:

'Some one with instant speed to Court retire
And fetch Demodocus his soundfull lyre.'
    This said the God-grac't king, and quicke resort
Pontonous made for that fair harpe to Court.
    Nine of the lot-chusde publique Rulers rose,
That all in those contentions did dispose,
Commanding a most smooth ground, and a wide,
And all the people in faire game aside.
    Then with the rich harpe came Pontonous,
And in the midst took place Demodocus.
About him then stood forth the choise yong men
That on man's first youth made fresh entry then,
Had Art to make their naturall motion sweet
And shooke a most divine dance from their feete,
That twinckld Star-like, mov'd as swift and fine,
And beat the aire so thinne they made it shine.
Ulysses wonderd at it, but amazd
He stood in minde to hear the dance so phras'd.

Chapman

Perhaps that ideal age constituted a Minoan haunting, a nostalgia for the already gone. The last line here is most interesting. Perhaps it is simply Chapman's version of the Greek, but what it suggests is the reverse of how one might have supposed it. Surely it implies that it is not the dancers who are accompanying the rhythm of the words with their feet; it is the singer who is fitting his words to their steps, finding his phrases through their dancing. So it is not that their movements are attuned to the rhythm of his words, their feet marking the ictus (or accent) of his verbal foot, instead it is that his expressions are attuned to the stamp of their feet, finding the rhythm of his poem through their dancing. This makes sense of the hint we get that the dancing group was initially silent and that it was the entire community gathered there at the dancing space who originally voiced the refrains and responses. It was only later that the dancers started to speak in unison as they danced, and became the chorus, which was another mile-stone on the road to drama—marking an initial division of voices, the single voice speaking, and chosen voices in unison responding to it before an audience. Later still, there came about a separation into specialised roles, dancers and singers, and these groups might be further subdivided into first chorus and second or even third chorus, each with its own conductor.

An alternative translation of the passage from the Odyssey quoted above suggests that "first the divine ground must be smoothed and prepared for the dancing." Gilbert Murray, in *The Classical Tradition in Poetry*, expresses surprise at this. He also finds it curious that, "Demodocus did not sing a lyric or a mere song; he sang a regular lay or a narrative poem." The blind Demodocus sings for Ulysses of Venus and Mars and their clandestine affair (Chapman utilises the Latin names for Homer's characters, so I'll do the same for now). The lay he recites is 125 lines long. Being blind, he hears the rhythm as the dancers stamp it out, feels it through the vibrations caused by their feet, feels it through the soles of his own feet. No wonder the floor is divine, for it communicates. Think how often dance generates sound without the need for extrinsic musical accompaniment: the heels of flamenco stamping out a *zapateado*, the chinking ankle bells of Kathakali. Dance is often percussive, utilising the floor as its drum.

❧

APOLLO IS SPOKEN OF AS "Striking his lyre, stepping fair and high." In these ancient times the recitation seems also to have been danced by the bard. Gilbert Murray tells us:

> The dancing was as integral a part of the bard's duty as his singing or his invention. That explains the punishment of Thamyris the Thracian, who boasted with his new-fangled sort of poetry to surpass the Muses: "And they in wrath made him a maimed man, and took away from him his heavenly Song and made him forget his harping." Scholars have taken the word πηρόν, maimed or lame, to mean something different, because to later ages lameness was no great disqualification to a poet. They thought Thamyris must have been struck blind or dumb. But a passage in Aratus' poem about the stars really settles the matter. He describes there a constellation called *The Man on his Knees*, and explains how this man trails wearily on one knee because he is lame; and the scholiast explains that the man is Thamyris. The curse of the Muses was terribly complete. Thamyris used to sing, to harp, and to dance; and they disabled him from all three.

Gilbert Murray, *The Classical Tradition in Poetry, p.33*

Stepping was high to mark what was then identified as the *ársis*—from the Ancient Greek verb "to lift". It signifies "the lifting of the foot, its removal from the ground, raised in order to supply the measure of the metre." The ancient Greek word *thésis* means "I put, set, place," and it signifies "the setting down, the placing of the foot on the ground." In Greek scansion *arsis* is an unaccented note, the upbeat or the "and"—but Ancient Greek was unaccented and depended on long and short syllables. However, this sense of quantity is difficult to utilise in Latin and in English poetry which are both definitely accented. So a reversal has taken place, and in Latin and English poetry *arsis* is the stressed syllable, that is, the *ictus*—the syllable upon which the stress falls. For the Greeks, I guess the raising would have taken longer than the placing, so it marked the long syllable. We now "sense" the stress with the "drop" into the step. The drop denotes the accent. In English orthometry, *arsis* or *ictus* refers to the stressed syllable, *thesis* refers to the unstressed syllable.

The accent in metre refers to metrical quality (is it stressed or unstressed?). Quantity refers to length—so *moon* is longer than *tip*. But in English it is often debatable whether a syllable is long or short, so scansion by quantity has largely been neglected by our poets—it's considered unworkable in an accented language. Robert Bridges made a valiant attempt to work with quantity in his *Poems in Classical Prosody,* published in 1903. At the time these experiments were dismissed as failures, but I find much to recommend lines such as these:

My Japanese paintings, my fair blue Cheney, Hellenic
Statues and Caroline silver, my beautiful Aldines,
Prized more highly because so few, so fondly familiar,
Need no tongue to defend them against rude hands, that assail them
Only because their name is RARITY; hands insensate,
Rending away pitilessly the fair embroideries of life,
That close-clustering man, his comfort pared to the outskirts
Of his discomfort, may share in meanness unenvied
But what if I unveil the figure that closely beside you
Half hides his Hell-charred skeleton with mysteries obscene,
That foul one, that Moloch of all Utopias, ancient
Poisoner and destroyer-elect of innumerous unborn?

Epistle 2—To a Socialist in London

In the main, critics have ridiculed attempts to utilise quantity when composing poetry in English. Thomas E. Jenkins points out that:

The difficulties involved are numerous. Greek and Roman poetry was based on quantitative metres, in which syllables are considered long or short depending on vowel length. Traditional English prosody, by contrast, is usually regulated by accent and line length; syllable length is at best a tertiary consideration. The least effective way to duplicate classical metres, then, is to compose English poetry by counting the vowel length of individual syllables.

In his devastating review of W. J. Stone's *On the Use of Classical Metre in English,* the distinguished classicist and poet A. E. Housman declared that Stone's method (of counting English "long" and "short" syllables) created "verses of no sort, but prose in ribands"; he further demonstrated the folly of Stone's *vade mecum* on "classical metres" by hilariously imposing a weakly accented native French metre, the Alexandrine, onto ordinarily strongly accented English words.

Why does not a lobster ever climb trees or fly?
Can he not? Or does he think it would look silly?
I have made these verses as well as I am able
You must be to blame if they sound disagreeable.

(*Antiquity Now: The Classical World in the Contemporary American Imagination,* Cambridge University Press, 2015)

The ridicule is undeserved, if applied to the experiments by Bridges, since these produce fascinating and unusual results, even if they hardly prove that quantity "works" in English. I like Housman's observation (which he makes elsewhere) that "English quantities really die into each other like the hues of the rainbow."

Quantity is very affected by the formants we use to create vowel sounds. Formants concern the several prominent bands of frequency that determine the phonetic quality of a vowel. The dominant harmonic that is augmented by a resonance in our larynx dictates what we hear as an A, an E, an I, an O or a U. As children we learn to make capital *A* sounds, short flat *a* sounds, and long *aah* sounds—all of which have their uses, as with the same variations of every vowel. The different frequencies of the vowel sounds, doubled vowels and vowel shifts as in dipthongs all create a sensation of varying lengths (quantities)—and this length may be shortened or extended by the consonants that introduce or complete the vowel. "Sh" will seem longer than "K", "M" will seem longer than "P"—because we form some consonants with plosive lip movements and some with open or mildly compressed lip movements. "Shawl" sounds longer than "Tip". "Moon" sounds longer than "Bet". While it may seem absurd to martial these varying lengths into some measurable system, there is no doubt that poets make use of these differences to create onomatopoeic effects. Think of Tennyson's:

The moan of doves in immemorial elms,
And murmuring of innumerable bees.

Or the contrast implicit in MacBeth's attempt to wash the guilt from his
bloody hands that can only implicate him further:

The multitudinous seas incarnadine,
Making the green one red.

My view is that a "feel" for quantity is a useful attribute. *Myrrh* seems a
word that can last forever. Doubled vowels—as in *moon*—or words with
two vowels, as in *cairn*—certainly feel longer as they are enunciated, and
"U" is quite often a vowel sound that seems lengthy. U, O, A, E, I might
be an interesting way to think of vowel sounds and their heights. Yes, I said
heights. As well as a difference in length there seems to me a difference in
their vertical stretch. This accesses a physicality about word-weaving. And
poets (Clark Coolidge for example) can immerse themselves in this material physicality, just as Jackson Pollock or Frank Auerbach may immerse
their painting in the physicality of paint and colour. W. J. Stone's mistake
was to attempt to develop a system out of all this.

Perhaps we are now considering poetry as a dance in itself, a physical dance of our lips and our throats. In the preamble, we considered
how the Spondee (two strong syllables) and the Pyrrhic (two unstressed
syllables) metres that were commonly used in the quantitive verse of the
ancient Greeks seem hard to fit into the verse of an accented language
such as English, but we should acknowledge that Gerard Manley Hopkins
made these metrical units come alive in English, with his notion of "sprung
rhythm":

I caught this morning morning's minion, king-
dom of daylight's dauphin, dapple-dawn-drawn Falcon, in his riding
Of the rolling level underneath him steady air, and striding
High there, how he rung upon the rein of a wimpling wing
In his ecstasy! then off, off forth on swing,
As a skate's heel sweeps smooth on a bow-bend: the hurl and gliding

Rebuffed the big wind. My heart in hiding
Stirred for a bird,—the achieve of; the mastery of the thing!

Brute beauty and valour and act, oh, air, pride, plume, here
Buckle! AND the fire that breaks from thee then, a billion
Times told lovelier, more dangerous, O my chevalier!

No wonder of it: shéer plód makes plough down sillion
Shine, and blue-bleak embers, ah my dear,
Fall, gall themselves, and gash gold-vermillion.

(To Christ our Lord)

These days, measuring line length by syllable-count (syllabics) has a well-respected modernist reputation, and was often used by the brilliant, but all too often unacknowledged F. T Prince. When quantity is taken into account, lines of an equal syllable count will not be heard to balance each other exactly. The number of stresses per line may also vary. I can see why this appeals to modernists. On the one hand, there is a regularity—the common number of syllables per line—but it constitutes a formal regularity that deliberately allows for variety. This modifies the threat of monotony that all too often affects verse with some traditionally regular scansion and ABAB rhyme scheme. Here Dylan Thomas uses a seven-syllable line:

In my craft or sullen art
Exercised in the still night
When only the moon rages
And the lovers lie abed
With all their griefs in their arms…

Syllabic poetry can also take a stanzaic form, as in Marianne Moore's poem "No Swan So Fine", in which the corresponding lines of each stanza have the same number of syllables.

"No water so still as the
    dead fountains of Versailles." No swan,

with swart blind look askance
and gondoliering legs, so fine
    as the chintz china one with fawn-
brown eyes and toothed gold
collar on to show whose bird it was.

Lodged in the Louis Fifteenth
    Candelabrum-tree of cockscomb-
tinted buttons, dahlias,
sea urchins, and everlastings,
    it perches on the branching foam
of polished sculptured
flowers—at ease and tall. The king is dead.

In an article in the Guardian, James Fenton pointed out that W. H. Auden once wrote a poem where each line had the same number of words. Forms can become quite arbitrary; limitations, artificially imposed. Such limitations may work, or they may not. It depends on the genius of the poet.

❦

AS APOLLO, OR HIS SURROGATE THE BARD, steps high in their midst, Murray identifies the Molpê with the worship of nature, which is unsurprising considering the dancing-ground's origin in the threshing-floor. The singing and the dancing might be tragic or comedic—the tragedy connected to the "death" of the old year and the comic with the birth of the new one—and he points out that most tragedies end in a death and most comedies culminate in a wedding. Here we might note an affinity with the notions prompted by that eternal feeling epitomised by the stillness of Egyptian stone sculpture, for rhythm also brings us back to the same place. It is created by repetition, and repetition is reiteration. I am reminded of Alice and the Red Queen, running to stay on the same spot.

This recurrence also brings to mind Nietzsche's concept of the eternal return. In psychoanalysis, it is often observed that the symptom is returned to again and again. The return of the repressed, the return of the drive, the return of desire, may all feature in the landscape of psychological suffering, the melancholy landscape of Milton's *Il Penseroso*—but repetition also features in the dancing that spreads out across the joyous landscape of *L'Allegro*. As Murray puts it: "Human nature loves imitating and loves rhythm." Rhythm reiterates the moment, and thus poetry may suspend time just as artistic representation may suspend it in two or in three dimensions. The songs and dances of Spring must be repeated in order that Spring may return and Dionysus be reborn. Perhaps all development is rehearsal, the step practised in order that the final step may become the acme of all previous stepping, just as the last line is ultimately the epitome of the poem. One of my own earliest poems seeks to express this notion:

THE MOLPÊ

You cannot be sure at which of his seats of worship your god will be, and you may be crying to an empty throne. Gilbert Murray

Dressed in the evening, shall Osiris roar
    For one step, perfect in its final prance,
    Repeatingly, to modify advance,
While nine au pair girls scrub His magic floor?
    The Daemon swarms with nard, with myrrh;
    Flora not to be hoped for here.

Tradition's methods, not tradition's gear,
    Invoke old corn to greet new season.
  Moved by temperament not reason,
Shrill winds plane at the indented year.
    Mountain to mountain, He walks air.
    We are one remove from His musical chair.

(From *Inside the Castle*, Barrie & Rockliffe the Cresset Press, 1969)

But it is not simply that imitation concerns visual art and rhythm concerns poetry. When we look at Minoan art, we are constantly made aware of the rhythm of the beings that are depicted, and their movements, from the curving leaps of dolphins to the curled tails of blue monkeys and the solemn processions of gift-bearers. Equally, the bardic narrative imitates in verse an action that may be mythic or may have actually occurred. The bard recreates history as his fiction. This notion of imitation in words is vital to the ceremonies of Spring and Winter and to the drama that later came into being.

When I was teaching a writing class in Wandsworth jail, there was a young man there who was serving a sentence for criminal assault. Recalcitrant and defensive at first, he plunged into writing when I asked him to describe a violent incident, either actual or imagined. He chose to set down a story describing a fight in a pub which culminated in someone getting "glassed" with a broken bottle. He wrote steadily for a good part of an hour, then read out his account. At the end of his reading he looked elated. He told me that doing this bit of writing was the most exciting thing he had ever done.

The boy had discovered fiction for himself, just as the Greeks discovered it for humanity. Whether "actual" or imagined, the glassing became fiction by being put into words. The actions had become more than facts, mythic, if you like. The Greeks had rules for the dramas which they made out of imagined actualities; rules which kept the action credible, such as the stricture that death must occur offstage—in all probability too many soldiers in the audience would have scoffed at the ketchup, had a death been "faked". But the god, whichever it was, who bestowed upon us the gift of creating fiction deserves our highest praise. It's the invention of "as if"—*as if* we were fighting, *as if* we had married our own mother, *as if* we had killed our children, *as if* we were forbidden to bury our dead. "As if" enables us to imagine even an enemy's point-of-view, even a rival's perspective. Small wonder drama and democracy emerged together. Drama enables a difference to be "entertained", registered, that is, just as hostile points of view have equal rights to an airing in the house. To encourage this acceptance of the other is the deep task of dramatic "entertainment", just as to accept the registration of difference is a vital aspect of democracy. Views hostile to each other may be expressed, and verse may even invest both views with rhythmic beauty, so that a view one does not share may be appreciated for the aptness of its dramatic expression in the play.

It is likely that some mimesis akin to fiction established the art of dancing. We have mentioned the imitation of the dances of birds and noted dance's origins in the Minoan threshing-circle, where Cora Greenhill has suggested that, "the criss-crossing steps that still characterise Greek dance were originally the kicking of the grain to separate it from the straw." Here we are dancing "as if" we were threshing. *Mimesis* is an alchemical quality. War is unpleasant, but to "play" at war is fun—as every child knows. Drama is deeply entertaining, even when it deals with what would be some monstrous act in actuality. In a similar way, toil is unpleasant, but to mimic toil turns out to be a pleasure. Morris dances have planting, reaping and shooting actions, while age-old dances with wooden staves known as "sword-play" dances may be connected with actions concerned with sheep-shearing. And then there is the Crane dance and the Eagle dance—which can be found in Greece today as well as in the repertoire of the dances of native Americans.

Poetic drama and mimetic dance both stimulate our imaginations, and imagining is vital to our evolution. We would never have built a house, had we not been able to imagine it before it was built.

As the bronze age evolved, the nature of the ground evolved also. For the Egyptians, in the land of the flooding Nile, the ground was ultimate stability: something so firm a pyramid could be built on it. It was horizontal: a level. For the Minoans, the floor was the sea threshing the waves into the chaff of spume, as the chaff was tossed to the wind on the threshing floor. To the Greeks, the floor was a fiction: it could be the shore outside mythic Troy, it could be Lemnos in bygone days, where Philoctetes has been abandoned. The ground was both sea and land. For the Greeks, it was the stage.

And it is interesting also that the nine "umpires" presiding over the Molpê given for Ulysses were "lot-chusde"—chosen by chance. Perhaps democracy evolved out of the lottery. People have always gambled—that goes back to the caves.

※

DANCERS CAN STEP IN TIME OR BE OUT OF TIME. A line of poetry can scan or it can be said not to scan. Let us explore this notion of "scansion". What exactly is meant by it? The received opinion is that it refers to the process of counting the metrical feet in a line, so that we would expect five in pentameter, six in hexameter. We might say that this line of pentameter scans with that when looking at two lines both with five feet in them. If one of the lines proved to be hexameter rather than pentameter, we might say, these lines do not scan.

> Shall I compare thee to a summer's day
> While the nine umpires happen to preside over the Molpê?

Here the second line does not scan with the first, not only because there are more than five stressed syllables in it but also because its prose rhythm (1 _11_1_ _11_ _ 1_) does not conform to the iambic pentameter of the first line. So, as well as not agreeing with the line above, it does not scan in itself: it does not obey the pattern of iambic metre.

An understanding of the nature of the foot, and how there must be some agreement to the number of feet in each line, is essential if one wants to understand metre and the notion of lines scanning. Each line in a true quatrain has four feet, that is the nature of their agreement. Of course you could also have four line stanzas of pentameter. However, it is worth bearing in mind that often, at the beginning of an iambic line, the iambic foot may be reversed, as we have seen in Milton, and that Edmund Spenser, in *The Faerie Queen* (1596) and in other poems, would add a six-stress hexameter line to each of his eight-lines of pentameter (the stanzas therefore consisting of nine lines). Since this happens in each stanza, our ear soon grows accustomed to this winding up of the stanza with an extra foot, so the stanzas scan, even if the eighth line of each stanza does not scan with the ninth. His follower Phineas Fletcher used a similar technique with his seven-line stanzas in *The Purple Island:*

> This drum is made of substance hard and thin:
> Which if some falling moisture chance to wet,
> The loudest sound is hardly heard within:
> But if it once grows thick, with stubborn let,
> It bars all passage to the inner room;

No sounding voice unto his seat may come:
The lazy sense still sleeps, unsummon'd with his drum.

Fletcher is describing the ear-drum in this book-length poem which maps out the human anatomy as if this were an island and the poem its geographic record. The poem admits of a wonderful game-like pastime: read your friend a passage, and see if he or she can guess which anatomical part of the body is being described. The Elizabethans had a penchant for this sort of poem that would actively engage reader and listener, in an age when poetry itself was far more popular than prose—perhaps because recitation was more common since it was a time when fewer people could read or write. Another example is Michael Drayton's *Poly-Olbion*—another geographical poem, this time a tour around the whole of England. Here you could read your friend the passage about where you came from, and then she could read you the passage about where she came from. As "pastime" poems, both *The Purple Island* and *Poly-Olbion* work just as well, in my opinion, now as they did then.

Returning to scansion, what is interesting about this sense of agreement is that, when experimenting with the madrigal, Drummond of Hawthornden discovered that prime numbers also scan *with each other* (here it is difference being scanned, whereas in the quatrain it is repetition). What I mean is that there proves to be an aptness about pentameter mixed with trimeter, or even with heptameter. More about primes in later chapters. It should also be noted that in the sixteenth and seventeenth centuries, while poetry was only beginning to emerge from the lutenist's accompaniment, mixed metre of all varieties was fairly commonly in use by poets who were composing lyrics—which were often actually sung—as can be seen in Henry Vaughan's lyrics, and those by Thomas Campion. Lutenists might through compose, taking each syllable of the lyric into account.

But this was indeed an experimental age that eventually emancipated poetry from musical accompaniment. Certain verses by Campion use mixed metre and even do away with rhyme. This could be the first example of free verse.

Rose-cheek'd Laura, come,
Sing thou smoothly with thy beauty's
Silent music, either other
Sweetly gracing.

Lovely forms do flow
From consent divinely framed;
Heav'n is music, and thy beauty's
Birth is heavenly.

These dull notes we sing
Discords need for helps to grace them;
Only beauty purely loving
Knows no discord,

But still moves delight,
Like clear springs renew'd by flowing,
Ever perfect, ever in them-
Selves eternal.

Campion's lines are a refreshing antidote to the tight stanza forms more commonly used by the Elizabethans, which are so ideal for "lyric poetry". I detect that the tighter the form, the simpler the content—not in terms of simplicity of thought, but in terms of their requiring a limitation of content to a single specific idea—abuse, melancholy, love. The taut pattern allows the poet to elaborate upon the theme. It was a particular aspect of the originality of Lady Mary Wroth that she insisted on choosing elaborate issues of emotional psychology, in a thoroughly contemporary way, while refusing to jettison the strictures of the pattern she had chosen (though I think that she may have finally abandoned her arch-lute).

᷁

WHY IS GREEK METRE SO OFTEN STUDIED as a key to English poetics? Gilbert Murray tells us that originally, when Ancient Greek was spoken:

One syllable in any long word was apt to be spoken on a note higher than the rest; our authorities say that in extreme cases it could be higher by a whole fifth. This peculiarity had apparently no effect on metre in classical times and was not marked in any way in the script. But during the Hellenistic period, when the civilization and language of Greece were spreading rapidly over all the Mediterranean world, foreigners found this "tone" difficult to reproduce. Hence the marks of acute, grave, and circumflex "accents," or "tones," were introduced into Greek writing in order to help the barbarians to speak correctly; and, as one might have expected, the barbarians first carefully learned their accents and then pronounced them all wrong. Instead of speaking the "tone" syllable on a higher musical note they merely spoke it with a violent stress. And this stress-accent, apparently unknown to classical Greece, gradually prevailed in most parts of the Mediterranean world, and had completely driven out quantity from the spoken language by about the fourth century A.D. It is extremely strong in modern Greek.

The Classical Tradition in Poetry, p.86

Because its long and short syllables and its tones evolved into the accented stress of Latin verse which generally accords with the *arsis* and *thesis* to be found in our own words and phrases, ancient Greek poetry has provided us with a model. Other early languages have characteristics that differ from this analysis of the *ictus*. Gilbert Murray has this to say about Hebrew poetry.

A great deal has been written of late years about Hebrew metre, and it may be that some discovery will be made which will completely change our conception of it. But, on the existing evidence, it seems that the verse of the ancient Hebrews cannot be called metrical. It had not really analysed words into syllables. Following ancient Babylonian models, it was content with the rhythm produced by parallel clauses, generally in sets of two; true, these clauses are expected to be approximately equal in length, but it is equally important for them to be cognate in meaning and parallel in grammatical structure. Thus it is not the metre that makes the verse: it is a general parallelism, in which a rough similarity of length is one factor. For example, Job, xxii, 9:

Thou hast sent widows away empty,
>And the arms of the fatherless have been broken.
>Therefore snares are round about thee
>>And sudden fear troubleth thee.
>Or darkness that thou canst not see
And abundance of waters cover thee.

In Hebrew it is probable, although not traditionally assured, that each line has three strong stresses, and therefore each couplet equals 3+3. This rule is said to hold throughout the book of Job, whereas in Lamentations and elsewhere a long line is followed by a shorter one, probably three stresses by two; as in Amos, v, 2:

>She is fallen to rise no more:
>>The virgin of Israel.
>She is forsaken upon her land:
>>None to raise her.

It is worth remarking that Josephus, who had the Greek conception of metre and was anxious to argue that his own nation was quite equal to the Greeks, describes the 3 + 3 form of Hebrew poetry as a hexameter. It is curious to see how Hebrew poetry was held back in its development by this initial lack of artistic analysis: it never analysed words into syllables.

The Classical Tradition in Poetry, p.87-8

Nevertheless, of course, Smart, Whitman and Ginsberg have all made great gains through an understanding of these cadences in Hebrew verse. It is as if there is a genre somewhere between prose and poetry best illustrated by King James's Version of the Bible.

Murray also takes a stab at elucidating the nature of Chinese poetry: Chinese poetry—so far as one entirely ignorant of the language can understand what scholars say of it—has no syntax, no inflections, no words longer than monosyllables, and no metre beyond a plain counting of words—or of syllables, since there is no distinction between the two. No lines are longer than seven syllables, while five-syllable lines are the commonest, and four-syllable lines are recognized as classic. The seven-syllable and five-syllable lines are divided by a regular caesura. So far it would seem as if Chinese poetry was deficient in almost all the elements that to us make rhythm or music in verse. On the other hand, it insists on rhyme, presumably because it has so little metrical structure that even a poem of four-syllable lines cannot maintain itself to the ear without rhyme. And it also insists on a quality which has no equivalent at all in our verse: every syllable has to have its musical "tone," and the sequence of tones has to follow definite rules. This sequence and alternation of tones must, one would imagine, be the main difficulty in composing Chinese verse, and must make the most essential and obvious difference between verse and prose. Yet it is a property which our European poetry does not possess at all.

The Classical Tradition in Poetry, p. 89-90

Earlier, though, I mentioned how, to my ear, when Chinese poetry is being recited—four short words or syllables followed by a long syllable—the tick-tock effect causes a stress to fall on the first and the third short syllable. Verse retains the downbeat and upbeat of the walk, and its rhythm can still be felt.

※

THE CONNECTION BETWEEN STEP AND FOOT is particularly applicable to the notion of stressed and unstressed syllables that ultimately emerged out of the classic tradition of Greece and Rome. We need to bear in mind that the poetry of other cultures may depend on different language structures, and that Hebrew and Chinese poetry, for instance, may have developed in different ways because poetic composition was less associated with pedestrian movement in their cultures; more with being seated, perhaps, an instrument in the hands.

Here, it is worth citing a difference noted in Persian poetry between walking and sedentary poets. Rumi (1207 to 1273), for instance, is considered a walker. This celebrated Sufi poet was born in the east of Persia, but his family fled west during the Mongol invasion, and he lived most

of his life in the Sultanate of Rum, in present-day Turkey. A great travel-
ler, he came under the influence of Greek culture, and composed several
verses in Graeco-Persian. Hearing the tapping of goldsmiths near Konya,
he went into an ecstatic state, whirling and spinning as he improvised. He
wrote plenty of mystical love-lyrics, but also the *Mathnawi*: an exhaustive
companion to plumbing one's potential in full awareness of the external
world and its realities. Its poetic structure is the rubā'iyāt—quatrains utilising rhyming couplets, and as a whole the poem is structured as a journey
from the beginning of awareness and continuing through to the process of
removing the will to permit one's essential humanity to express itself. His
poetry abounds in walking imagery: "As you start to walk on the way, the
way appears." "Keep walking, though there's no place to get to."

Hafiz (1320 to 1389), by contrast, may be considered a sedentary poet.
He lived most of his life in Shiraz. He is considered one of the finest lyricists in the Persian language. A devout Sufi, he lived about the same time
as Chaucer in England. At 60, he is said to have begun a *Chilla-nashini*,
a 40-day-and-night vigil by sitting in a circle that he had drawn for himself. On the 40th day, he met with the physician Zayn al-Attar and was
offered a cup of wine. It was then that he is said to have attained "Cosmic
Consciousness". He hints at this episode in one of his verses in which he
advises the reader to attain "clarity of wine" by letting it "sit for 40 days".
He wrote no more than ten ghazels (mystical lyrics) per year. The structural requirements of the ghazal are similar in stringency to those of the
Petrarchan sonnet.

Hafiz uses a variety of terms to indicate words set to music and/or
the melodies that accompany lyrics. The Persian ghazal emerged in the
Ghaznavid period as a verse composed by poets for singers to perform, and
he frequently associates the words *ḡaz*al and qawl with music, singers and
songbirds. He is pictured sitting near a chang-player (a form of harp). His
poetry is carefully crafted—utilising fricatives, onomatopoeia, word music
and extra-prosodic sonorities. The poetics of Hafez depends on a sensuality
of language and imagery. Smell, taste, texture, colour and sound imagery abound, often mixed together. The ghazel was also influenced by the
west, its setting being the mystic wine symposium, with its *locus classicus* in
Athens, an influence established in Persia during the Hellenistic period and

later developed into the *kamriyāt* of the Islamic tradition. Nevertheless, the sedentary inclination may have originated in the unaccentuated but musical East rather than in the footsteps of the West.

So the difference between Rumi and Hafiz could be compared to the difference between Dante and Petrarch, or Chaucer and Wyatt, or Ginsberg and Allen Tate.

The connection to walking and stepping is of particular interest to poetry in English, however, and our language owes much to the chorus that continued, in the wake of the Minoans, to physically step out its recitations. That chorus received its first full development in the Doric states, and in them it was particularly connected with the military organisation of these tough Northern Greeks, who had come down from even further north. The Dorians give their name to Doric architecture, the minimalist, essentially functional and unashamed older style of Greek architecture, which was far less fussy than the later Corinthian style with its fluted effeminacy. The Dorian chorus was composed of the same persons who formed their battle-array: the best dancers and the best fighters were called by the same name. This link between warriors and dancers persists throughout history. The Scots and the Cossacks are great dancers, as are Israeli soldiers. *Pedes* in Latin means "foot soldier, one who goes on foot." We now encounter a fifth meaning for "foot"—infantry.

War has always been in as mimetic a relation to drama as drama has been to war. To this day war takes place in theatres. The theatre of the Classic age was capable of describing battle without the presence of death on stage, and its violence was projected through poetry. There were warriors in the audience. Down the ages, soldiers have remained great lovers of poetry. Sir Philip Sidney was a commander on the battlefield and the major poet of his day. Poetry and war have rhythm in common. Rhythm is essential to most martial arts, from fencing to capoeira. Rhythm is synonymous with practice. And practice is essential—if you wish your troops to be successful in any theatre of operations. Drill expresses the essence of practice. Military drill is a form of walking dance. It's a dance in honour of discipline itself, and very much a preparation for the discipline required when the regiment goes into action and comes under fire. As a dance, it places great emphasis on measure and exactitude and essentially on unity and moving in unison.

The bagpipes may accompany the drum; essentially an outdoor instrument because of their loudness. Tunes may be learnt by walking to their rhythm as the pipes do not admit of reading the music as you play. The tunes are in all rhythms (and it is interesting to note how musical notation mirrors poetic form—4/4 rhythm, for instance, is 4 beats to a bar in a phrase of 4 bars, equivalent to 4 feet to a line in a 4-line verse). There's a skirling of the pipes for advancing, for going over the top and for retreating. The art of war is very much a dance. But it was the dances on the threshing floor which first equated words and walking. And then the generals were quick to take advantage of the connection and military drill evolved out of the stepping dance of the chorus.

At the moment that the unit does come under fire, the game is on against chaos and catastrophe. Inconsistency determines to overwhelm repetition. Here the practised drill empowers the improvisation which may be necessary to get out of a tricky situation. Contemporary dancers and performance artists need to be trained as much in improvisation as in the acquisition of specific skills. In Russia the armed services are as much performers as the Bolshoi.

When a sergeant major barks "Left, left, left, right, left," at his squad, his "left" is on the downbeat while his "right" is on the upbeat. The upbeat is the musical "and". Therefore, it corresponds to the *thesis*—our unaccented syllable—while the *arsis* (the strong beat, the *ictus*) falls on the left. Scansion, as we know it, and as we have seen, comes from this connection of the marching step with the metrical foot known as the trochee.

Taking a slower pace, "Left and right and left and right puts the upbeat on the *and*, and now, while both left and right steps are on the downbeat, the first and the third downbeats (the left steps) are the strong beats. This can be sensed in many a melody—the last step of the bar being onto the right foot. It is as if the strong beat always evoked a response from the subsidiary beat. One senses this particularly strongly with trochaic verse.

The pastoral impulse in poetry sometimes manages to utilise this martial rhythm with considerable subtlety.

> Though my carriage be but careless,
>> Though my looks be of the sternest,

Yet my passions are compareless;
    When I love, I love in earnest.

No; my wits are not so wild,
    But a gentle soul may yoke me;
Nor my heart so hard compiled,
    But it melts, if love provoke me

From Thomas Weelkes' *Airs or Fantastic Spirits*, 1608

We have seen trochees used before, by Lady Mary Wroth. Does the trochaic, a march-like rarity compared to iambic verse, appeal to poets who happen to be women? Even this poem attributed to Thomas Weelkes suggests to me a female protagonist. It is tempting to call this an 'ironic' use, and risk accusations of sexism. However, in the mainstream of so many previous centuries women have been seen as filling a role other than warlike, so there is an irony, even if it is historical. Of course, in the pastoral undercurrent, idyllic Arcadias and Uranias abound in helmeted heroines, fierce huntresses and companions of Diana. Here, in the trochaic mode, I sense an almost suffragette emphasis. Yes, I'm a woman, and yes, I've got strong opinions. This is what the metre says to me.

TRADITION,
MODERNISM,
FUSION

1. THE ACCUMULATION OF TRADITION
From the "Unities" of Aristotle to the épaulement of Le Roi Soleil/ The accumulation of tradition in verse and dance.

WHAT HAPPENS WHEN METRE IS ABANDONED; when poets seek to free themselves from a pattern of stressed and unstressed syllables and the regulated rhythm that "conventional" verse imposes on the text? In the ongoing stream that is artistic and literary practice, insight has its heyday with some fresh innovation and then this innovation gets imitated and eventually it becomes an oppressive formula. There is a constant need to overturn accepted requirements when their dynamic fails to deliver, and when they seem to have become travesties of themselves.

For many poets emerging out of the shadow of Swinburne and the Victorian age after a devastating war, rhythm, especially when accompanied by rhyme, seemed old hat, and metre a galloping, non-ironic invitation to participate in heroic feelings of empire—take *The Charge of the Light Brigade* as an example. Metre inferred jingoism. Scansion had been applied by many Victorians with a thumping monotony, obliging meaning to kow-tow to automatically overpowering schemes. Time-honoured though it might have been, scansion now threatened to overwhelm the integrity of thought and image—just as the need for the poem to be "attuned" to the lute threatened to constrain the thorny metaphysics of John Donne and his contemporaries in the seventeenth century, so that eventually the instrument fell out of use.

But feeling was under attack as well. Wilfred Owen was not included in the first edition of the *Oxford Book of Modern Verse,* edited by W. B. Yeats in 1936, despite the anguish of his war poems. Absent from the pages of this anthology were all the poets of The Great War—Owen, Sassoon, Blunden, Rosenberg and all their comrades who had written and, in some cases, died during the war. Yeats explains his editorial decision in this passage from the introduction:

> I have a distaste for certain poems written in the midst of the great war; they are in all anthologies, but I have substituted Herbert Read's 'End of the War' written long after. The writers of these poems were invariably officers of exceptional courage and capacity, one a man constantly selected for dangerous work, all, I think, had the Military Cross; their letters are vivid and humorous, they were not without joy—for all skill is joyful—but felt bound, in the words of the best known, to plead the suffering of their men. In poems that had for a time considerable fame, written in the first person, they made that suffering their own. I have rejected these poems for the same reason that made Arnold withdraw his "Empedocles on Etna" from circulation; passive suffering is not a theme for poetry. In all the great tragedies, tragedy is a joy to the man who dies; in Greece the tragic chorus danced
>
> (From the *Introduction*, p. xxxiv).

Yeats was in all likelihood reacting to the words of Wilfred Owen. In June, 1918, a few months before he was killed at the front, Owen was preparing *Disabled and Other Poems* for publication. He was drafting these comments as a preface for the book:

> This book is not about heroes. English poetry is not yet fit to speak of them. Nor is it about deeds, or land, nor anything about glory, honour, might, majesty, dominion, or power, except War. Above all I am not concerned with Poetry. My subject is War, and the pity of War. The Poetry is in the pity.

But for the emerging modern sensibility, this was still old-fashioned, sentimental. The poems of the war poets could be seen as just as guilty of instigating an appeal to humanity and emotion as Tennyson's glorification of heroics. Yeats explains, in a letter to Dorothy Wellesley:

> When I excluded Wilfred Owen, whom I consider unworthy of the poets' corner of a country newspaper, I did not know I was excluding a revered sandwich-board Man of the revolution & that somebody has put his worst & most famous poem in a glass-case in the British Museum—however if I had known it I would have excluded him just the same. He is all blood, dirt & sucked sugar stick (look at the selection in Faber's anthology—he calls poets 'bards,' a girl a 'maid,' & talks about 'Titanic wars'). There is every excuse for him but none for those who like him.

Yeats is complaining about antiquated verbiage, and this raises an age-old source of friction between tradition and invention. Ezra Pound's dictum, "Make it new," was a clarion call to the writers of his generation; a phrase that expressed the desire to get right away from old-fashioned language and any appeal to sentiment, to shake off the shackles of played out patterns, to discover new ones or bring back unusual forms that had long been forgotten.

But today, what is difficult to comprehend is how the moderns failed to grasp that the reality of war had abruptly shifted the gears of poetry. In 1909, a love-lorn C.K. Scott-Moncrieff could write:

> Thinking Love's Empire lay along that way
> Where the new-duggen grave of friendship gaped,
> We fell therein, and, weary, slept till day.
> But with the sun you rose, and clean escaped,
> Strode honourably homewards…

> Poetry notebook, Lanark, april 1909, quoted in *Chasing Lost Time: the Life of C.K. Scott-Moncrieff* by Jean Findlay, *p.59* (Vintage) 2014

However, by 2018, having experienced warfare, and invalided out, he would write, in *Silver Badgeman*:

Houses I hate now, who have seen houses strewn,
A bitter matter for battle, by sun and by moon,
Stones crumbled, bricks broken, timbers charred and rotten,
And the smell of a ghost of a house; these are ill-forgotten.

Gardens too, I hate; for I have seen gardens going
Into green slime and brown swamp, no flowers growing
In pits where old rains linger, stale snows harden,
And only graves, where roses grew, still tell of garden.
And I hate ploughed lands, who have been set a-ploughing
Crooked furrows to fight in, where the guns go sowing
Bodies of men in the trenches, and grey mud covers
Fools, philosophers, failures, labourers, lovers.

Ibid, p.134

Obsolete words, drowsy abstractions and sentiment have given way to an
immediacy of image and an insistence on the reality of what has been gone
through. The wartime experience demanded vividness, and so it tempered
"Georgian" vapourishness—as verse moved deeper into the twentieth century.

All that remained of sentiment was the reality of bitterness. But, for the
most radical of the moderns, even this was suspect. There was an iciness to
their new aesthetic, a concentration on the material quality of each medium.
Writers, artists and composers all felt a need to abandon over-trodden ways
and explore new paths or make fresh tracks. This impulse towards "freedom" was the fanfare sounded by modernism that sent seismic waves of
upheaval through the earlier part of the twentieth century—in tandem
with the actual devastation of its wars. But to fully understand that rebellion against aesthetic conformity, we need to familiarise ourselves with the
deeper nature of the tradition from whose harness the modernists sought
to free themselves.

❧

FIRST OF ALL, THEREFORE, WE MUST DEFINE or at least describe what it
was that modernism was rebelling most deeply against. This will entail

a preliminary review of the history of poetics, of theatre and the dance, the relevant arts for our purposes, to grasp the state these arts were in before modernism. Actually, we need to start our sweep through history way back—with the views of Aristotle.

Aristotle had a flair for categorisation (it was his speciality), and he lists the ingredients that go into a well-made tragedy. He sees verse as a team player in the collaborative work of creating it. He defines tragic drama as mimesis of an action, which should be elevated, complete, and of magnitude, if it is to have its cathartic effect, purging its audience of the ills that led to the awful consequences the play lays before us. He identifies the drama's six components: plot, character, diction, thought, spectacle and lyric poetry. Tragedy has to be a whole, with a beginning, a middle and an end, and it should exhibit a unity of time, space and action. Tragedy is an art of representation that Aristotle considers superior to the epic poem, since it is vivid in performance and achieves the goal of its mimesis in a shorter space of time than the epic and has the capacity to move us more effectively.

In his *Poetics,* therefore, Aristotle is suggesting that poetry, along with the other arts, should seek to serve the noble condition of tragic humanity, as expressed through theatre, for all the arts achieve their culmination in this drama, which is a team effort mutually created by the playwright and his patron and the actors, as well as by the costumier, the architect of the amphitheatre and the musicians.

In the classical period, drama was either comic or tragic. Through the insight of anthropologists like J. G. Frazer, who investigated the origins of these terms in *The Golden Bough,* we get the sense that essentially there is one tragedy and one comedy. As already noted, tragedy is the death of the year, while comedy is its birth: ritualised death is followed by ritualised mating. The "discovery" of drama in ancient Greece came about through the ever more complex combining of artistic, literary and choreographic skills. In drama, as on the threshing floor, the poetry is accompanied by movement. However, it is now more than the stepping of the chorus and the stepping of a principle bard. Dancers need not be linked by the arms. There are solo dancers, while the bardic role has been divided among the actors. Ode and dithyramb have evolved. There is dialogue.

In some ways the drama attests to a loosening of the power of religion, since now the actor can take on the role of one who is dead, or even the role of a god: an appropriation which might have been considered sacrilege in an earlier, more pious age. But what has been retained is the fusion of speech and action. The actors accompany the text through ritualized movements demonstrative of the action; movements such as the Japanese Noh theatre continues to employ today. In ancient Greece, the playwrights themselves were well-versed in dancing: at the age of fifteen, Sophocles was the chief dancer at the triumph of Salamis in 480 BC.

The plots of the ancient Greek plays have to do with heroic characters, that is, larger than life figures, noble spirits who have passed on, for the heroes are always long dead. Certain heroes exert a particular fascination—both Oedipus and Hercules have several plays concerning what happens during their lives or afterwards. In classical drama, the whole is greater than the sum of its parts. This is Aristotle's main contention. The whole that constitutes each play is bound together by those three unities—of time, place and action—and all the components that make up that play are expected to serve its plot and its plot's significance. He felt the same way about sculpture, observing that a sculpture was more than merely that which it might be made out of. Its form, into which it had been hewn, had to be taken into account.

In his meticulously detailed book, *The Ancient Classical Drama: a Study in Literary Evolution*, Oxford 1890, Richard G. Moulton identifies four "Plots of Passion" and two "Plots of Action"—which may take place within the strictures of these unities:

Plots of Passion:

1. An Opening Situation developed to a Climax
2. Development of a Final Situation
3. Development from one situation to another
4. An Opening Situation developed to its reversal

Plots of Action:

5. Complication and Resolution
6. The Pendulum Plot, or Plot of Fortune Turns

Let us look at the last of these, by way of example—the Pendulum Plot. It shapes the development of *Iphigenia in Tauris, Hercules Mad* and *Philoctetes.* In *Philoctetes* by Sophocles (the action concerns a man suffering from an evil-smelling foot!) the plot swings from complication to resolution and then back again to complication. What Moulton has to say about this play can be found in *Appendix 1.* His remarkable analysis cannot be bettered. But here we can see that action may swing back and forth, just as the chorus might sway forward and back, and that *action,* as one of the unities, is integral to the development of the drama.

Taking another play—*Hercules Mad* by Euripides—which also has a pendulum plot, Moulton shows how, when properly used, poetic rhythm mirrors and indeed enhances the action of a play, for instance, when Madness, at the behest of Hera, resolves to send the returning hero mad. As Moulton puts it: "Especially powerful is the transition from blank verse to accelerated rhythm, as handled by Euripides. The typical example in his *Hercules* may be appreciated by the English reader with peculiar force in the translation of Robert Browning. The scene represents the personification of Madness reluctantly dragged by the messenger of heaven to the task of afflicting the hero. As long as Madness hesitates, she speaks blank verse; when at last she yields, and abandons herself to her awful work, the metre bounds into the rapid rhythm, which is made still wilder in the translation."

Madness. This man, the house of whom ye hound me to,
Is not unfamed on earth, nor gods among;
Since, having quelled waste land and savage sea,
He alone raised again the falling rights
Of gods—gone ruinous through impious men.
Desire no mighty mischief, I advise!
Iris. Give thou no thought to Heré's faulty schemes!
Madness. Changing her step from faulty to fault-free!
Iris. Not to be wise did Zeus' wife send thee here!

Madness. Sun, thee I cite to witness—doing what I loathe to do!
But since indeed to Heré and thyself I must subserve,
And follow you quick, with a whizz, as the hounds a-hunt with the huntsman,
Go I will! and neither the sea, as it groans with its waves so furiously,
Nor earthquake, no, nor the bolt of thunder gasping out earth's labour-throe
Shall cover the ground as I, at a bound, rush into the bosom of Herakles.
And home I scatter, and house I batter,
Having first of all made the children fall,—
And he who felled them is never to know
He gave birth to each child that received the blow,
Till the Madness I am have let him go!
Ha, behold, already he rocks his head—he is off from the starting-place!
Not a word, as he rolls his frightful orbs, from their sockets wrenched in the
    ghastly race!
And the breathings of him he tempers and times no more than a bull in the
    act to toss,
And hideously he bellows, invoking the Keres, daughters of Tartaros.
Ay, and I soon will dance thee madder, and pipe thee quite out of thy mind
    with fear!
So, up with the famous foot, thou Iris, march to Olumpos, leave me here!
Me and mine, who now combine, in the dreadful shape no mortal sees,
And now are about to pass, from without, inside of the home of Herakles [1].

We can imagine how the shift in the metre might be mirrored by the actor scurrying to and fro, becoming ever more frenzied. Movement quickens the heart of mimesis. It can be seen that the action can scarcely by separated from the poetry—both in plot construction and in the actual texture of the verse.

Later, the Romans appropriated Greek culture and shaped it to their own requirements. But now mimesis was more sophisticated and incorporated "fake news". Theirs was the first mass culture, and to the cunning of the Greeks, as epitomised by Odysseus, they added hyper-real counterfeits and even more complex deception—just as their cement and brick construction techniques could create architectural fantasy a far cry from the

---

1   It will be observed, of course, that Browning does not use the exact metre of the original, but the literary effect of the transition is maintained and enhanced—as can be said also of Christopher Logue's versions of Homer.

structure sustaining the building (whereas, the doric temples of ancient Greece were their structure and the structure alone). Encolpius, the narrator of *The Satyricon* by Petronius, is invited to dine at the house of Trimalchio, who serves dishes which are not at all what they seem. A fat goose, with fishes and all kind of fowl round it, turns out to be made of pork.

> "Whatever you see here," said Trimalchio, "is of the same substance…" "My Cook made all of it out of one Hog; there is not an excellenter fellow than himself; he shall if he please, make thee a Poll of Ling of a Sow's Tripe; a Wood-Culver of fat bacon; a Turtle of a Spring of Pork; and a Hen of a Collar of Brawn; and therefore of my own fancy, I gave him a Name proper to him, for he is called Daedalus."

Satyricon, Burnaby's translation 1694, p 103.

A similar sense of fraud informs the comedy *Amphitryon* by Plautus, which describes how Alcmena, the wife of Amphitryon, commander of the Theban army, is seduced by Jupiter, who comes to her in the guise of her husband. It is just so unfair! After all, she would have known it was Jupiter if he had come in the shape of a bull or an eagle. The trickster is aided and abetted by Mercury, who visits the commander's residence as the spitting image of the house-slave, Sosia. The play is wonderfully constructed, as regards its action. It requires that the cast must include a pair of twins—to play Sosia and Mercury in the shape of Sosia—for these two characters appear on stage at the same time, while one actor takes the role of Jupiter and Amphitryon himself, since these two characters never appear on stage at the same time. The outcome of this deception is that Alcmena gives birth to Hercules. To a modern sensibility there is a further layer to this game of disguise, for the parts of Alcmena, and that of Bromia, the nurse who delivers Hercules, would have been played by men rather than women.

As a form, the "play" has survived many centuries, forever adapting to its times. By expanding its fiction into magnificent displays, Nero proved himself to be one of the first to understand the power of art as a spectacular, big-budget product aimed at a mass market. Later on, in the mystery plays, the Church realised the potential of drama for delivering a religious message. Poetry itself was inexorably moulded by immersion in the Thespian crucible, and Aristotle's view that the arts—poetry, dance (as action), image and music—are at their best when they all come together to serve the common purpose of a plot, and that the plot concerns some moral significance, still persists—in plays put on at experimental theatres as much as in Hollywood block-busters.

That is not to say that its predominance as a form has not been seriously questioned, especially by the modernists of the last century and by the minimalist ethos of very recent times, given a contemporary tendency to focus on one particular speciality. We should recognise, however, that, earlier on, the arts were more intent on mimesis, and more knit together than they are today. We have seen how, at its gestation, dance was matched to the recitation of the chorus and how each dancer stepped and spoke in unison—though later, for efficiency's sake, a division of the chorus came about, the activation of one chorus enabling recovery time for another; this in turn leading to the possibility of dialogue between choruses, but all in the service of a purpose.

At first poetry was sung or recited with attention paid to vocal pitch, and it was accompanied by the lyre or the cithara. One can imagine Apollo, the divine bard, stepping as high as the chorus of the muses that inspired him. Repetition, reflection and coherence gave aesthetics their initial impetus, and then, as a moral outcome seemed necessary (perhaps because there was now an audience) poetry, song and dance were expected to serve each other in the common purpose that led in the direction of theatre, so that dance's role became lessened. Difference, opacity, separation and confusion have largely been explored only in more recent times, while dance is returning via performance art.

In European poetry, the sung aspect persisted through the middle ages. As has been shown, verse was first sung by the bards to the sound of their harps, and then, from the Middle Ages to the Renaissance, "lyric" poetry was accompanied by the lute, the practice only dying out after the reign of Elizabeth I. Centuries before that, troubadour poems were sung by the jongleurs of aristocratic troubadours who travelled the country disseminating the poem and its melody. The jongleurs were proficient with the lute or with the viol. The poem of the courtly Languedoc was a collaboration between the troubadour or the trobairitz (a female troubadour) and the jongleur, who may often have contributed the melody as well as acting as distributor.

The more they are the result of collaboration, the more some mutual purpose is served, the more the arts project or maintain a society. Here we readily comprehend the notion of "agreement". From this "integrated" viewpoint, what art is, what it is for, how it is made, is a matter of consensus. It is consensual, rather than some solitary pursuit, which society might denounce as onanist. Consensual art is a social product. Aristotle understands this and therefore he considers that all the arts aspire to the condition of theatre, serving the story as their communal purpose. Consensus establishes its rules, such as the stricture in classical tragedy that the actors should wear masks.

Later, consensus dictated that the twelve-syllable Alexandrine line (hexameter), derived from a twelfth-century romance about Alexander the Great and then promoted by Ronsard and the poets of La Pléiade in sixteenth century France, should become *de rigeur* for French verse until the mid-eighteenth century.

OF COURSE, WHAT IS MEANT BY SOCIETY, and social product, will always need to be defined. Are we talking about "high society" or "the peasantry"?

Even within the high society of courts and courtiers there can be conflicts. The Cathar "heresy"—which gave us the troubadours—called into question the Church of Rome and patriarchal succession. Tracing descent from the "Bulgars" of the Caucasus, the Cathar's beliefs incorporated "dualism"—a notion of conflicting forces of good and evil—derived possibly from Zoroastrian thought. This was at odds with the catholic notion of a single all-powerful god who has created Hell for sinners to burn in till the end of time. Inheritance among the Cathars passed to the eldest of one's offspring, even if the eldest was female—hence the wealth of Eleanor of Aquitaine, mother of the Lionheart, who inherited her Duchy from her father, William. It was the cultivated courts of powerful women such as Eleanor that gave rise to male and female troubadours. Their promotion of courtly love was a step in the direction of women's emancipation, since, in the patriarchal tradition of Rome and the rest of Europe, women were chattels merely, part of the property of the males. The Cathars were experts at contraception too, from the use of pigs' bladders to anal sex (we get "buggar" from Bulgar). These notions were all anathema to the Roman faith.

The Cathars of the Languedoc were wiped out by the Albigensian Crusade which began in 1208 and was led by the sadistic Simon de Montfort. Like all crusades it was a war, declared by the Pope, and backed by the Roman Church with promises of remission of sins and a guaranteed place in heaven. A few survivors managed to make it to Northern Italy, where the poetry of the language of "Oc" was appreciated by Dante. Provencal courtly love provided the kernel of the "sweet new style"—the *dolce stil novo*—which was pioneered by Dante and his contemporary Cavalcante, and by Petrarch of course. This ensured that such love and its significant appreciation of women was not simply reversed by the patriarchal attitude of the likes of de Montfort.

But while it might have been a step in the right direction, this was still essentially a poetics for the privileged few. Dante, and poets who shared his aesthetic worshipped their ladies from afar, as emblems of femininity, or as a feminine principal of inspiration, rather than as flesh-and-blood women. Often, they were married to someone other than their "saint".

However, an acquaintance of Dante's, one Cecco Angiolieri, saw things rather differently.

So bitterly indeed have I lamented
To have kept loving when my love was spurned,
That like a heavy stone at last I'm turned,
Although too late I've probably repented.
Had I foreseen how I'd be discontented,
I might have bought such wisdom at less cost;
For while so much of blood and breath I've lost,
It's very sure my honour's not augmented.
But anyhow the moral's clear as day,
To love those only who are fond of me:

Henceforward in this view I'm firmly anchored.
And, for whoever thinks the other way
(Unless he changes quickly), it will be
A miracle if his whole life's not cankered.

Sonnet XI (*Sonnets of Cecco Angiolieri* translated by C. H. Scott and Anthony Mortimer, Oneworldclassics, 2008)

"To love those only who are fond of me" sounds like common sense. Unfortunately, Cecco is in love with an ungrateful slut called Becchina. He's too broke to woo her successfully. His father wears a cassock and has become a member of a religious order known as the "joyful friars" (sounds a bit as if he had become a "born again" Christian). He's a mean old bastard, far from joyful, and he keeps his son short of cash. Cecco has a sonnet in which he wishes him dead.

Unlike the courtly sonnets, with their Aristotelian sense of a unified ideal—a relationship of shared virtue—Cecco's work has its origins in a more vulgar style:

> The poetry of Angiolieri has some of its roots in the old medieval Latin Goliardic tradition still familiar to many readers through Helen Waddell's *The Wandering Scholars* (1926) or through the lyrics that Carl Orff set to music in *Carmina Burana*. The addiction to "woman, the tavern and a game of dice" (LXXXVII), the denunciation of poverty as the worst of ills and the frequent juxtaposition of religious imagery with decidedly secular sentiments—these were already the stock-in-trade of the Archpoet and his contemporaries more than a century before Angiolieri exploited them in the new vernacular... His work needs to be seen in the context of a whole current of thirteenth-century poetry that Italian criticism labels as "comic", "realist" or "burlesque..."

Ibid, p. 273

This burlesque way of writing derives from the entertainments of the under-privileged, from the belly laugh, slapstick, the routines of street and fair. It is verse as removed from the court as music hall antics are from ballet. It provides us with an example of how there has always been a "Satyricon" to offset some paean to the sublime. The topic is well articulated by Mikhail Bakhtin in his work on *Rabelais and his World* (Indiana University Press, 1984). And this binary aspect of culture, that there are usually two currents—an elite, not necessarily popular, expression and a fart-punctuated, peasant earthiness generating something altogether less sophisticated—has affected the history of dance just as it has the history of poetry.

※

THE TROUBLE WITH THE HISTORY OF DANCE is that all too often it is "water under the bridge". It proves to be a history that can be gleaned more from visual art than from literature—until the sixteenth century, at least. Prior to that it's a history that relies on a fair amount of guesswork. From visual representation we can see that scantily dressed females danced in front of pharaohs, and that "striptease" tradition seems borne out by the biblical account of Salome dancing before Herod to secure the head of John the Baptist. The dances of Crete and the dances of classical Greece were often "choric"—as we have seen—with lines of chanting dancers linked by the hands or elbows. Because such dances demanded the coordination of a number of people they were taken up by the military and evolved into drill. It may be presumed that the Dionysian dance of the revel after the banquet was a pretty liberated affair, generally processional in character. Dances accompanying the drama that subsequently evolved would have been choreographed to suit the tenor of the action.

The dance of the middle ages known as the Branle had its origins in the thumping and stamping dances enjoyed by the peasantry from as early as the twelfth century. In its origins, it was a chain dance, for men alternating with women, the last person to join the dance taking the free hand of the first, so that the line becomes a circle. Couple dancing seems to have emerged from this arrangement, as during the dance the hands get freed, and each couple may circle each other or perform steps opposite each other before the hands join up again and the circle is re-formed. Named for its characteristic side-to-side movement (French *branler*, "to sway"), the lowly origins of this dance are emphasised by the fact that it was known as a "brawl" in English translation.

By the sixteenth century though, the dance had become associated with aristocratic etiquette. In France and in England, the branle was taken up by the court, and it is said that the Branle of the Torch was danced admirably by Marguerite de Valois and her courtiers. A similar dance, the Branle des Brandens, was danced on the first Sunday in Lent with a lighted torch in the dancer's hand. According to Sonny Watson, an expert on the history of dance from Ancient Greece to Swing:

> Probably this was a remnant of an old superstitious practice of the Gauls. During the month of February, which was the last of the solar year, the ancient inhabitants of France ran about the forests at night with lighted torches and danced a rite which was supposed to be one of purification, and also a ceremony which was meant to bring rest to their departed relatives and friends. This custom was founded in a utilitarian spirit by the Druidic priests, who knew that to run about with lights in the woods would free the trees from caterpillars, which generally emerge from their eggs in Spring.

It sounds as if this branle had affiliations with Comus, the god of revelry, and the comedic impulse of a Spring ceremony—as in the earliest dances of antiquity. In the renaissance, courtiers frequently performed pantomimic branles, scolding each other like washerwomen, or kicking up their heels in imitation of the kick of a cow. Thus many movements were mimetic.

Catherine de Medici insisted on her courtiers being able to dance with great proficiency—in order perhaps that they should not have time on their hands in which to plot and meddle in politics. Elizabeth I may have demanded sonnets from her courtiers for the same reason. Catherine was responsible for staging the *Ballet Comique de la Reine*—in 1581—the first ballet with a libretto that has come down to us—though danced pageants and ballets were often staged in Italy before that date (and Catherine, after all, was brought up in Italy). Meanwhile courtly dance was becoming ever more sophisticated, and the structure of these dances influenced the development of musical forms such as the sonata.

Thoinot Arbeau, the lively canon of Langres, born at Dijon in 1519, is our best source of information regarding dance in his time, and much can be learnt from his *Orchesography—a treatise in the form of a dialogue, whereby all may easily learn and practise the honourable exercise of dancing.* Arbeau says that the order in which the dances were performed takes the differences among the dancers into account. He says that "Musicians are all accustomed to beginning the dances at a feast" with a certain Suite of Branles, which are performed by various groups. "The elderly solemnly dance the double and single branles; the young married dance the gay branle; and the youngest of all lightly dance the Burgundy branle."

In order to explain dancing, Arbeau initially emphasises the value of steps regulated by the drum for drilling the infantry and timing how long it will take a battalion to march a league. These calculations were as precise then as they are today—and the influence of notions expressed by Arbeau can be felt in any contemporary manual on drill. Asked by his interlocutor, Capriol, why soldiers set out on the left foot, Arbeau answers, "Because most men are right footed and the left foot is the weaker, so if it should come about that the left foot were to falter for any reason the right foot would immediately be ready to support it."

Capriol: Would it not be the same if the soldier brought his right foot down on the first note?

Arbeau: Plainly not, because assuming most soldiers to be right-footed they march with the left foot first. If any of them were to start with the right and finish with the left foot they would knock shoulders when in close formation and hinder one another, because we turn the shoulder slightly to the side of the foot that is leading. If, therefore, one soldier were to start on the left foot, his shoulder would swing towards the left and the shoulder of another who had started on the right foot would swing towards the right and they would collide. This does not happen when they march in step, as all the shoulders incline first to one side and then to the other without jostling or hindering one another, a thing you can easily prove for yourself by walking with someone.

Orchesography—translated by Mary Stewart Evans, Noverre Press 2012, p. 37

Here, again, we see how intimately dance is connected with the martial science of drill, and indeed how marching conforms to metre. We have seen how *Pedes*, meaning "foot" is the Latin for foot-soldier—and incorporated into this martial science is the notion of the foot as a measure. Setting the pace of the marching step enables a general to know how long it will take to march a given distance. The drum is the instrument by which orders are communicated, and the metre beaten out dictates the nature of the formation, and it is "a great help in evolutions." When his pupil asks him, what is meant by an "evolution", Arbeau refers him to the writings of Aelian Taticus. Aelian's treatise on the manoeuvres of the Greeks, *On the tactical arrays of the Greeks*, dated 106 A.D., is an exhaustive handbook of Greek precedents and technical details in matters of drill. The Byzantines and the Arabs translated his work, and it was highly valued in sixteenth century Europe.

A body of soldiers "evolves" from one formation to another, from an open formation to a closed formation, for instance. The Macedonian phalanx described by Aelian had many points of resemblance to the solid masses of pikemen and the squadrons of cavalry of the Spanish and Dutch armies. The drum represents the order given by the commander in metrical terms. When the order is obeyed precisely the length of the pace will be defined and the speed of the step. It is thus that the time it will take to march a league may be calculated.

Having demonstrated how the length of a march can be timed, Arbeau moves on to courtly dance, and he is careful to stress how vital it is to dance to the music's rhythm.

> Without this rhythmic quality dancing would be dull and confused inasmuch as the movements of the limbs must follow the rhythm of the music, for the foot must not tell of one thing and the music of another.

Ibid, p. 16

From the point of view of our enquiry into the relationship between dance and verbal expression, what he has to say is interesting:

…Most of the authorities hold that dancing is a kind of mute rhetoric by which the orator, without uttering a word, can make himself understood by his movements and persuade the spectators that he is gallant and worthy to be acclaimed, admired and loved. Are you not of the opinion that this is the dancer's own language, expressed by his feet and in a convincing manner? Does he not plead tacitly with his mistress, who marks the seemliness and grace of his dancing, 'Love me. Desire me'? And, when miming is added, she has the power to stir his emotions, now to anger, now to pity and commiseration, now to hate, now to love. Even as we read of the daughter of Herodias, who obtained her wish from Herod Antipas by dancing before him at the magnificent banquet he offered to the princes of his realm on his birthday. So it was also with Roscius, who proved to Cicero that, by his employment of gesture and dumb show he could move the spectators, in the judgment of the arbiters, as much or more than Cicero had been able to by his eloquent orations.

Ibid.

Then, later:

…You know, in the art of grammar the pupil first amasses nouns, verbs and other components of speech and then learns to link them together with congruity. So it is in the art of dancing, you must first learn a variety of separate movements and then by means of the music you will be given, together with the tabular arrangements of movements, you will grasp it all.

Ibid, p. 84

This suggests that music is in a similar relationship to the steps in dance as meaning is to the words in poetry. It reminds me of Walter Pater's notion, that "All art constantly aspires to the condition of music." Here the definition of mimesis needs elaboration: if poetry "represents" meaning, dance "represents" music—at least within that traditional view first laid out by Aristotle which perceives mimesis as an essential component of art.

❧

SIMILARITY IN UNLIKE THINGS, as conceived by mimesis, may produce metaphor, but it can also be seen as at the root of all rhyming. And here the music of words truly enters the fray. The alikeness of vowel sound and ending is offset by a dissimilarity in the opening consonant; a coincidence it takes considerable skill to organise so that the coincidence reads as such. Here one sound is set up to agree except for its prefatory sibilant or plosive.

But why should the sound of a word have bearing on the rhythm? To examine sound instead of accent might seem like a red herring in a book about the step and its relation to the metrical foot, since it might seem that the inquiry concerns rhythm purely, or rhythm most specifically, rather than tone. However, I think it's right, at this juncture, to introduce rhyme into the discussion.

First, let us acknowledge that rhyming is difficult.

Difficulty has a role to play in art. In dance, there has always been a fascination with the difficult step, the tricky sequence, the elaboration within some magnificent leap. Difficulty has just as significant a role to play in the creation of verse. In the first place, there's the difficulty that can deliver the triumph of one getting just *how* to scan the passage with the apparently boggling phrase in it. The Italians had a word for this. They called it *asprezza*—asperity, harshness of tone or manner:

> …This roughness or "effort" may be contrasted and placed in opposition to *sprezzatura*—a quality cited by Baldassare Castiglione in his *Book of the Courtier*, where it is defined as "a certain nonchalance, so as to conceal all art and make whatever one does or says appear to be without effort and almost without any thought about it". It suggests a certain smoothness in the diction. You can see how Dryden rejects Donne's harsher tones for increased *sprezzatura*, nonchalant flow.
>
> From *Asprezza, a Paean to the Pioneer of the Madrigal*, A.H., (Fortnightly Review) 2015

So as well as making the difficult look easy (often cited as a received opinion these days), art can make the easy tough, or at least a degree more pungent than might be expected, creating a difficulty which adds the piquant touch;

a place where the reader could stumble, though it works! Can you surmount its difficulty when reciting it? That is, can you master the asprezza?

There is also the effort that can be put into making the whole poem more difficult to bring off. Lady Mary Wroth rhymes the first two quatrains of any of her sonnets using only two rhyme sounds. This means that she has to rhyme four times on one word. Now *Terza rima*—ABA BCB CDC—the stanza structure favoured by Dante, which rhymes three times on any end word, is far more difficult to do in English than it is in Italian, so four-words-a-rhyme is serious virtuosity. We can feel the same level of virtuosity in a villanelle, if all its rules are rigorously adhered to. Note how William Empson is restricted to there being only two rhyme sounds (the correct way to do it), in *Missing Dates:*

Slowly the poison the whole blood stream fills.
It is not the effort nor the failure tires.
The waste remains, the waste remains and kills.

It is not your system or clear sight that mills
Down small to the consequence a life requires;
Slowly the poison the whole blood stream fills.

They bled an old dog dry yet the exchange rills
Of young dog blood gave but a month's desires.
The waste remains, the waste remains and kills.

It is the Chinese tombs and the slag hills
Usurp the soil, and not the soil retires.
Slowly the poison the whole blood stream fills.

Not to have fire is to be a skin that shrills.
The complete fire is death. From partial fires
The waste remains, the waste remains and kills.

It is the poems you have lost, the ills
From missing dates, at which the heart expires.
Slowly the poison the whole blood stream fills.
The waste remains, the waste remains and kills.

Wroth's message *is* her difficulty. She is the pioneer of an economic, almost Spartan style, stripped of all ornament—so *night* becomes a psychic force rather than some paraphernalia brought in to make up a line. The limitation on her vocabulary makes the rhyming even more problematic to accomplish, but the musical gain is extraordinary. When I say her message is her difficulty, I mean that the added difficulty of finding the rhyme necessitates the bending of syntax—with limited words and only words to the point—as Japanese trees may be coached into extraordinary angles. Out of this bending and twisting, dreamy phrases—simple yet magical—appear—"weeping afternoons". Today, her lyrical work seems modern by comparison to many of her contemporaries. It is minimalist in its language and devious in its intricate rhyming.

> Leave me vaine Hope, too long thou hast possest
> My mind, made subject to thy flattring skill,
> While Aprill mornings did my pleasures fill,
> But cloudy dayes soone changd me from that rest;
>
> And weeping afternoones to me adrest,
> My utter ruin framd by Fortunes will,
> When knowledge said Hope did but breed, and kill,
> Producing only shadowes at the best.

From *Lindamira's Complaint*, Sonnet 5, *The Countesse of Montgomery's Urania*.

But rhyme needs rhythm to bring itself off. A random use of rhyme, allowing it to pepper the poem, can prove irritating and at times may seem too convenient. To work as a harmonic agent, rhyme can't do without the coincidence of ultimate sounds when two lines of an equal number of feet agree, or when they don't agree but aptly so, since both lengths are participating in some wider agreement governing the stanza—trimeter and pentameter, for instance, in a madrigal, or an ultimate extra foot in the last line of a stanza, as we find in Spenser and the Fletchers.

Wroth also wrote a fascinating sequence of autobiographical sonnets (which appear in her *Urania)* and a *corona* of sonnets "dedicated to love".

It was Sir Philip Sydney (her uncle) who introduced this form in English with a sequence of ten linked *dizains*. The *corona,* or crown, is of Italian origin. In this form, the last line of one sonnet serves as the first line of the next. So, the last line of Wroth's fourteenth sonnet—"In this strange labourinth how shall I turn?" is also the first line of the entire sequence. Josephine A. Roberts has edited Wroth's poems with a useful introduction and notes (published 1983, Louisiana State University Press). The *corona* was also used by John Donne. It has been revived recently (very effectively) by Martyn Crucefix and by Jacqueline Saphra.

ART VERY OFTEN DERIVES STIMULUS FROM CONSTRAINT. Poetry may "represent" meaning while demonstrating how difficult it can be to achieve it when constricted by the strait-jacket of a tough rhyme scheme which may constitute the structure for its courtly stays. And dance may "represent" music—at least within that traditional view first laid out by Aristotle which perceives mimesis as an essential component of art. But dance also can have its laces drawn in at the back, in order to demonstrate a courtliness of posture.

By the time Louis XIV, Le Roi Soleil, held court at Versailles in the seventeenth century, dance had become a highly sophisticated component in the etiquette of the court. Dance ability therefore designated status. The pantomimic dance moves cited above were a useful form of mockery, disdainfully accentuating the difference between the aristocracy and the common people—an accentuation that was eventually to lead to the guillotine. Courtiers strutted stiltedly down the allées of the palace gardens, walking with *épaulement effacé.* This would be a posed method of strolling, placing emphasis on "shouldering". The line of the shoulders would abandon the swing of the walk, and instead be shaded effacé, emphasizing the open side of the step, placing the right shoulder back as one stepped onto the left foot, thus associating the left shoulder with that left foot. Such a courtly walk showed how different aristocrats were from ordinary folk.

Épaulement indicates a movement of the torso from the waist upward, bringing one shoulder forward and the other back with the head turned to the open display side of the step. Come to think of it, aren't we back to the triangular torso and foot by foot pose of the Pharaohs?

The two fundamental positions of épaulement are croisé and effacé. When épaulement is used the position of the head depends upon the position of the shoulders and the shoulder position depends upon the position of the legs. Épaulement would give the finishing artistic touch to the courtiers' every movement, that is, swinging the left shoulder forward as they stepped forward onto the left toe. Nothing could be further from the natural way of walking, where, as Arbeau points out, "we turn the shoulder slightly to the side of the foot that is leading". In other words, when our left foot goes forward, our left shoulder swings slightly back. We have mentioned this disassociation before when discussing gait and evolution. But this "natural" walk was linked to peasant and foot-soldier, and therefore inappropriate for the higher beings divinely ushered into the company of the Sun King—in all probability to recite some pompous dithyrambic ode, written according to an elaborately stilted metrical scheme, in the grandest manner of Le Brun.

Out of an aristocratic cultural milieu the ballet emerged, while courtly partner dancing refined the peasant stomping, which re-appeared transformed—only to mingle again with the crowd and evolve into the myriad forms partnership could take in the nineteenth century—deriving fresh content and new moves from different countries as ethnicities mingled more and more in the cities. The Polka mania of the eighteen-forties led to a flowering of other couple dances, including the Schottische, the Valse à Deux Temps, the Five-Step Waltz and the Varsouvienne, plus new variations on the earlier Waltz, Mazurka and Galop. Back in the sixteenth century, Arbeau complained that the dances of his fathers were forgotten, and that new forms were forever emerging.

This seems to have always been the case, as it is in our day. By the 1950s, for instance, many of the Victorian dances had been abandoned. A broader, more expressive repertoire had taken their place with the advent of radio. New dance crazes were emerging out of the need for immediate contact between the sexes which a catastrophic war can only promote.

But if we turn back to the latter half of the nineteenth century, it can now be seen how rule-bound everything had become, in that period of

Classical revival, some time prior to the liberating explosion of modernism. Stultifying times, these, with the traditionalists among the poets insisting on an exhaustive knowledge of orthometric form, with neo-classicism instituting a revival of rules that demanded that figuration should be idealized and that all the arts should act as components of a story with an approved moral aim (this being epitomised by tragedy, as understood by Aristotle).

At the same time, there were academics steeped in baggy and outmoded values who insisted on an authoritative acquaintance with historical precedent, while dance was increasingly defined as a traditional skill executed by professional dancers who utilized a technique with elaborate physical demands. Even social dance required an intensive course with a ballroom dancing instructor—one among a number of skills concerning etiquette and deportment which might be acquired at a "finishing school". And this insistence on learning an acceptable form or adhering to some rigid style continued well into the twentieth century with the popularity of Victor Sylvester and his dance manuals, mapped out step by step.

2. LOOSENING THE STAYS
Mick Jagger dancing on his own/Metre abandoned/Free verse and abstraction.

We offer an evolutionary logic in which function arises in structures that are already complex, sometimes more complex than they need to be. Natural selection then favours a reduction in the complexity of these structures. They lose parts, to produce structures that are still functional, sometimes improvements, and often still sporting considerable residual complexity. There is nothing undarwinian about this route. It relies heavily on the principle of natural selection…

Complexity is easy. It is spontaneous. No special mechanism beyond the simple tendency for parts to become different from each other is needed to account for it. No selective advantage to complexity needs to be invoked. Of course, selection can favour complexity, in which case one would expect differentiation to occur even more quickly, but a rapid rise in complexity is not, all by itself, evidence for a selective advantage…

Consider a cartoon version of the problem, the construction of a stone arch. Arches are stable and weight supporting only when completed, when the keystone is finally lowered into place. And so in the standard method of building an arch, intermediates require scaffolding for support. But there is another route…. Start with a large pile of stones of various shapes. Within a sufficiently large pile, weight supporting structures are likely to be present.

The engineer's job, then, is not to build an arch out of stones but to remove the excess, the stones that do not participate in the already existing arch (and perhaps to reshape the remaining stones). The resulting structure is still complex, although obviously reduced from what might be called the "excessive complexity" of the structure it arose from.

Complexity by Subtraction—Daniel W. McShea and Wim Hordijk

These quotes from a recent article on evolution, have some bearing on how innovation works in the arts. When a genre is clearly defined, as with Aristotle's exhaustive categorisation of the elements required by tragedy or Corelli's shaping of the early concerto in the late Baroque period, that genre will be elaborated upon and develop through complexity. But at some point, innovation may be better served if some stricture dictated by the tradition is sacrificed. Innovation then proceeds by subtraction. In ancient times, tragic actors wore buskins on their feet—calf-length boots laced across the shins but open across the toes. To wear these "bare buskins" was evidence that you were to die a tragic death. You don't see a lot of buskins these days, though tragedies are still being written and performed. The gold that made a medieval painting precious was put aside as sophisticated Renaissance artists began depicting opulence or splendour via a more dynamic use of colour.

In the twentieth century, Aristotle's belief that art aspires to a goal defined by the arts working as a team (each serving a higher purpose, and that purpose being the illustration of some significant action) is a view that gets challenged by the minimalist painter Ad Reinhardt's dictum that each art strives for emancipation from any other; to be the painting which cannot even be photographed, for instance. It is a contemporary commonplace, that things progress by abandonment. For instance, the abandonment of figuration aligned to reality allowed abstract art to come into its own. In order for art to grow, something time-honoured may well have to be jettisoned.

Evidently, this jettisoning of restriction is by no means an impulse that should be thought of as reserved for the twentieth century. The Elizabethan age was highly innovative, and the flourishing of drama that it fostered represents a notable loosening of the stays, not only by assuming the licence to deal with uncomfortable subjects such as contemporary murder trials, courtly corruption and enforced marriages, but also by making blank verse its principle mode of expression. Shakespeare's mannerist dramas also do away with those unities dear to classical drama. His plays are not limited to a single action happening on a single day in one particular locale.

Where poetry was concerned the sixteenth century was an age of contrasts—highly wrought *coronas* of sonnets on the one hand, and dramatic speeches in blank verse on the other, where rhyme was the element abandoned and even the relation to scansion could be casual:

> Now, my co-mates and brothers in exile,
> Hath not old custom made this life more sweet
> Than that of painted pomp? Are not these woods
> More free from peril than the envious court?
> Here feel we but the penalty of Adam,
> The seasons' difference, as the icy fang
> And churlish chiding of the winter's wind,
> Which, when it bites and blows upon my body,
> Even till I shrink with cold, I smile and say
> 'This is no flattery: these are counsellors
> That feelingly persuade me what I am.'
> Sweet are the uses of adversity,
> Which, like the toad, ugly and venomous,
> Wears yet a precious jewel in his head;
> And this our life exempt from public haunt
> Finds tongues in trees, books in the running brooks,
> Sermons in stones and good in every thing.
> I would not change it.

As You Like It, Act II, scene 1

❧

A KEY DEVELOPMENT, prompted by the abandoning of an element, was the decline of the lute during the seventeenth century—which enabled poetry to go forward in its own right. In the Elizabethan age, a lyric poem was sung—to the accompaniment of this instrument (which had its origins in the Arabic "oud"). Thomas Campion's song-books contain fine poems which all have tunes, so that they can be sung. He died in 1620, and the song-books for lute and voice had all but disappeared some eighty years later. The Puritan aesthetic which swept in with the Civil War (1642-51) incorporated a distaste for the courtly, profane lyrics sung in the times of Charles 1. Declamatory poetry was of course already thriving on the stage, as it was in satires and elegies where rhyming couplets provided columns of verse; however, it is with John Donne that one senses that the lyric poem has been liberated from the need for a musical complement, though musical accompaniment may have persisted for the lyrics of Robert Herrick.

Lady Mary Wroth danced with Anne of Denmark, consort of James I, as one of the twelve Ethiopian princesses in *The Masque of Blackness* – performed at the Stuart Court in the Banqueting Hall of Whitehall Palace on Twelfth Night, 6 January 1605. This masque commissioned by the Queen was ultimately to lead to actresses appearing on the English stage in 1629, though it took another thirty years before a representation of *Othello* could take place in which the role of *Desdemona* was performed by a woman. The full-length portrait of Lady Mary in Penshurst Place shows her with an archlute practically as tall as she is, so she came of age at a time when the lyric poem was still accompanied by the instrument. However, one senses that by the time the seventeenth century had established itself, the new "metaphysical" poetry of John Donne, George Herbert, Henry Vaughan, Andrew Marvell and Richard Crashaw, and indeed the sonnets of Lady Mary herself, no longer required accompaniment. It is true that she rhymes the two quatrains of a sonnet with just two rhyme sounds, so the "word music" is of great importance to her, but her thought does away with those ornaments which her uncle, Sir Philip Sidney, might have used. She employs a simple vocabulary limited to its key words, while her thought has all the twists and quiddities which epitomise that new age of lawyers and divines rather than courtiers, and this suggests a deepening preoccupation with ideas, and a waning of the obligation to create rhythmic patterns that aptly balanced each other and a decorative vocabulary that leant itself to song.

Thomas Mace has the instrument complain in *The Decline of the Lute in England after 1660:*

Lute: Despair I doe.
Old Dowland he is Dead; R. Johnson too;
Two Famous Men; Great Masters in My Art;
In each of Them I had more than One Part,
Or Two or Three; They were not Single-Soul'd,
As most our Upstarts are, and too too bold.
Soon after them, that Famous man Gotiere
Did make me grateful in each Noble Ear;
He's likewise gone: I fear me much that I
Am not Long-liv'd, but shortly too shall Dye.

Musick's Monument, p. 34

As the age of enlightenment swept along, to be followed by industrialisation, innovation gained momentum, and former manners of making were abandoned with increased rapidity. Ultimately, we see this process amount to an explosion of "advances" when modernism gets broached towards the end of the nineteenth century. I use the term "advances" ironically, since in my view art changes rather than improves.

An historical view may insist on development. It's perhaps better to think of the cultural sphere as one in which two forces are pretty constantly sparring with each other, tradition versus innovation, rule adherence versus the relinquishing of rules, Apollo versus Dionysus. To take one example, in the heyday of the lute-accompanied lyric poem, lutenists would "through compose"—devising notation for every phrase of each verse of a poem rather than simply fitting it to a tune. However much we may seem to have grown away from such a process, consider the Manhattan Transfer. This formidable jazz vocal group use "vocalese". Vocalese is defined as words that are sung to melodies or improvisational solos that were originally part of an all-instrumental composition. So now the singers are through composing in reverse: fitting words to each nuance of a jazz solo by Miles Davies or Clifford Brown or Louis Armstrong.

Nevertheless, Modernism was a mighty shift of gears, and its rejection of much of what had gone before is evident in all the contemporary arts, though sometimes, frankly, you might not know it. After all, in the sphere of "entertainment", comedies and "moving" dramas that express human predicaments remain a staple for the film industry and for television serials. Tragedies are still being written for the stage. A sector of the British literary establishment likes to imagine that modernism and abstraction never happened. Yet, when one thinks of *Ubu Roi, Rhinoceros* and *Waiting for Godot*, one can see how modernism has not been slow to repudiate the traditional approach to theatre, while Gertrude Stein, Edith Sitwell, Leonora Carrington and William Burroughs, to name but a few, have pioneered a writing that treats words as a material stuff—as plastic, as fluid, as violent and as vital as a painting by Picasso, or more recently by Basquiat. In his seminal essay, *On the Dehumanisation of Art,* (1925) Ortega Y Gasset, pioneer of modernist theory, called both tragedy and comedy into question. Stipulating that the true business of art was art itself rather than the mimesis of the human condition, Ortega favoured an art that prompted one *neither to laugh nor to cry*, opposing this difficult and often unpopular modern art to the popular products of the romantics that persisted in glorifying emotion:

This can be seen very clearly in music and poetry. From Beethoven to Wagner, the theme of music was the expression of personal feelings. The lyric artist composed grand edifices of sound in order to fill them with his autobiography. Art was more or less confession. There was no other way of aesthetic enjoyment other than by contagion of feelings. Even Nietzsche said, 'In music, the passions take pleasure from themselves'. Wagner injects his adultery with La Wesendonck into *Tristan,* and leaves us with no other remedy, if we wish to enjoy his work, than to become vaguely adulterous for a couple of hours. That music fills us with compunction, and to enjoy it we have to weep, suffer anguish, or melt with love in spasmodic voluptuousness. All the music of Beethoven or Wagner is melodrama.

The modern artist would say that this is treachery; that it plays on man's noble weakness whereby he becomes infected by the pain or joy of his fellows. This contagion is not of a spiritual order, it is merely a reflex reaction, as when one's teeth are set on edge by a knife scraped on glass, an instinctive response, no more. It is no good confusing the effect of tickling with the experience of gladness. Art cannot be subject to unconscious phenomenon for it ought to be all clarity, the high noon of cerebration. Weeping and laughter are aesthetically fraudulent. The expression of beauty never goes beyond a smile, whether melancholy or delight, and is better still without either. *'Toute maîtrise jette le froid'* (Mallarmé).

Ortega Y Gasset (1925)—edited version—the full text can be found in *On the Dehumanisation of Art and other writings on art and culture*, Anchor Books NY, 1956.

The generation in their late twenties in the sixties and early seventies of the last century (my generation), felt, as the modernists had before them, that in order to make art or poetry which was vitally new, they needed to continue to dismantle the notions prevalent in the nineteenth century. After all, the Victorians had melted things together in nostalgic mush that looked back to antiquity for musicality, dabbling in poetic "quantity" to generate a lyric tonality they felt that the satirical and analytic poetry of Pope had overlooked (for to some extent each age overturns the values of its predecessor).

More overtly melodic than that previous age, but even more caught up in large scale artistic teamwork—from Wagner, and the emergence of classical ballet, to melodrama and the operas of Gilbert and Sullivan—romantic art turned away from the satire that had characterised the eighteenth century and courted empathy and popularity. Their sparring partners, the realists, were as keen on "moving" their readership as the romantics. In general, the trend in creativity was not as insistent on "wit", and that rigour of thought that distinguished the Augustan age. Moving one's audience was the aim, and it was the start of mass markets for art, but, in Lefebvre's terms, art thus became more of a product, less of a work.

Anathema to the moderns, this Victorian emphasis on the *humanity* of art seemed to have turned poetry into persuasion; an innately dangerous force that could summon millions to battle. "Dulce et Decorum est, pro patria mori!" Thus goes the old lie denigrated by Wilfred Owen. But even Owen deals in pathos, as we have seen, and the moderns needed to deconstruct that lie and take matters still further *away* from emotion. Gertrude Stein challenged the very notion of coherent narrative, and in opposition to the "rousing" metre of Tennyson's *Charge of the Light Brigade,* the twentieth century challenge was *vers libre.*

All this had happened before my time, for by the sixties, modernism was already 70 years old (if we date its inception from 1891 when George Meredith published his highly innovative sixteen-line sonnet sequence *Modern Love*).

In dance, an urge towards improvisation had begun with Isadora Duncan. Here was dance freeing itself from choreography, from the barre, from expertise, particularly as exemplified by the ballet. For my generation, the moderns were instigators of a new tradition, a tradition which had validity for us. Coming of age in the sixties, I could not help but be steeped in modernism, despite my soppy verse. A love of gymnastics coupled with an overriding interest in the arts had led me in my teens to dedicate myself to ballet. But being in the Royal Ballet corps was a regimental experience. An agreed technique in an approved style was rigorously driven towards virtuosity—all in the service of confection: *Sleeping Beauty, The Nutcracker, La Fille mal Gardée.* The appeal of ballet's major works was to the emotions in a chintzy and sentimental way, coupled with this emphasis on a consensually approved skill. Many a young intellectual would turn, as I did, to Ortega and to the dehumanisation of art, to Wittgenstein and his notion that "ethics is aesthetics"—thus rejecting the sentiment of my juvenilia.

Meanwhile Mick Jagger danced on his own. He made up his movements. He jerked and shrugged to his own music. He "did his own thing". As his contemporaries, we had already rebelled against the fixed repertoire of ballroom dancing—as it was then—waltz, quickstep and cha-cha-cha (interspersed at hunt balls with the Gay Gordons on evenings culminating in the conga and the hokey-cokey). We danced rock-and-roll with enthusiasm if not with the technique which is obligatory for today's Lindi-hoppers. But Mick Jagger took the revolt from set moves much further. His was a revolt from partner dancing itself, and that enabled millions to swarm into nightclubs and simply groove on their own, yet all together; moving any which way to the beat. It was "Move it like you feel!" Nightclub dance music was actually merely a background thud in a space so dark that no one noticed if you merely shuffled. The disco was a new dance product, mass produced, and serviced by "Top of the Pops". We thought of it as a Dionysiac impulse. And it was black—as we perceived it—black as in Black American (James Brown). And Black African—again as we perceived it—with the power of mask and fetish—what Picasso was getting at with *Les Demoiselles de Avignon*.

Of course, I saw this as a revolt as far more than my own reaction to a discipline which seemed to give me no room for expression, though in point of fact this dancing as one "felt" was romantic at its core; as was the poetry of "the Beats"—which became popular at that time. I saw modernism as an impulse to get away from the sentimentality of Landseer, from the overstated rhythm of Swinburne's poetry, from the fussy elaboration of choreographers who clung on to setting their choreography. Merce Cunningham was loosening the ties of dance to notated music and instead opting for the felicities of chance and coincidence, while John Cage created random sounds that might or might not interface simultaneously with an action by one of the dancers.

I wasn't that keen on the Beats. While identifying poetry that scanned and used rhyme as a cliché—just as the ballet was "old hat"—I didn't readily buy the notion of "free expression". I liked to work on my poems, just as I had enjoyed executing a pirouette, even if it was a cliché. "Mastery projects a coldness," says Mallarmé, and I wasn't prepared to throw out the baby with the bath-water: mastery there had to be. I began to work on pieces of writing that I thought of as "Limited Vocabularies". These required their own technique, as is demonstrated by a prose-poem completed in 1972, which uses exactly the same words and punctuation as a passage by Henry James:

MAISIE RECONSTITUTED

'It was by no means, however, that his presence, in any degree, ceased to prevail; for there were minutes during which her face, the only thing in her that moved, turning with his turns and following his glances, actually had a look inconsistent with anything but submission to almost any accident. It might have expressed a desire for his talk to last and last, an acceptance of any treatment of the hour or any version, or want of version, of her act that would best suit his ease, even in fact a resigned prevision of the occurrence of something that would leave her, quenched and blank, with the appearance of having made him come simply that she might look at him.'

(Henry James)

'His last appearance in his best suit, his want of any desire, was inconsistent with the version of that presence following, that her occurrence with him by accident almost might come to something, for even were no act to prevail there it would leave him; a thing, or fact, that anything but a version might at least talk of, however simply, having her look turning, in degree, for means. And that ease with which she would have expressed her acceptance of the prevision, or any, had actually only made of his face a blank, quenched his glances, and moved in her look the resigned submission to any treatment of the turns of an hour and any minutes that ceased during it.'

(James Henry)

❧

I WAS TWENTY-SEVEN. It was the year of Bloody Sunday. Unemployment exceeded one million for the first time since the second world war. But who wanted a job? You could be a drop-out and go on the dole. That gave you time to create art in a squatted building. Culture had gone underground. I was a roadie for a brilliant jazz musician, the Hammond organist Robert Stuckey, and he was playing with South African jazzmen, black and white, brilliant musicians who had been flung out of their country for playing together. After their gig had finished at Ronnie Scott's old place, we would head off to the Count Suckle Cue Club in Praed Street, or the Golden Star somewhere north of Islington—darkest London in those days—and dance to reggae till dawn, endlessly repeating a double-dip of the hip this way and then that. Repetition provided an escape from representation. In 1975, Philip Glass brought his musicians over to play "Music for Changing Parts" in London, and the group stayed on the floor of my studio during their brief visit.

Looking back now, I see this as a confusing time. There was so much to rebel against, and most of us were rebelling, but were we all rebelling against the same thing? I am not so sure. Everyone was engaged in their own personal rebellion. Perhaps that is just how it is when one is in one's twenties. For me, it was being fed up with classical ballet, Swinburne and Aristotle! Even serious theatre seemed to set up a dogma of illustration that was at the service of its tragic ideal or its social message. Illustration was a dirty word for the progressive artists seeking to "make it new" in these confusing times. But was it actually no more than a revolt from the team product into doing your own thing and pursuing form for its own sake? No. The Philip Glass Ensemble was a team and so was Chris McGregor's Brotherhood of Breath—formed with the same musicians who played with my Hammond organist friend. It was traditional structures that needed to change, as well as traditional intent.

In 1970 *An Anthology of New York Poets* came out, edited by Ron Padgett and David Shapiro. It is difficult, in the current climate, to convey how important this anthology was, at least for me and for several of my contemporaries. At the time, New York was the cultural capital of the world—as Paris had been in the twenties. We all tried to get over there at least once a year. Several of us moved over there permanently and became American citizens. The anthology drew on a network of writers that had grown up around magazines such as *Locus Solus* and *Art & Literature*—both published during the sixties in Paris—and was often influenced by the poetry of French writers such as Denis Roche, Yves Bonnefoy and Marcelin Pleynet, who were in turn developing a poetics pioneered by Mallarmé, Éluard and Reverdy.

In the UK, this modernist poetry was mocked or ignored by the establishment which had grown up around Faber and Faber, the school curriculum and mass circulation newspapers. Nothing much has changed in forty years. The result of this narrow-mindedness has been that the arts in Britain have become isolated from each other, since modernism was embraced by visual artists and the art-schools but not by the British literary establishment dominated by Faber, not by a publishing industry that was becoming ever more corporate, as small independent firms were swallowed up by syndicates.

Odd this, that Ad Reinhardt's notion of the emancipation of the arts from each other could be accepted by a consensus of poets, visual artists and musicians in New York—for although separation and specialisation was what was being promoted, practitioners in various arts nevertheless felt close to each other because they shared this new aesthetic notion. Here in the UK, however, the arts became ever more divorced from each other. Caught between tradition and innovation, artists and poets here were unable to agree on an aesthetic. In itself, the "tradition" espoused by the traditionalists was unashamedly nationalist, essentially concerned with "British" poetry. The innovators were seen as associating themselves with Europe and the States.

John Ashbery was a key player when it came to introducing up-to-date French poetics to an American readership and to his more isolated admirers "across the pond". He had been an editor on both *Locus Plus* and *Art & Literature*. He had also been the art critic for the Paris Edition of the *New York Herald Tribune*.

The poets of the New York School, as the poets associated with the New York anthology came to be known, were a mixed bunch. Many, but by no means all, called narrative representation (mimesis) into question as well as the strictures of scanned verse. When the verse did represent some aspect of life, it was often "significance" which was removed. Take this prose poem by Lewis MacAdams:

THE DAZZLING DAY

The shopping cart clatters out of the Safeway, a young man with a black tie, loose at the collar but tucked in to his long white apron tilts the cart up to ease it over a curb. A small pamphlet is stuck behind the windshield wiper in front of the driver's side. The metal light pole is fiery to touch except for the shards of an old political sign. Someone has been in the car, the glove compartment is open, a box of Kleenex on the dashboard, the chrome end of the steering wheel is hot.

The groceries, in thick brown paper sacks lean against each other in the back seat. I tip the boy and get in the car. The ice cream bars are melting, I must turn on the air conditioner and drive back toward the house.

We have no difficulty understanding it. But the significance, the *import* of its meaning, eludes us. It is *purely* description; as icily exact as anything by Mallarmé. But it is actually an emphasis on significance which betrays a poem as traditionalist, intent on the poignant human homily it illustrates, that being its purpose rather than its purpose being its own making, its own poetic existence. And it is here that the line of battle is drawn. Should the poem move us to a comprehension of some extra-poetic "humanizing" significance or should it only succeed in its own terms in being a poem and a poem alone?

Ashbery posited the poem as a flow of mellifluous syntax that felt as if it could or might be articulating something, if only one could grasp what it was, if only the meaning did not seem to evaporate behind one as one moved on to the next sentence. Clark Coolidge, also included in that anthology, attacked the sentence itself, rather as Jackson Pollock refused to allow line to delineate a shape in his most energetic abstract paintings. With experience as a jazz percussionist, Coolidge's lines are almost syncopated, as can be felt here:

MANGROVE IN CHROME

gas sigh invert balk
caball ants too
    trunk
        if so, in case, sat soon
sump, pro
       down
    lump, lung, in toe, if is
saturday flirt
       sank echo chiming dreg, it
sank down dream so, concert your so self sue, if

Benny's charts so pipe bark, kids cramp
back trudging allergic, stamp snapping
       fired
shark 'lastic keeled in, ramp dun bird so?
whiskered die & plectrum

roll of ouvre   (Premium)
                  clatter punt & echo

shoot   shot   shout
                                  scup

As with much of Coolidge's work, this is less opaquely abstract than it may first appear. One gets the sense of a nature walk, a school trip, perhaps to the mangrove swamps, complaining kids getting cramps from all the trudging: a trip perceived through all the senses—*plectrum* suggests what—a campfire guitar? Coolidge cuts down on all parts of speech except nouns and verbs, which makes both these parts of speech ambivalent: context does not show us when a word is being used as a noun or when it is being used as a verb. The result is a percussive rattle of language, a stark spikiness that recalls the music of the serial composers—Berg and Webern.

But where is the role of metre in all this—or the notion of steps? Lefebvre remarks on the 'violence of abstraction'. And indeed, abstraction represented a pretty savage rupture with the past, as first exemplified by Picasso's *Demoiselles d'Avignon.* But that was painted in 1907. Half a century later, a young poet or artist would equate abstraction with 'freedom', and that also meant a freedom to demonstrate, as with the protests of '68; and this accompanied an impulse to break free from a tradition which, in the London literary world at least, was still trying to maintain a coherent unity of form and content, meaning and verse-form. Meanwhile a youthful generation were immersed in exploring a freedom to experiment with drugs, politics, clothing and relationships.

It was indeed an emancipation from pre-ordained procedures. However, it led to a general sense of formlessness and a state of flux. A large portion of the era that began in the mid-sixties and tailed off as the seventies took over seemed to be no more than just grooving to reggae down a club while trying to write with no form and no meaning, as if it were a point of honour to be able to do this, to work with no rules and no message. When free verse was allied to abstraction from reality did it become a bridge too far?

Not entirely. It was simply that one was not trying to "fill up" a recognised verse-structure as one might fill a jug with a liquid. Nor was one certain in advance what it was one was writing "about". There was no "about". Somehow or other, a body of words emerged; partly collage perhaps, partly stream of consciousness or chosen at random from a dictionary or a text—every seventh word perhaps, or only the words found within brackets. But then, the etiquette of prosody took over, and one employed all the myriad tactics of rhetoric, albeit one might be doing so unconsciously: never starting a word with an "S" when the word preceding it ended in an "S", never allowing a phrase in which three unstressed syllables followed each other—niggly rules one had set for oneself.

With free verse, previously unconsidered strategies may emerge, such as noting the assonance that can be generated by vowel sounds and developing that assonance from line to line—or cutting across it. One may always find a synonym for a word one wishes to refer to or never seek a synonym for a word one wishes to repeat. It can be a matter of always prohibiting an accidental rhyme or generating as many accidental rhymes as possible. Or it can be an instinctual wariness: finding a way around an expression if that expression feels like "a mouthful"—or, with *asprezza* in mind, making a mouthful of the next line. Ashbery has a poem entitled *And Ut Pictura Poesis is her Name* which plays with what might or might not go into the making of a poem:

> You can't say it that way any more.
> Bothered about beauty you have to
> Come out into the open, into a clearing,
> And rest. Certainly whatever funny happens to you
> Is OK. To demand more than this would be strange
> Of you, you who have so many lovers,
> People who look up to you and are willing
> To do things for you, but you think
> It's not right, that if they really knew you . . .
> So much for self-analysis. Now,
> About what to put in your poem-painting:
> Flowers are always nice, particularly delphinium.
> Names of boys you once knew and their sleds,
> Skyrockets are good—do they still exist?
> There are a lot of other things of the same quality

As those I've mentioned. Now one must
Find a few important words, and a lot of low-keyed,
Dull-sounding ones. She approached me
About buying her desk. Suddenly the street was
Bananas and the clangor of Japanese instruments.
Humdrum testaments were scattered around. His head
Locked into mine. We were a seesaw. Something
Ought to be written about how this affects
You when you write poetry:
The extreme austerity of an almost empty mind
Colliding with the lush, Rousseau-like foliage of its desire to communicate
Something between breaths, if only for the sake
Of others and their desire to understand you and desert you
For other centers of communication, so that understanding
May begin, and in doing so be undone.

***

BACK IN THE SIXTIES, the poetry world was polarised, in several directions, traditionalists were opposed to beat poets, and "abstract" poets were opposed to both beats and traditionalists. While for several years I considered myself entrenched in the modernist camp, these days my position has mellowed. Perhaps it is because my writing is less theoretically driven than it was in the sixties, or perhaps it is simply that I have, through the law of having done that already, eventually been led to explore areas I have not dealt with so thoroughly, including satirical poetry, simply because of Pound's "Make it new!" dictum, to which I have always adhered. Now making it new must also refer to one's work. One needs to be new to oneself.

I feel that the main difference between what I was doing in the 60s and 70s and what I have been attempting more recently has to do with uncertainty. Back then, the issue was polarised: you were either in the traditionalist camp or in the modernist one. Today, both positions strike me as lacking in ambivalence. More and more, I find myself concerned with not being sure. I am interested in leaving it to the reader to make up his or her mind as to whether I am writing in an abstract way or in a narrative way. In an uncertain age, it feels appropriate to come to terms with doubt.

In the sixties though, one felt that one was free to break any rule: to try following a word that ended with an "S" with a word which began with an "S"—slurring your words, as it were. Or you could see if you could always separate a stressed syllable by three unstressed syllables. There were plenty of things to do still. You could invent new rules, following the example of Raymond Roussel, every word of whose opening sentence might rhyme, all the way through, with every word of his concluding sentence—while a seamless narrative linked the two sentences.

The poem, or indeed the artwork or performance, was the result of your concept of what the mechanism was that might bring it about. And the process of writing became very specifically focused on the text as a text, on the poem as the body of its words. In this new domain of poetic abstraction, language was not designed to communicate so much as to resonate—aspiring to the condition of music, yes, but to the experimental music of our century, from the serial syntax of Webern to the permutations of Philip Glass.

But meaning (in the service of communication) has never been as concise in English poetry as the Augustans might have wished it to be. Our language abounds in words which have more than one meaning. In *Seven Types of Ambiguity*, William Empson suggests that the multifarious readings, double meanings and ambiguities which are to be found in English verse differentiate the language of this island from other European languages. This is perhaps the result of wave after wave of conquest or immigration—Romans, Vikings, Saxons, Normans, Huguenots, Jews and Jamaicans—their vocabularies have enriched our language, and added new meanings to existing words. Suggested secondary meanings to the line give English verse a sense of being haunted by alternative senses: a quality the modernists were happy to exploit.

And in the dance studio and the night-club? In these locations also the sixties introduced new ways of thinking. Experimentation and new methods of expression hit the dance world as hard as they hit the literary environment. For instance, the double sidestep used in dancing to reggae allowed an S to weave its way through the spine with a snaky undulation as one pushed off on the second beat from one foot onto the other, introducing an Afro quality that altered the way society jigged about. This was a movement alien to the upright and remorselessly symmetrical protocol of ballroom dancing and the ballet. The use of the spine and its ability to be snake-like was exploited by Martha Graham, who made the spine central to her innovative new choreography, with arches and contractions that drew in the limbs or emanated outwards to the rest of the body. And then there was Simone Forti, drawing inspiration from the movements of animals.

For me, I realise, night-clubs such as the Cue Club in Praed Street, where reggae was danced till dawn, provided an introduction to improvisation. I admired my jazz musician friends for this ability. After all, I had spent years learning set enchainments and working with elaborate sestinas and villanelles. Now I learnt to simply allow my body to move with the music—perhaps it sounds obvious now, but back then it was a personal revolution. I tried improvising on the page as well, generating automatic writing. The results were hardly impressive, but later this appreciation of improvisation was exactly what made dancing the tango so exciting for me, since the tango is the "jazz" of dance—in the sense that it is the most developed system of improvisation to be offered by a dance-form.

The liberation from mimesis, from illustration, and the freedom from adherence to some preordained unity concerning the human spirit, opened up new possibilities, new techniques, and a fresh sense of art as art. It allowed poetry to regain the sense that a poem could be read purely as a poem, and movement could be understood as located at its core rather than at its delicate extensions; an activity that could be improvised as well as contrived. Spectacle was challenged by a more private creativity, appealing to a smaller audience. Ultimately, that abandonment of the necessity for art to act as humanity's advertisement, that liberation of each art from any necessity to act as another arts accompaniment, that urge to emancipate each art from all others, ushered in the era of minimalism.

It also had a sort of rebound effect on forms of creativity that did rely on teamwork and a fusion of artistic endeavour. These arts were obliged to become more adventurous, to explore more dynamic options. Robert Wilson, one of the greatest innovators in theatre at this time, mounted a play at the Persepolis festival in Iran in 1972 that lasted 168 hours:

I had an idea to do a play that would be performed continuously for seven days, a kind of window to a world where ordinary and extraordinary events could be seen together. One could see the work at 8 a.m., 3 p.m., or midnight, and the play would always be there, a twenty-four-hour clock composed of natural time interrupted by supernatural time. It would be a bit like going to a park where you could daydream, watch clouds change, observe people passing, and even read a book, then suddenly there would appear a prepared stage work combining the real with the surreal....

I first thought to present the work in Persepolis, and so I went to Iran in 1971 to find a location for my proposal. On the way there I visited a garden where seven Sufi poets were buried. After leaving this beautiful oasis, I noticed seven foothills that rose progressively higher. I was immediately attracted to this barren landscape that reminded me of my home state of Texas, with a garden at the base....

I could not possibly write and direct a play that was seven days long, so I created a mega-structure that I divided into hours, with twenty-four segments a day. I worked with an international core group of over 100 people and in the end we had over 700 people participating, including local students, people I had met in the bazaar in Shiraz, and people who lived in the foothills who had never been to Shiraz and did not know man had been to the moon, as well as people I had invited from Latin America, the United States, and the Far East. I wanted to stage large crowd scenes, and so it was suggested that I work with the Iranian army, and I gladly accepted. I divided the play into seven themes over a week. Day one took place on hill one, day two on hill two, so by the seventh day there were activities on all seven hills. The participants were divided into groups and each group had a time slot and that would repeat and run throughout the week....

At the base of the first hill I erected a sort of tower of Babel that had seven levels. Walking up this scaffolding structure, one could sit and converse with a wide range of people: artists, housewives, teachers, scholars, shepherds, etc. People were talking about anything and everything: politics, art, how to make a pizza, and how to build a house. There was an elderly storyteller from the bazaar telling stories from the past and a housewife from New Jersey conversing with local women from the city of Shiraz. It was a real cross-cultural view of the East and West. The entire seven-day play brought together a mix of extraordinary people. There were some with formal education and some with no education. Looking back at it now I think this was the most interesting aspect of the work. I cannot imagine anyone today taking such a risk and commissioning a piece like this. There was no censorship, no one telling me I could not do what we did....

I often think of this work as a cross-section of people with very different political, religious, social, and cultural backgrounds working together for an event that would happen only once, like a shooting star. We were like a large family evolving.

Excerpted from *KA MOUNTAIN AND GUARDenia TERRACE: a story about a family and SOME people changing, a 168-hour play for the 1972 Festival of Shiraz* by Robert Wilson, in the catalogue accompanying Asia Society Museum's exhibition Iran Modern, on view through January 5, 2014.

⁂

SUCH DIVERSITY MARKED THE NEW YORK ART SCENE in the 60s and early 70s. The exuberant creativity generated there spilled over into England and Europe, South America and Asia. I was immersed in what I conceived as "abstract poetry"—and exploring this notion now plunged me into a nebula of systems and permutations, concepts and manifestations that led me away from the page. For instance, at the opposite extreme to Wilson's mega-productions, Yoko Ono was creating instruction art on tiny scraps of paper. One of her friends visited Bernard Stone's Turret Bookshop in Kensington Church Walk, where I was working, and she presented me with an instruction.

Dawn Piece

Take the first word that comes across
your mind.
Repeat the word until dawn

1963 winter
From *Grapefruit, a Book of Instruction and Drawings,* Yoko Ono, (Simon and Schuster)

Yoko Ono's instruction art proved a radical inspiration. I began writing instruction poetry. Several of these instructions for generating poems are included later in *Elements of Performance Art,* which I wrote in collaboration with Fiona Templeton when we worked together in The Theatre of Mistakes:

Extending Sentence Duet

One performer says a word. The second performer repeats the word and adds another word, either before or after the original word. The first performer repeats the first two words and adds a further word either before or after them—and so on.

Depending on the conditions of the performance decide whether to add words before or after or before and after the original word so that the word string extends according to a chosen method.

Do not add words between words already spoken.

Sounds may be employed instead of words.

Now I found myself led back in the world of performance—after several years concentrating exclusively on poetry. Initially speech and action coincided in these performances but were generated by independent groups of performers, as in my *Birth Ballet Chorale,* in which an invited chorus of pregnant ladies read passages from a text I had written, while performers carried out simple instructions on the space in front of them.

But having been inspired by Yoko Ono's initiative to create instruction poems, I soon realised I could create what I termed at the time "instruction art performances". These were performances derived from recipes, inviting the participants to improvise within a set of simple strictures similar to those used in the 'instruction poems'.

It was this realisation that opened up the notion of an art of action. Since that time, I have often been asked to define the "performance art" in which I became engaged. My reply has been, 'Think of this definition as a wedge: the wide end of the wedge is the idea that performance art can be a term for art as a "catch all"—with everything thrown in—dance, mime, conjuring, opera, circus, slapstick—mixed up in any way you wish; the narrow end of the wedge is action freed from any need to be accompanied by any other art, so not opera (action accompanied by song), not dance (action accompanied by music), not theatre (action accompanied by words).'

Action for itself. Actions structured so that they create their own homeostasis, their own wholeness, their own development. A new art. Action emancipated from all other arts.

The wide end of the wedge might be epitomised by the Cirque du Soleil, the narrow end by the performances of the late Stuart Sherman.

My own inclination was towards the narrower definition; a minimalist vision of performance art. Such minimalist and conceptual ideas were part and parcel of the energetic enquiry that drove a posse of teachers in the fine art department run by Jon Thomson and Michael Craig-Martin at Goldsmiths College of Art in the late sixties and the early seventies. I was honoured to be one of the tutors on that course, and I sensed I fitted into this world of concepts with my notion of what performance art might achieve. It was performance versus story, integrity versus illustration.

I CAME TO REALISE THAT THE MINIMALIST AESTHETIC had carried me a long way from the ballet, and theoretically-speaking, a long way from Aristotle. However, it enabled me to invent a career for myself—the artist as a body, engaged in the art of action. Now here was a dynamic that seemed appropriate for me. A new freedom. But a freedom that entailed a discipline. Recently, I have reviewed this position and see it as an extension of the poet's role: the poet as a body. What I realise now is that this allies me to the high-stepping poet, who took on the role of Apollo among his muses, on the threshing floor, and later in the amphitheatre. Remember that Thamyris used to sing, to harp, and to dance; and it was these *three* abilities that defined him as a poet.

Minimalism enabled my poetry to become performative when I created instruction pieces that concerned language. It also enabled me to hit upon an art of action I had been unable to locate since leaving the ballet. But where was the foot in all this? What of orthometry, the artifice that transmuted the poem and turned it into rhythmically enhanced resonance? It took the Theatre of Mistakes to restore the rhythm of the spoken phrase to my work as well as the rhythmic action of stepping.

3. THE THEATRE OF MISTAKES
Fusion /The notion of the action phrase a new way of bringing words and action together/ walking as art, and poetry as 90 degree turns.

THIS CHAPTER CONTAINS A LOT OF MATERIAL ABOUT ME. But in the nineteen-seventies there was almost no notion of performance poetry, though Mike Horowitz was pioneering beat poetry at gigs such as the Albert Hall extravaganza—which very definitely emphasised the impact of the declaimed poem—as did the poets of the "Liverpool Scene". Performance art was unheard of here, though elsewhere in Europe, actionists were creating seminal work. Being a founder member of *Wallpaper*—a magazine with wallpaper covers edited by poets, conceptual artists and musicians, I was very much involved in a sector of the artworld that sought to pioneer performance poetry, performance art and the inter-action of artistic disciplines, so, if I am to bring my enquiry into the fusion of the step and the foot up-to-date, having looked pretty thoroughly at its archeological roots and its history, I am going to have to refer to my own undertakings in this period. I hope that my readers will bear with me.

❧

BACK IN THE SEVENTIES, Lucinda Childs was renowned for dancing to the sound of her own feet. She was the first 'systems' dancer. Systemic music had already gained fair headway through the work of composers such as Steve Reich and Philip Glass in America, and Michael Nyman, John White and Chris Hobbs in England. In dance, Lucinda Childs would repeat a limited vocabulary of steps until every juxtaposition of the chosen steps had been shown. She created solos with no music other than the sound of her feet.

Performers often derive their aesthetic motivation from the visual arts. In my own case, the idea that objects have more than one side from which to be viewed has intrigued me ever since I saw the work of the cubists and felt this to underpin their art. I first considered a form of performative cubism after watching these solo dances by Lucinda Childs. The sequential context of the movement, what it came before, what it followed, still didn't tell the whole story—each variation needed to be seen from every angle. Like systemic music, systemic dance was often hypnotic.

As one sat watching, her dance grew resonant with suggestions and associations. Gertrude Stein maintained that no repetition is the same as another—it's either earlier or later in a sequence of repetitions, and so one is less saturated with one image during early repetitions of it, more so later, and each repetition slightly changes one's view. Ideas suggested first may fade, and then deeper insights may stir in the mind. Now I think of the complex permutations in the song of the Bengalese Finch, and of Brian Eno suggesting that a simple formula may grow a complex "foliage" of permutation, as a plant develops from a seed.

The thoroughness of the activity and the precision of the execution brought something to Childs' work which was almost like punctuation, as if she had dotted each *i*, employed semi-colons exactly where appropriate.

We have seen how modernism broke away from the tradition of humanitarian purpose to create an ethos where each art was focused on the materiality of its own presence—music on the sheer reality of time and sound, painting on its ingredients, space, mark and colour—and this is how we get a dancer like Childs focusing on the sound of her dancing feet. However, since well before the millennium, the dichotomy of oppositions, tradition versus modernism, Apollo versus Dionysus, abstract versus figurative, and the material of language versus narrative poetry, has been losing ground to an awareness of how the pipe can be permitted to play along with the lyre.

Fusion is possible. Lessons learnt from working with abstraction can provide a vital new approach to representation, to tragedy even. This brings about the cross-fertilisation of seemingly irreconcilable opposites. Pattern and shape for its own sake can be recruited for a purpose. Picasso remarked to Gertrude Stein that he and his fellow artists had paved the way for camouflage. Abstraction thus took on meaning in a military application. Paul Nash designed the camouflage for the Navy in the second world war.

Similarly, poetic structures pioneered in a non-narrative context can find a way to be employed by some new method of telling a story. A good example is Jorie Graham's poem *Fast*—the title poem of a recent collection from Carcanet—for here, what seems to start out densely, even obscurely, abstract eventuates in narrative, so that one re-reads the beginning again, in the light of that meaningful ending.

Abstraction, as pioneered by Gertrude Stein, the surreal dislocation of sense, the notion of a "game" of creation introduced by Raymond Roussel, and the delight in musicality emphasised in the work of Edith Sitwell and Dylan Thomas, may all serve to restore repetition, sound, surprise and rhythm to a poetics that tries not to sacrifice meaning altogether; though these values may be dismissed by those who adhere too strictly to the social purpose required by F. R. Leavis. The insights of abstraction may also go unappreciated by those whose poems are simply prose chopped into lines.

The difficulty facing any poet is how to steer a distinctive course. Poetry is not a genre in itself. Each poet must invent a genre within the wide range of poetic possibilities; must find a language. With the prevalence of "plurality" in the new century, with the synthesis of Apollo and Dionysus, it is tempting to become tolerant of all movements. Still, it is hardly wise to make oneself an all-inclusive omelette of trends. A painter knows that to mix too many colours together results in dullness. Perhaps, though, it is courtesy to refrain from overt hostility to what one cannot use.

Nevertheless, these are days when fusion is in the air: days of marrying unlikely partners and merging fields ostensibly far apart. Perhaps a historical view that plots a course from one development to another—modernism supposedly "leading" to post-modernism, for instance—is outmoded. Perhaps in the arts, we should not trace the profile of each success, and insist that this grew out of that: instead, we should consider that at all times, almost all possibilities of artistic and creative practice are being exploited, by someone somewhere. Within the sphere of what might be termed "Beauty and the Sublime", the notion of the picture within the picture, of "innocuous art" done simply for the art's sake, the notion of grandeur or of *non-finito* (the art of incompletion) have for centuries intrigued artistic practitioners, while within the sphere of "Ugliness and the Abject"—immoralism, the grotesque, fetishism, the uncanny and the capricious all have their creative adherents, as they have also had for a very long time. Essays of mine concerning these diverse "rivers of art" can be found on my blog: https://anthonyhowelljournal.wordpress.com/2013/07/06/art-and-its-dark-side-introduction/

The instruction art exercises that developed out of my engagement with performance, eventually enabled me to bring about a fusion of two aspects of my endeavours, the dance aspect and the poetic aspect. Through the mnemonics of the "action phrase", I was able to find a way of bringing together action and language.

≈

MY OWN INVOLVEMENT IN PERFORMANCE ART properly began in 1973 when my choric song, *Essora Tessorio*, was performed at The Whitechapel Gallery during Ed Meneely's exhibition there. This was primarily a verbal event, supplemented by dancers—Fergus Early and Jackie Lansley—who created an accompanying choreography. The audience was invited to recite the song. Those reciting were asked to intone its lines in staggered unison—holding a line for a minimum of fifteen counts, but joined by a second reciter after 5 counts, so the lines overlapped:

EEEEEEEEEEEEEEEEEEEEEEEEEEEEEEEEEEEEEEEEEEEEEEEEEEE
S-S-S-S-S-S-S-S-S-S-S-S-S-S-S-S-S-S-S-S-S-S-S-S-S-S-S-S-S-S-S-S-
iiiiiiiiiiiiiiiiiiiiiiiiiiiiiiiiiiiiiiiiiiiiiiiiiiiiiiiiiiiiiiiiiiiiiiiiiiiiiiiiiiiiiiiiiiii
zzzzzzzzzzzzzzzzzzzzzzzzzzzzzzzzzzzzzzzzzzzzzzzzzzzzzzzzzz
L-L-L-L-L-L-L-L-L-L-L-L-L-L-L-L-L-L-L-L-L-L-L-L-L-L-L-L-L-L-L
sssssssssssssssssssssssssssssssssssssssssssssssssssssssssssss
iyeh   iyeh   iyeh   iyeh   iyeh   iyeh   iyeh   iyeh   iyeh   iyeh   iyeh   iy

yes is less is yes is less is yes is less is yes is less is yes is less is yes is
eeeeeeeeeeeeeeeeeeeeeeeeeeeeeeeeeeeeeeeeeeeeeeeeeeeeeeeeeeeeeeee
th-th-th-th-th-th-th-th-th-th-th-th-th-th-th-th-th-th-th-th-th-th-th-

There are some two hundred and twenty lines in the complete song.

In the same year, I was invited to join the International Writers' program at the University of Iowa, thanks to my versions of the pre-Islamic poetry of Imr-al-Kais *(Imruil)*. In Iowa, I experimented with systemic writing; working through rigorously computed variations of a number of key sentences, using pronouns that could be varied rather than nouns:

I do more deeply than anyone else ever could. You don't more deeply than anyone else ever could. You silence me. Don't think I don't silence you. So. Not so because of me. Not under one. Under one because of you. Oh do I? Oh don't you? Not more deeply by never. Don't think more deeply by never because of me. All of me feels so. All of you does not feel so. To going with you and someone else. To not going with me and someone else. I do by not. You don't by not. Don't think I don't by not. To going with me and someone else. To not going with you and someone else. All of you feels so. All of me does not feel so. More deeply by never. Not more deeply by never because of you. Oh do you? Oh don't I don't you think? Under one. Not under one because of me. Not so. So because of you. I silence you. You don't silence me. You do more deeply than anyone else ever could. Don't think I don't more deeply than anyone else ever could.

You have left thousands on me. I have left thousands on you. I have left thousands on you. You have not left thousands on me.

From *Hot Damn, a Poetic Rage*

Calder and Boyars published one of the systemic texts I wrote in this period—*Oslo, a Tantric Ode*. This received an encouraging review by Robert Nye in *The Times,* but was otherwise ignored.

IN 1974, I FOUNDED THE THEATRE OF MISTAKES, an ironic name for a performance art initiative, and the work the company was pioneering initially occupied a territory shared by poetry and live art. I worked with "a tribe" of performers and the performances were generated by performance instruction exercises put together rather in the way one chooses dishes from a menu in a Chinese restaurant. There was always a performance space, even if it was a sitting-room. We had this idea that the space could be *on* or *off*, or we might designate where "off" was, much like a child's game. Thirty counts after a clap, the space would be "On!" In no way did it need to be a conventional theatre or dance space. And we sought out performance spaces, from the Corn Exchange in Cambridge to a village green and the fields of Purdies Farm. That this work was a fusion of action and poetry is born out by the fact that one of our performances—*Going*—was first performed at the Cambridge Poetry Festival.

The tribal stage of the company's development culminated in the performance of *The Street* in July, 1975. It was devised by members of the company nucleus—myself, Fiona Templeton, Michael Greenall and Patricia Murphy. Drawing from "The Gymnasium"—a comprehensive collection of performance exercises devised by the company—an engagement was created which required some nine weeks of rehearsal on the same London locale—Ascham Street in Kentish Town. The culminating performance featured a chorus of performers in the first-floor windows of my house, and any passer-by walking up the pavement on the left would trigger closure of the windows—which in turn caused the performers in the street to fall to the ground. A passer-by walking up the pavement on the right would trigger the opening of the windows and the continuation of the chorus which in turn triggered the continuation of the performance. The chorus itself was created out of snippets of conversation overheard from passers-by in the street below.

When we first started rehearsing for this piece, we distributed leaflets through letter-boxes, outlining our intentions. A local landlord clearly disapproved and got a tenant of his to voice disapproval by shouting at us as we started to perform, "Wipe your arses with your fucking brochures!" Well, this got repeated by the chorus in additive waves: "Wipe, wipe your, wipe your arses, wipe your arses with etc." After an hour and a half of this, everyone on the street saw the joke, and from then on, the people who lived on it very willingly collaborated with our efforts.

So these snippets were repeated additively in instant, repetitive sonnet forms. On the day of the actual show, the performance also featured the externalisation of residents' living rooms (their furniture including carpets and televisions got placed outside on the pavements). There was also an interior decorated skip, and slow-motion children who followed a slow-motion ice-cream van into the deepening twilight.

After this, the work of the company became more refined and the concern of a core group rather than a tribe. This smaller group initiated the fusion of serial poetry with serial actions. Performance art in those days was very much in the process of defining itself and, in our case at least, of distancing itself from the expressive rituals of Hermann Nitsch and the autobiographical shamanism of Joseph Beuys. Stuart Sherman, Gilbert and George, Bruce McLean (with Nice Style) and Min Tanaka, among others, were some of the key players promoting a more conceptual approach, which explored irony rather than imitating the excessive expressions of the earlier actionists, and this brought about a new diversity of specialization and preoccupation which took action as an art in itself forward at this time, in tandem with that complete reinvention of theatre and spectacle pioneered by Robert Wilson and the large scale-wrapping projects of Christo. The history of performance in this period can be found in *Performance: Live Art since the 60s* by Roselee Goldberg (Thames and Hudson 1998) and my own book: *The Analysis of Performance Art: a guide to its theory and Practice* (Routledge 1999).

Functional action became the domain of The Theatre of Mistakes. This was a notion of action emancipated from gesture—much as the austere paintings of Michael Craig-Martin, delineated with architectural tape, freed painting from the notion that gestural brushwork defined artistry; while the strict conceptual instructions that might generate a work by Sol Lewitt would be uninfluenced by the idiosyncrasy of any personal gesture.

By functional action, what do I mean?

The actions that we used in our performances were those commonly used in everyday life: picking up a chair and putting it down somewhere else, moving a table, taking off a jacket, or walking over to a pull switch light and pulling the chord. There was no music—unless we sang. The majority of these actions was accompanied by a word or phrase. Were we to vary the order of any sequence of actions, then the order of the phrases associated with the actions would be varied as well. The results were rhythmic and hypnotic.

We stressed the point that we were not "acting". We were ourselves—we were performers. But then we became pre-occupied with copying each other's actions and "being each other". The culmination of this dynamic activity came with the performance called *Going*—in which each performer copied the actions of a previous performer.

> GOING is a five-act performance. In it, the performers have to learn all the parts, while trying to be each other rather than presuming to enact characters. It is a fugue put together out of the mannerisms of departure. It concerns going, or attempting to go when the participants are bound together as closely as the strands of a knotted ring. Each weaves a role identical to that of the others into different moments of the same role.

> (From a statement on a poster for the performance of *Going* in New York.)

The notion of a performance where the early scenes of an act are instigated by one performer with subsequent performers trying to repeat the actions instigated had for a long time been a preoccupation of the company. Here is how *Going* is structured:

> There are five acts in the play. Each of the five acts is a repetition of the first act, and each is instigated by a different performer. In each act a further element is introduced by the first performer to enter in that act. Each new element is repeated in all subsequent acts.

The text was learnt by all the performers—but it was only heard in its entirety in the very last act. It is not a monologue but a three-way conversation accompanied by actions:

> I do think I'd better be going now because I ...
> Oh, don't be so silly.

Really, I must go.
Tell her she ought to stay.
Ahem.
I do have to go now.
You don't have to go.
Are you sure?
She doesn't have to go, does she?
'Fraid so.
I can't stand it.
Tell me, does she have to go?
I just think it's better to.
Why do you have to go?
If you must, you must.
Goodbye.
'Bye.
Really.
I can't stand it either.
That's why I have to go.
Do you think I ought to stay?
Are you just afraid to tell me …?
Oh, don't be so silly.

Going: The Theatre of Mistakes, Grey Suit Editions, 2007

What is significant from the perspective of our theme is that each phrase is only said when performing the action that always goes with that phrase. Thus, *I do think I'd better be going now because I …* is always said by a seated person resting one elbow on a table who rises from the chair while speaking those words. *Oh, don't be so silly,* is said by someone who rushes onto the space and pulls the person who said *I do think I'd better be going now because I …* back into the chair.

Just as the relation of the signifier to the signified has been described as that of a sheet of paper to its own back, each action was welded to its phrase. This way of constructing a performance sequence that could then be systemically subjected to variation grew out of the discovery of the *word unit*, where a word was always accompanied by a unit of action. If that word or phrase got repeated then so did the action welded to it. In retrospect, immersed in writing this book, I realise that we had, by some circuitous route, returned to the notion of the ancient chorus stepping to the metre of the verse. The work was mutually created by its performers, and I do recall that while we aligned ourselves to the minimal artists and the conceptual artists who were our contemporaries, we sensed also a kinship with the Noh, and we certainly felt that our endeavours restored to theatre the *action* of the chorus in Greek drama and restored to poetry a sense of the physicality that came from the accompanying action.

The notion evolved into the *action phrase*—which is what we called the unification of phrase and action that was employed in *Going*. A very grainy video of the piece can be found here: https://theatreofmistakes.wordpress.com/2017/11/13/going/

Each act was timed by "the metronome"—a performer who slowly paced the perimeter of the performance space. One at a time, each performer became the metronome. Ultimately, however, everything about *Going* is synchronised—so the metronome was as much timed by the action as the action was timed by the metronome. Time became a substance for the company. This is very apparent in another piece—*The Waterfall*. It was created for a terrace at the Hayward Gallery during the first Hayward Annual in 1977. There was a different performance for each day of this 48-day exhibition. The piece was originally based on a timing device for another performance. You could say that the form of the Theatre of Mistakes was space, but the content was time.

On the first day, a single performer sat cross-legged on the ground between two buckets. She held a cup in each hand. She scooped water out of the first pail into one cup, poured it into the other cup, then poured it out of the second cup into the second pail. Each action lasted for twenty counts—so transference of water took 60 seconds per cupful. There were sixty cups of water in the first pail—so to empty it took an hour. Her last action was to stand, pick up the now full bucket, and to pour all the water in the second pail back into the first pail.

On the second day a second performer was added as well as a chair and the second performer, seated on the chair, held the second bucket between his legs—now the last action of the first performer was to pour water from the second cup into the first cup of the second performer. The last action of the second performer was to stand on the chair and pour the contents of the filled bucket back into the bucket on the floor. Thus a pouring chain was established. On the third day a table was added and a third performer. By the twelfth day there were twelve performers arranged vertically above each other on a structure made of tables balanced on chairs balanced on top of other tables.

Performances happened at a different hour each day, sometimes as the sun rose, sometimes as it set. The synchronisation of arm-movements for the pouring was achieved by the recitation of chants known as "Koans"—and all these chants were based on weather reports from off-shore regions of the British Isles. The Koans linked repetitive actions (of pouring water) with metrically scanned verse "Koans" which progressed from simple to elaborate metrical feet, and these could be overlaid so as to coincide with the culmination of a group action. Koans were recited additively—line 1, then 1 + 2, 1 + 2 + 3 etc—and lasted the length of a pour. When you poured into another performer's cup you shared the koan with that performer.

The first Koan was simple (spondees):

Blue Sky
Rough sea
High winds
Cold front
Gale force
Eight knots

However, the last was elaborately complex:

The Hebrides will
Be sweltering if
As thundery as
Snowdonia or
As variable
As yesterday was.

See *Appendix 6*—for the complete set of Waterfall Koans.

Each day's performance culminated in the pouring of the water in the top bucket into the lower bucket—which was quite a feat at the height of the structure—so at every stage the lower bucket had to be within range of the upper pouring position—this dictated the nature of the construction. After twelve days, the performer cross-legged on the ground was removed and the lower bucket raised onto the first chair—so by the twenty-fourth day there was again only one performer, this time sitting at the height of the completed edifice of chair on chair on table on chairs on tables on chairs on tables, with a bucket on either side. For the next twenty-four days, the entire sequence of performance was reversed, and so the structure was dismantled and the last day was a reflection of the first.

⁂

INCREASINGLY, MNEMONICS INTERESTED THE COMPANY, and it became a focused preoccupation of Peter Stickland, an architect who had joined the company early and created drafted drawings and diagrams of our structures. He went on to create mnemonic performances of his own. We devised increasingly complex pieces that utilised memory by ascribing a phrase to an external prompt brought about through the action with which it was associated. One piece used each action-associated phrase or sentence as a palimpsest that could generate other sentences exactly matching the ictic stresses of the initial phrase or sentence. This was *Orpheus and Hermes*— one of our last performances. Julian Maynard Smith and Miranda Payne performed in it: and they went on to create *Station House Opera*—a company which has carried the flame of team performance art ever since.

The set for *Orpheus and Hermes* was two free-standing doors set at right-angles to each other. Opening a door and stepping beyond it while still holding onto its handle involved the performer in a sequence of small actions, each situated in a slightly different location. These locations became associated with poetic sentences, so one memorised what was said at the location as you took the steps required to open a door and walk through the doorway. Each location was thus invested with sentences (which altered, depending on whether one was going through the door into the space the door opened into or back the other way). It was thus that the space in which one found oneself, in relation to the door, prompted the memory of the sentence appropriate to that place and direction. Again, we were utilising the fusion of poetry with actions.

Hermes was the guide of Orpheus when he went to the underworld to rescue Euridice. There were forty-eight sentences concerned with not looking back (Don't look back. Take another step. Go on. Aim into the future. Aim into the iron wind etc). These were said additively as one opened a door and walked through it. Each move required its subtraction before progress could be made, so there were twelve sentences advocating looking back (After all I must look back. How can I be certain? etc). The performer used the forward-looking sentences while opening the door to go through it, the backward-looking sentences when reversing. Performers alternated their actions, and this generated the exchange of sentences as if having a conversation. Memory of which sentence to use was fused with where precisely one was on the set.

Not only that. There were also these palimpsests I've mentioned. While writing the piece, I would white out a sentence and replace it with another that scanned exactly with the original "root" sentence. Thus each position was the repository of all sentences that scanned with its root sentence, and all sentences on that spot in the reversed direction. Each sentence was overlaid with other versions which scanned with it. I called this method of generating poetry "Sentence Scansion". The sentences became more and more complex, and each sentence had a feminine version and a masculine version—beginnings adjusted to start on or off the ictus or the ends adjusted in the same manner. Finally the piece generated negative versions of positive sentences and positive versions of negative sentences. Here is an example of how one sentence could be altered.

Driving on with deliberate devilry into dangers,
      baffle analysis with your *joie de vivre!*
Nullify your neurotically Narcissistic reflections
        —why make of messages a *roman des lettres?*
Naturally the negation of nervousness at an absence
      must add an elegance to the *je ne sais quoi.*

Competence in complicity conjures up our excitement
      —should the wife deputise for a *femme de chambre?*

A readiness to revivify vivisected reactions
      sullies the finery of *Les Fleurs du Mal.*
Play the pipe with particular prettiness in the twilight
      —scorn the proximity of *le pays ténebreux,*
Regurgitated remembering rummages in an attic
      —down with the preference for *les neiges d'antan.*

Orpheus and Hermes amounted to the baroque culmination of the company's endeavours. We did not survive this devastating accumulation of complexity, and soon after the performers went their separate ways.

⁂

THE ACTION PHRASE AMOUNTED TO A FUSION OF ACTION and poetry. Sentence scansion generated a peculiar and ultimately ornate versification. Indeed, this was theatre transformed into *musical* structure—drama as fugue, our actions often generating harmonising duets, as in opera. Other work included *The Table Moves* and *Homage to Morandi*—which were both works which developed from similar principles.

Performance art was engaged in freeing movement from simply being an illustration of a score, as in ballet, and it allowed the emancipation of action as an art in itself, while the *action phrase* sought to explore a new way of connecting words to action. But there was no articulated dialectics, no theory, back in the seventies, for performance art itself—unlike film, which had a robust body of thought generating theories and suggesting strategies such as "expanded cinema"—which is well covered in Peter Gidal's *Materialist Film* (Routledge 1989). Using the films of Andy Warhol, Jean-Luc Goddard and Malcolm LeGrice, his book explores questions of film form and cinematic meaning within avant-garde cinema, with particular reference to fusions of film projection and performance, as exemplified by the 'solid light' pieces by Anthony McCall and the work of Annabel Nicholson (threading a film of herself at a sewing machine through a sewing machine she was working at, so as it was projected we watched it being progressively destroyed).

Fiona Templeton and I wrote *Elements of Performance Art* (Theatre of Mistakes Edition 1976), in response to this perceived lack of a theory of performance. The book was a pedagogical tool, basically a compilation of exercises the company had generated during its tribal beginnings. Later, I evolved a theory of the primaries of performance—stillness, repetition and, inconsistency—compare Deleuze: *Difference and Repetition*—and these are discussed in depth in my own book, *The Analysis of Performance Art* (Harwood/Routledge 1999).

It was at the end of the 70s that the core-members of The Theatre of Mistakes separated and began creating solo performances.

※

I FOUND MYSELF PERFORMING AND LECTURING IN AUSTRALIA at the invitation of Sydney College of the Arts. The inspiration of this desert country stimulated a resurgence of writing poetry unaccompanied by performance. For some seven years, my own writing, apart from what was written for the company, had focused on writing freed from narrative signification. I thought of this poetry as "abstract". In Australia, I became interested in writing poetry that was descriptive but without significance. I've referred to this aspect of modernist poetry earlier. It was in Australia that it occurred to me that significance could be removed, just as narrative or figuration could be abandoned, and that narrative description could be retained by modernism if the significance was drained out of it—as in *The Dazzling Day* by Lewis MacAdams, quoted in the preceding chapter.

Why? Because perhaps the most urgent issue modernism faced was the need to get away from the belief that "coherent" language was a "true" mirror of life that could communicate the moral and social significance of the issues to which it alluded. It's a view propounded by Leavis, and it is still the dominating orthodoxy of the British literary establishment. Leavis believed that literature should be closely related to criticism of life and that it was therefore a critic's duty to assess works according to the author's and society's moral position. But his pragmatic judgement fails to take into account the difference between object and description. As Marcel Duchamp shows us, *Ceci n'est pas une pipe*. A painting of a pipe is not a pipe. It's a painting. And in a similar way, a poem is a thing in itself, it is not that to which it refers. It cannot be defined by its meaning. I can describe a pipe in words. That description is not a pipe. Leavis fails to comprehend the artifice of art. Moral and social significance are matters extrinsic to the stuff of poetry, and a work without such significance may emerge with a presence which is purely its own, and that presence is its poetry, compounded of its material existence as a thing of words. This was something that I. A. Richards understood when he promoted a "practical criticism" that stressed the way a poem was constructed; which is more relevant to grasping its nature than searching for whether it has fulfilled some moral or social obligation. The only British critic who understood this, and championed a position similar to my own and to several of the "language" poets deliberately marginalised by the establishment, was Veronica Forrest-Thomson in her seminal book *Poetic Artifice: a theory of twentieth century poetry* (Shearsman 2016—posthumous publication).

As a poet, I was as influenced by the ideas that had revolutionised visual art as I was by poetic theory. Just as Richard Long might create a verbal art piece listing the objects in his line of sight, I tried to write a poetry which simply generated descriptive sentences from observation, but without seeking *justification* by attaching a motive, moral or ethical, to the process. I identified this avoidance of significance with the writing of J-K Huysmans, tracing from his work a thread that led to *A Nest of Ninnies* by John Ashbery and Jimmy Schuyler, which is a collage of dinner-table conversations, and I also took as my model *Une Vue* by Raymond Roussel, which is basically the exhaustive and meticulous description of a tiny photograph mounted in a pen-holder. This line-of-sight writing was exemplified in my poem, *The Age of the Street*, which begins:

> Here is the passing of an uneventful hour
> In a backwater of the town, above a backwater of the bay
> Behind the containers brought to this faraway shore.
> Wall-to-wall carpet, sweet-smelling dust in the air,

The gloss of doors, each knob a scintilla of day,
Rackets and hats, glimpses of sash and pane
Through the blinds, flaws troubling the picture-plane:
Then lengths of railing, kerb and the grey camber
Levelling off into gutters lead the eye away
With the newsboy's whistle as he tugs his trolley of papers
Up the shallow incline punctuated by some blooms.
An hour between darkness and light for overcast portions
Of changeable afternoons; monochrome, khaki and amber
Moments with no more definition than a reproduction
In the discarded volume: vacant chairs and rooms,
Reticent gardens, phones unanswered, pasted-over heaven,
Locked factory gates…

(From *Why I May Never See The Walls of China*, Anthony Howell, Anvil 1986)

However, describing Australia rarely felt as if one were reproducing the ordinary. Describing Australia often felt surreal! The ground was red, the leaves were grey, and the trees lost their bark instead of their leaves. It got hotter in the North. Andre Breton felt a similar sensation when experiencing the jungle of the Amazon and observed that had he known about the nature of the jungle he would not have needed surrealism at all. To a westerner brought up in a temperate climate, there is something dreamlike about these faraway and dissimilar environments.

What was significant, for my own development, was coming across the work of Bruce Chatwin. Reading his *Song Lines* in Australia strongly reinforced an interest in walking as fundamental both to the human condition and to the generation of poetry. The interest in walking—and the possibility of working in vast spaces—led me to re-create a piece called *Active Circles,* devised by The Theatre of Mistakes a few years earlier. This came about because, after performing my *Table Move Solos* at the Biennale of Sydney in April, 1982, I was invited to Perth, Western Australia, by the art organisation *Praxis*. From Perth, an expedition was set up to go out to the dry lakes of the goldfields, to research the largest available performance spaces in that desert region. Another group, *Media Space*, collaborated with *Praxis* in creating a team of six performers in addition to myself, and it included my host, Allan Vizents, who met me at the airport.

I decided to keep a log of this expedition. Here are some passages from that log:

...In the afternoon I sit re-reading the instructions for *Active Circles*. It's a performance The Theatre of Mistakes abandoned in 1977 because the company couldn't find a flat space in England large enough for it. It's like a game really, the performers forming two radii of a circle which can accelerate towards the centre or towards the perimeter—and when both radii form a single straight line, a new, larger circle can be started, with either end of the line-out as its pivot...

...In the long, hot summer of 1977 we did perform *Active Circles* on Hartley Wintney village-green, which has a sizeable cricket-pitch, as a dance to bring down the rain—or so we told the press! It had to be abandoned after 9 hours though, because performers were beginning to circumnavigate the village during their circling—thus losing sight of each other. However, as we packed it in, the first drops of rain fell—as the *Southern Evening Echo* duly noted— though the R.A.F Met. office claimed, post hoc, that they knew all along the weather was about to change...

...If we take seven people out into the desert and perform *Active Circles* as a five-performer piece, then we can count on two reserve players at all times, ensuring that everybody gets a two-hour break—but if we've only two women that'll mean that the girls never get a break. Finally, somebody somewhere in Perth says Yes, she'll bring a sleeping bag, warm clothing etc. and meet us at Media Space at 7 p.m....

...On the dune, red peelings, shards, husks of bark fall from each gumtree onto its black circle of dead leaves, and the burnt remnants of some former tree. The sand vividly red, the dead embers black, the peel grated on top of the embers vividly red again—while the naked orange trunks of the trees reach up out of the centres of these debris strewn circles, wrinkling like human skin at all joints and junctions...

...I suggest a few practice exercises—additive spins, when one revolves for one turn in one direction, two in the other direction, three in the original direction and so on—as a method of unwinding and rewinding when spinning fast in the centre of a circle…and we try changing instigation of the circles; gyrating at speed, or slowly, in the centre—or walking at speed, or slowly, around the circumference of a circle whose centre is your opposite number—a slow centre causing a fast perimeter, and vice-versa. I then teach everybody the rules of *Active Circles*, and by noon most of my performers have more or less got the hang of it. We break for lunch and a siesta, during which I write up the log.

After lunch, we venture out further onto the lake, which has dried up considerably in the noonday sun……Certain rules are changed, in particular the instructions for what happens after an audible line is called—denoting the moment when two radii are at 6 o'clock position…Also, we noted some tentative ratios for the vortex circling—when velocity increases towards the centre… So to get an audible line from a vortex—always more difficult than a 'clock-hands' type of circling:

5 walks ½ a circle; 4 walks a full circle- moving twice as fast as 5; 3 walks 1 ½ circles—moving two thirds faster than 4; 2 walks 2 circles—moving ¾ faster than 3; 1 spins on the spot.

As the sun goes down we break for 'tea', as the Australians call supper, and prepare for our night project... Five performers, each equipped with one of the five smaller gas-lamps, perform circling exercises and then specific moves from *Active Circles* on the flat sands below. Since there are seven of us, we still have one reserve performer, so everyone gets a chance to watch the torch-lit ellipses of our performance from the higher ground. I have the sensation that in a small way we are contributing to the universe, as our wheeling lights twinkle below the larger wheel of the milky way; our lamps adding to the general nebulosity. Inside the performance, during a vortex circling, one gets the impression that this lagoon of sand is a wide shadowy circus ring—all one can see are feet, lamps and the looming and veering shadows.

Working at night with lamps seems to me the best way to perform *Active Circles*. Only the arcs are visible; nothing distracts from the intention of the work. As Lindsay remarks, the afterimages keep burning in the back of the head. We also try an extended audible line, finishing up on the opposite headland to the camera, where Martin sets a tree alight. This 'burning bush' flickers at the far end of our line of lights which continues up into the stars. It keeps flaring and flickering as we make our way back to the tents…

(Extracts from an article first published in Performance Magazine, Issue 33— the full log may be found in Appendix 2)

ᚪᚪ

WITH THIS PERFORMANCE OF *ACTIVE CIRCLES*, the action of walking in itself took over from the "action phrase"—and the next performance I created, *The Tower,* used no words, while I had also returned to writing poetry which entailed no action. My two interests, poetry and dance, had once more separated into discrete pursuits. However, the experience of creating performances was still to have a bearing on my writing. Just as I had become interested in performances which might turn an arrangement of furniture through 90 degrees, as if trying to create a species of performance cubism, I became interested in what I termed "Ninety degree turn poems". In such a poem, one starts off writing descriptively about one subject, and then switches subject and continues writing descriptively about a completely different matter. I was interested in the moment of incomprehension that might occur at the "hinge": a disjunction that created abstraction at the seam where the two descriptions came together. Sometimes of course, after the poem had been written, a connection between the two subjects might be perceived, but this was always "after the event". I quote one of these 90-degree turn poems in its entirety:

UPWARDS

Telephone poles, their cable-mounts and coils
Fixed on quadrivial spars and cross-beams;
These are the totems raised along our ways,
Hung with our emblems, our street-signs,
With waste-paper bins also attached to them.
Boasting obscure number-plates, letters tacked on
Or stencilled over metal stamped with codes,

They exhibit gouged initials, adze-scars,
Blackened nail-heads where redundant data
Has been prised off at some time or another.
Never quite vertical, inclined towards the sag
In staves of wires, their makeshift scaffolds rise
From kerosene-soaked bases covered with elks,
With staghorns, birds' nests; leeches of root,
Extra-terrestrials clinging to rain-forest giants;
Their dinosaur trunks displacing painted leaves,
Low plants of the undergrowth, sodden logs
Disintegrating beneath moss and red earth.
Out of the overgrowth things occasionally drop:
Palm shards, centipede and earwig husk,
Spastic calf-supports—all on a grand scale
- Falling off and sliding through the slits
In fanlike greenery down onto the shadows below.
There are bird quivers and invisible sounds
Where the simply enormous arm of the Grandis
(The Flooded Gum) holds aloft a paraplegic
Fist of high branches, thumbs twisted
Into the heart of the hand in the tree's heartland.

The 90-degree turn could be compared to a single act of collage, except that in the visual field one can see both "pieces" simultaneously whereas in writing the turn comes as a surprise. When such a right angle happens in time (as in poetry) the sensation is like that of a cartoon character racing away to escape some predator and running off a cliff without realising that there is no longer any ground beneath him.

Would I have hit upon this idea without already having developed an interest in right-angles in my performances? I came to it partly through the cubists, by taking their theories into theatre, while the enthralling possibilities of turning things around emerged out of an engrossment in permutations and variations that was inspired by the systemic music of Philip Glass and the dances made by Lucinda Childs.

I also realise that the reader may ask, why the Theatre of Mistakes? Mistakes were the performance equivalent of dramatic catastrophe. Very often, our structures and instructions were complex. Suspense accrued to "getting it right." It was easy for a performer to go wrong and "jeopardise" the unfolding of the action. When this happened, a forfeit might have to be paid, a correction given—as can be seen happening in *Going*. The possibility of a mistake brought tension and uncertainty to the work. The mistake was performance art's answer to the *Deus ex Machina*.

EXILED SENSES

1. TANGO SHIVA
Exiled senses—smell, taste and touch/the tango as the feel of walking/ Weight as a tactile sensation and the physical sense of the metrical beat.

To speak like a river and to move like a panther: two ambitions that complement each other.

Essentially when we associate walking with scansion we are associating the tactile sense with the auditory one, connecting touch with sound. Of course, making a sound is also a tactile sensation.

However, as well as considering the pace and the sound, it has been fashionable (since Mallarmé) to take into account the "look" of the poem, how it presents itself on the white page. This may have been a preoccupation that recommended itself to the French because their poets were desperate to get away from the prevailing monopoly of the Alexandrine (the invention of the prose poem was another way of liberating French verse from this inherited formal strait-jacket). Nevertheless, consideration of the "look" of the poem made an impression on American writing—Cummings and Carlos Williams come to mind. Visual concerns influenced the structure of Pound's *Cantos*. The twentieth century was very much a visual century, and this emphasis has influenced poetry. But can the structure of a poem be founded on its look on the page? Or is the look simply its façade?

A fair amount of contemporary theoretical writing has been given over to questioning the prevailing emphasis on the visualising of concepts—particularly in architecture—a visualisation promoted at the expense of other senses:

> …The privileging of the sense of sight over the other senses is an inarguable theme in Western thought, and it is also an evident bias in the architecture of our century. The negative development in architecture is, of course, forcefully supported by forces and patterns of management, organisation and production as well as by the abstracting and universalising impact of technological rationality itself. The negative developments in the realm of the senses cannot, either, be directly attributed to the historical privileging of the sense of vision itself. The perception of sight as our most important sense is well grounded in physiological, perceptual and psychological facts. The problems arise from *the isolation of the eye outside its natural interaction with other sense modalities*, and from the elimination and suppression of other senses, which increasingly reduce and restrict the experience of the world into the sphere of vision. This separation and reduction fragments the innate complexity, comprehensiveness and plasticity of the perceptual system, reinforcing a sense of detachment and alienation.

> Juhani Pallasmaa. *The Eyes of the Skin; architecture and the senses,* p. 43.

Pallasmaa points out that, in contrast to such excessive visualisation, Merleau-Ponty's philosophy makes the human body the centre of the experiential world.

> I confront the city with my body; my legs measure the length of the arcade and the width of the square; my gaze unconsciously projects my body onto the facade of the cathedral, where it roams over the mouldings and contours, sensing the size of recesses and projections; my body weight meets the mass of the cathedral door, and my hand grasps the door pull as I enter the dark void behind. I experience myself in the city, and the city exists through my embodied experience. The city and my body supplement and define each other. I dwell in the city and the city dwells in me.

> *Ibid.* p. 43

Pallasmaa goes on to emphasise the importance of touch when it comes to comprehending our world:

> In accord with Berkeley, Hegel claimed that the only sense that can give a sensation of spatial depth is touch, because touch 'senses the weight, resistance, and three-dimensional shape (gestalt) of material bodies, and thus makes us aware that things extend away from us in all directions.'

Ibid. p. 45

Touch is a misleading term in many ways. The word suggests sensations received at the tips of fingers or the feeling of being touched by finger-tips. This tactile sense is more than that. It encompasses the entire sphere of sensation, of what we register through feeling, of what is felt inside the body as well as on its external surface. Pain is one of its components, and so is the orgasm. Laughter is experienced as a feeling and so are tears.

The feeling of walking is especially interesting. But initially, let us simply stand.

To stand up on two feet is one of our very first achievements. It is not learnt exactly, since nobody teaches us to do it and we do not as yet have the language to describe it to ourselves. We may be aided by the mirror neurons, which help us imitate what we see being performed. These neurons are one of the most important discoveries in neuroscience. Essentially, mirror neurons respond to actions that we observe in others. Mirror neurons fire in the same way when we actually recreate that action ourselves. Apart from imitation, they are responsible for plenty of other sophisticated human actions and thought processes. Defects in the mirror neuron system may be linked to disorders such as autism; so it may be responsible for an excessive reliance on visualisation since these neurons establish a major connection between sight and motor sensation.

But what do we feel when we stand? We feel gravity. We feel the pull of the mass of our planet. And as we balance on our two feet the vestibular system comes into play. This is well explained by the American Speech Language Hearing Association:

Balance and equilibrium help us stay upright when standing and know where we are in relation to gravity. Our balance system also helps us walk, run, and move without falling. Balance is controlled through signals to the brain from your eyes, the inner ear, and the sensory systems of the body (such as the skin, muscles, and joints). This balance system is also known as the vestibular system.

In the inner ear, the balance system consists of three semi-circular canals that contain fluid and "sensors" that detect rotational movement of the head. Each of the semi-circular canals lies at a different angle and is situated at a right angle to each other. The semi-circular canals deal with different movement: up-and-down, side-to-side, and tilting from one side to the other. All contain sensory hair cells that are activated by movement of inner ear fluid (endolymph). As the head moves, hair cells in the semi-circular canals send nerve impulses to the brain by way of the acoustic nerve. The nerve impulses are processed in the brain to help us know where we are in space or if we are moving.

Located near the semi-circular canals are the utricle and the saccule. The ends of the semi-circular canals connect with the utricle, and the utricle connects with the saccule. The semi-circular canals provide information about movement of the head. The sensory hair cells of the utricle and saccule provide information to the brain about head position when it is not moving. The utricle is sensitive to change in horizontal movement. The saccule is sensitive to the change in vertical acceleration (such as going up in an elevator).

So just as the mirror neurons associate seeing with feeling, the vestibular system associates the ear with physical balance—which we register through physical sensation. The semi-circular canals located within the ear constitute our personal spirit-levels.

Very much dependent on balance, walking, connected through the Greek chorus to poetry, may be proposed as being in a metaphorical relationship with talking, while standing may be likened to a pause. To stand is to listen. To walk is to express.

We experience the stillness of simply standing through tactile means; our sense of our weight in our soles, pressing us down against the floor.

It is through physical sensation that we experience not only our density, that is, our weight against the ground, but also our volume, however distorted a view some eating disorder may have warped this into. We have a *feeling* of our volume.

This volume can be conveyed through our feet. When we land from a jump, the floor responds. Elephants can hear through their feet. As well as their vast ears, they have extended pads to their soles and will use both to locate the presence of a rival herd or of danger. While trumpeting may be heard a good distance away, elephants can also communicate in a low rumble that can travel as far as 6 miles, and the elephant receiving the call picks it up through its feet. So when an elephant stomps when agitated, there's a purpose greater than just warning those in the immediate area—the elephant may also be warning other elephants many miles away. And when an elephant rumbles a call, it could be intended for family members far out of sight.

> It's believed that elephants can hear storms as much as 100 to 150 miles (160 to 240 kilometers) away," Michael Garstang, a meteorologist at the University of Virginia, Charlottesville, told National Geographic. "When culling was being done in some of the parks, the elephants could clearly detect and identify the thump-thump-thump sound of the helicopter blades from 80 to 90 miles (130 to 140 kilometers) away, identify it as danger, and take off in the opposite direction.

This space each inhabits is self-created, or rather each is it, that space uniquely his or hers. Its volume is pretty large, if you are an elephant. But does the elephant perceive it as large, or simply as itself, what it is? To be created is to create a space for oneself. And indeed, Lefebvre asks:

> Can the body, with its capacity for action, and its various energies, be said to create space? Assuredly, but not in the sense that occupation might be said to 'manufacture' spatiality; rather, there is an immediate relationship between the body and its space, between the body's deployment in space and its occupation of space. Before *producing* effects in the material realm (tools and objects), before *producing itself* by drawing nourishment from that realm, and before *reproducing itself* by generating other bodies, each living body *is* space and *has* its space: it produces itself in space and it also produces that space. This is a truly remarkable relationship: the body with the energies at

its disposal, the living body, creates or produces its own space; conversely, the laws of space, which is to say the laws of discrimination in space, also govern the living body and the deployment of its energies.

Lefebvre—p 170

Bend our knees as we stand, and we seem to press down more. But how can we press down more? Our weight is whatever it is, so we can't exert greater pressure. But bending the knees redistributes the location of the weight, puts more of it into the heel, in all likelihood, unless the heels are raised. And it also redistributes the tension between sinews and ligaments in the body itself. Now let the knees straighten, but keep the weight in the heels, now shift all the weight into one of the heels and push off. Walking alternates weight.

There's a sense of presence in the step, a spatial and tactile awareness of the self from which poetry profited, by being linked to the landing of the foot. Upbeat is linked to the push, downbeat to its grounding. Slow it right down, to feel each detail of the tread as it is taken by the foot; speed it up and experience the striking of each heel in succession. Strike and strike and strike and strike. Walking generates the stressed and unstressed components of metre. It is this that gives verse the dynamic of walking. Here touch links up with hearing, and we perceive how the senses weave a web among themselves—as Pallasmaa suggests.

I'm convinced that tactility is of a different order to the other four senses, as the thumb is of a different order to the four fingers. Touch is the thumb of the senses. You might lose a finger, but you wouldn't want to lose a thumb. For one thing, sight is specifically located, so is smell, hearing and taste. Touch is everywhere. It "embodies" the body.

The body is not a mere physical entity; it is enriched by both memory and dream, past and future. Edward S. Casey (*Remembering: A Phenomenological Study*, Indiana University Press, 2000, p. 172) even argues that our capacity for memory would be impossible without a body memory. The world is reflected in the body, and the body is projected onto the world. We remember through our bodies as much as through our nervous system and brain.

Juhani Pallasmaa. *The Eyes of the Skin; architecture and the senses,* p.49.

The subtle connections between the body's diverse forms of sensory input go further than vestibules and mirrors. There are nerves in the nose that connect the nose to the heart, so breathing and heart rate are "in touch" with each other.

Synaesthesia is an ever-popular arena for speculation—hearing colours and seeing sounds—but one could ask, what does that colour smell like? What sensation does that painting give you—heavy, light? A stroking or a jab? What colour is that taste? What sound does that smell make?

I leave such speculation aside. When I consider the literature of the senses, I am inevitably drawn to the writing of Joris-Karl Huysmans, especially to his novel À *Rebours*—"Against Nature" or "Against the Grain". Going "against the grain" of predictable "reality", Huysmans turned to an exploration of esoteric sensations and smells. He got labelled a decadent, but it would be more accurate to say that he was in fact seeking new spheres of perception. The hero of this novel, the retiring aesthete Des Esseintes, creates his own artificial paradise within the walls of his house in a suburb of Paris.

Writing in the twilight of the 19th century, Huysmans had initially embraced realism, admiring the work of Balzac, Zola and Flaubert. But he began to realise that reality had an irritating habit of repeating itself. Realism became tedious, since after all ordinary people lived out their normal lives accompanied by the usual upsets. Like any long-running soap, a celebration of the ordinary fell back onto the same stories. Adultery was a sin so common that it became a cliché. Suffering all too often came down to complications caused by over-eating. Seeking more novel experiences to describe, Huysmans became a pioneer of a writing removed from passion, forensic yet humorous, a style that was swiftly labled "decadent", However, it is writing which shows him to have been a precursor, or pioneer, of modernism. In his work he betrays a penchant for the tactile:

Ever since his early youth, he had been tormented by inexplicable feelings of revulsion, by shuddering spasms which left him chilled to the marrow, his teeth on edge, whenever, for instance, he saw wet laundry being wrung out by a servant; these reactions still persisted; even today it actually made him suffer to hear someone tearing up a cloth, or to rub his finger over a bit of chalk or run his hand over a piece of watered silk.

Against Nature, trans. Margaret Maulden, Oxford World's Classics, 1998

Des Esseintes has a cabinet of scents, capable in subtle combination of evoking a scene such as a hayfield in summer. He has a collection of the engravings of Christian martyrs by the Flemish artist Jan Luyken, depicting torture in a myriad of ingenious ways. He is an effete, sickly individual, immersed in all that the senses can offer, except that of taste—in that regard he subsists on a French version of Bovril. As a writer, he is significant for a sense of irony that heralded in the notion of the "absurd" and for his emphasis on sensory impressions.

In 1906, William James published *The Varieties of Religious Experience: A Study in Human Nature.* The purpose was by no means theological. James believed that religious experiences were simply physical experiences. This was a pragmatic approach that examined emotional states as sensations "Religious happiness is happiness. Religious trance is trance." His 'down-to-earth' view encouraged his pupil, Gertrude Stein to consider words as material things—and set her off on her quest to explore the sensation of that materiality through repetition and word order. In philosophy, Wittgenstein adopted a similar down-to-earth focus: "Words are pictures of facts". Allusion to the double-aspected coincidence of signifier and signified in the word is an attempt to define its material actuality. All these impulses are evidence of a twentieth-century zeitgeist which sought to get away from metaphysical, sentimental or political projection. A focus on our actual response to specific stimuli ushered in this new dawn.

The integrity of physical and emotional sensation, the input from our nose, from our taste-buds, from our sense of the ground under our feet—a groundedness in how things are—as gathered from all our senses—is of considerable relevance to poetry. Remember that we see nothing other than the words, when we read, and we hear no actual sounds, only the sounds associated with the signifier, the word itself—not the actual sound of a car shifting its gears or a nightingale elaborating on its song. Each art has its limitations, despite what may be claimed by enthusiasts of synaesthesia. We do not hear a painting. We do not see music. A description of a face in words cannot actually produce a likeness. However, good writing is capable of *evoking*, via its signifiers, all sounds, all sights, smells, flavours and tactile sensations. Proust recognised the evocative power of smell, and there is plenty of gustatory imagery in *The Debt to Pleasure* by John Lanchester, though much of it concerns food. There is more to taste than hunger, however, or more to hunger than simply food. Gold has a taste. In sexual terms, D. H. Lawrence made a heroic stab at conveying the hunger of the senses in *Lady Chatterley's Lover*. Inspired writing may offer an approximation of reality as perceived through the entire gamut of our sense impressions.

In this regard, Lefebvre offers a quotation from *Why we are in Viet-Nam* by Norman Mailer. Celebrating smell and taste and physical contact, this is writing immersed in guts, pong, sour sweat, scratches, spit, licking and sniffing:

> Next step, in they're plunged into some rot, some stump of dwarf birch, bark rubbed ass of raw by tail of bear or moose of caribou antlers eight years ago! like that! and dying over the years, cause a ring of bark had been cut and the skin of such dying tree go to rot beneath the trunk, fell down. Into the open mouth of that remaining stump came the years of snow, sun, little jewels of bird shit, cries of sap from the long dying roots, the monomaniacal electric yodelling of insects, and wood rotting into rotting wood, into gestures of wood, into powder and punk all wet and stinking with fracture between earth and sky, yeah, D.J. could smell the break, gangrene in the wood, electric rot cleaner than meat and sick shit smell and red-hot blood of your flesh in putrefaction, but a confirmed wood gangrene nonetheless, Burbank, a chaos of odor on the banks of the wound, nothing smells worse than half-life, life which has no life but don't know it—thank you, Mr. Philosopher, just show me the haemorrhoids of the academy, and on that rock! ... Next step was into a pool of odor which came from the sweets of the earth, sweet earth smell speaking of endless noncontemplative powers, beds of rest, burgeonings, spring of life, a nectar for the man's muscles on the odor of that breath, yeah, D.J. was breathing his last, he was in the vale of breath, every small smell counted....

Why we are in Viet-Nam, p. 139

Film, radio, television and sound relayed through speakers are these days the principle means by which, in a "hyper-real" sense, our world is represented. We may enjoy dramatic scenes of carnage in a movie, partly because we don't smell what that battlefield would be like in reality. If obliged to wade through some cinematic swamp, we don't feel the water soaking our boots. Poetry presents us with no actual image (as does a film). However, it can evoke an experience through reference to every one of the senses. Walter Owen's *The Cross of Carl* is writing which manages to do this for the experience of the trenches during the Great War:

> Carl is now mounting the ridge where the wire was, packed tight among a hustle of figures that bear him onward in their rush. He is treading on bodies on which his feet slip and blunder. It is like walking on bolsters full of stones. Bones pop underfoot. He looks down and sees a face give under his boot, then slides and comes down. A gnashing mouth closes on his leg; he frees himself and is up again. A lane crashes through the crowd, missing him narrowly, and a welter of fragments whirls round him. A man in front goes down on his knees and, shrieking, grabbles blindly at a stringy mass that pours downward from the lower part of his body, trying madly to mend that cruel hurt that is past all mending. Carl leaps over the man and goes on. He is nearing that dreadful edge where the crowd frays into a fringe of death. Hill 50, slavering at him with flaming breath, looms above.

The Cross of Carl, p. 49-50

Just as Ezra Pound advocated the search for the particular verb that might render an experience dynamic, seeking to crack open the image to get to its action, so, in the spirit of Huysmans, I advocate the employment of what I refer to as the three "exiled" senses—touch, smell and taste. Exiled, because left out by our narrative entertainment industry's reliance on audio/visual stimulus.

Say you are intent on describing a football match. It is not just a matter of the way the ball is passed from one player to another, the tackles, the saves, the blasts of the whistle. Consider the smell, of the turf, of the foggy afternoon, of the crowd pressing close to you, and note the physical shoving, the slightly acrid smell of the soft drink you were about to sip when someone jolted your elbow, the damp spread of the liquid into your scarf and down over your sternum. Consider your proximity to others. Our perception of that proximity concerns tactile sensation.

We sense where we are grounded through the soles of our feet. Thus it is that I stand at my own deictic centre. My love is my weight, says Saint Augustine, where it goes I go. I stand *here, now.* Given my perception of this, I can identify what is over there in terms of spatial deixis—which is actually the entire sphere of the space around me. And I can identify what happened before and expect what may happen next on the line of temporal deixis—before, recently, yesterday/later, tomorrow, soon—while in the space of otherness, other than where I am standing, that is, there is the presence or absence of you, or of him or her or them. All this awareness comes from where I stand, from where I am grounded. And when I move, I carry my deictic centre with me, as Augustine carries his love.

૨ૡ

LINKING POETRY WITH THIS IMPRESSION of groundedness can make our verse more tactile. Bernard Berenson identified a similar drive towards how things feel in visual art when he praised the work of early Florentine painters Masaccio and Giotto, who broke away from the purely visual formulae of the ikon painters, to establish "tactile values"; a term Berenson employed in his essay *Florentine Painters of the Renaissance* (1896) to describe those qualities in a painting that stimulate the sense of touch. It might be just how a disciple rests his hand on another's shoulder, how the robe of a kneeling figure spreads across the floor. Berenson thought that Giotto was the first master since classical antiquity whose painting demonstrated such tactile qualities, which he considered to be a distinctive feature of Florentine painting and held to be 'life enhancing'. "Even if our primary sensations of space be three dimensional (which I would not deny) the third dimension in precise form must largely be the result of tactile and locomotor sensations," he wrote to Mary Berenson in 1895.

Perhaps one of the greatest exponents of tactile imagery is Homer, in *The Iliad*; where every blow dealt out in battle is described, every wound, with an intensity of detail that has suggested to some that the epic was written by a military surgeon. But what is essential to bear in mind is that *pace is a tactile sensation*, thus metre enables the poem to appeal on a level that relates to action and gives impulse to meaning, helping us recall the physical sense of that meaning; and the rhythm of the poem draws us into an accompanying sense of movement, and of moving through space.

Dancing concerns transfer of weight without loss of balance. We do this without thinking when we walk, but the action is nevertheless complex. I now want to consider what balance means to poetry, and I want to relate this enquiry to our general perception of gravity and our sense of axis—drawing largely on my knowledge and experience of dance. Balance seems almost to be the very subject addressed by the tango, for instance. The dancers are constantly exploring their own axis and the axis of their partnership. Balance is the key to stability, and this is sagely epitomised by Shiva standing on one leg. Shiva also rotates his upper body in relation to his hips. He *disassociates*, as the tangueros would say.

Balance involves homeostasis, that is the removal of any excess, and where weight is concerned, lack of homeostasis is lack of balance, carrying an excess in any one direction only—without spreading it in two directions at once so that our axis is maintained. We cope with excess by apportioning it equally, "distributing our weight", or we eject it, rid our systems of its burden. The jettisoning of excess constitutes the basis of pleasure, and attaining balance is a pleasure for the child taking a first step or two as it is for an experienced dancer. But perhaps we should first familiarise ourselves more deeply with this term I have stolen from Freud, who uses it when defining the pleasure principle.

What is homeostasis? Certain observations concerning it appear in *The Analysis of Performance Art*:

Homeostasis: the maintenance of metabolic equilibrium within an organism by a tendency to compensate for disrupting changes.

Homeostasis: a universal tendency in all living matter to maintain constancy in the face of internal and external pressures.

The arts concern making, bringing something to life. As such, they are more aligned to growth than to communication. The wonder is that an inanimate creation can resemble an organism. Thus the "integrity" of an artwork, including a performance, suggests this condition of homeostasis that Freud identifies with the living being.

Deleuze maintains that in addition to an 'aesthetic' there is an 'analytic' (*Difference and Repetition*, page 109). Now the analytic examines the 'integrity' of the work—its wholeness, its soundness—rather than its beauty, which concerns its aesthetic, though one might argue that our contemporary aesthetic *is* the analytic (as Wittgenstein argued that 'ethics is aesthetics'). If this is the case, the notion of homeostasis has replaced the notion of beauty, or we could say that the ideal homeostasis of a piece constitutes its beauty. In art, therefore, homeostasis, or something very similar to the homeostasis of an organism, is achieved by creating a situation where each element or action is under as much tension as any other, and where no element or action is subservient to another or merely there as a support, and where each part is essential to the whole. An artwork "holds itself together".

Joel Fisher is a sculptor who draws his inspiration from filaments discovered in paper which he has made himself. Paper is made by lifting the pulp fibres out of the water where they float in dispersion, using a filter mesh, in order to deposit them onto some base where the fibres may dry out. Fisher has observed that "the tiny cellulose fibres interlock, fibre upon fibre, each holding a place in turn being held by others. There is no glue for it is unnecessary; it is a self-structuring surface maintaining itself."

Analysis of Performance Art, p. 54/56

※

TO JETTISON EXCESS WHERE BALANCE IS CONCERNED is not necessarily to discard the weight of it. Rather it involves shifting some weight to the other side, balancing the equation, as it were: shifting just as much as you need to shift. However, balance is not just something to consider when in a static pose. Balance is required when we walk. To attain the grace of balance we must understand our relationship to the floor, get to know our free leg, and how we push from the base leg's foot, from that foot's area of contact with the gravitational base which is the floor.

Imagine you are seated in a rowing boat beside the bank of a river, and you wish to go across to the other bank. No amount of reaching for it will make this happen. Instead, you push off from the bank, and thus enter the stream. Showing this to people suffering from Parkinson's and other disorders can improve their walking.

When we walk we are on one leg and then the other. A step can take us forwards, backwards, or sideways. The tango explores every nuance of this, even that instant, which may be extended in slow-motion, where the transference occurs and the weight is distributed between both feet. The dancing may look rehearsed but for the most skilled partnerships what is going on is improvisation. The couple's understanding of each other's weight and where it is located—in the partner's ball or in their heel, and in which foot—allows them to dance from a deep understanding of how our body works as a grammar of articulations. This is a more atomic approach than dancing in a molecular sequence that fits together one complex figure after another.

Axis is demanded by sculpture as well as by the human body. Equally we can make use of the axis and the spiral in architecture, and sense the weight, the gravity, the feel of a building. Then Julio Balmaceda uses body circles to teach tango movement and explains the workings of what might be thought of as the human gyroscope. Circles can be made in time as well as in space. Dancing with a partner adds complexity to such notions, think of gyroscopes working in tandem.

Why is partnership important for this investigation into the notion of a fusion of step and phrase? Because partner dancing is a matter of mutual equilibrium and can be deeply communicative. We have seen in a previous chapter how ritual song and dance may have created an aural unison before noise-making with the mouth had evolved into verbal communication. When dancing in a chorus, the performers stand next to each other: all movement is parallel—that is, the dancers take a step to the left at the same time. We get the dance of the cygnets from this choric linkage. To dance in chorus develops memory and coheres the community. Linked arm-to-arm, a chorus repeatedly steps in unison, they all do the same thing. It's a line-dance, all the more so if you are carrying a snake!

In social dance, partners face each other: a movement forward for one is a movement back for the other. In such a dance, we communicate by dove-tailing our movements together. If I go forward, you go back and vice versa. In this way, a model for verbal proposal and response (as in conversation) may have emerged from what was once a physical link. Language as expression, though a notion rejected by the theories of Chomsky and Bickerton, is still worth considering, since it may have provided an "emotive" syntax of sounds and steps in which we responded to each other before precise signification was established.

Conversation allows us to agree, differ, disagree; to argue as well as to affirm. In the tango, however, the follower is not arguing with the leader, nor is she doing what the leader does. She is following the proposal of his lead. It is like a conversation that consists of affirmatives. In poetic terms, it is an eclogue between lovers.

Devout feminists may insist that the tango demeans women. These days there is plenty of queer tango, and women may lead, just as men may follow. However, the nature of the relationship of "the lead" to "the follow" is complex. The investigation it provokes can last a lifetime. A single movement performed by two bodies, that is the ideal sensation the *parechas* (the partners) aim to achieve. It is as if one person instigated the expression of a word or a sentence and the other person completed it. There is an equilibrium to this: one gets to start but not to finish, the other may not initiate but always has the last word.

Let me reiterate that essentially the tango is a walking dance. Walking can be performed at several speeds. Normal walking happens at the pace of the heart's beat, the tango walk is half that speed, but that generic walk can be slowed down, becoming twice as slow, or speeded up, to become double-time (the pace of the normal walk). In the generic tango walk, the upbeat happens as one ankle brushes past the other. Walking only on the downbeat gives us the tango walk, walking on up and down beat gives us a double-time walk.

Recently I have experimented with fitting words to the rhythms the feet are capable of generating, the downbeat being the stressed syllable.

Slow slow:	Bay Leaf
Slow, quick, slow:	Frankincense
Slow, quick, slow, quick:	Milk-and-honey
Long (two slows):	Myrrh

※

CAN A WORD HURT ME? Plenty of contemporary legislation concerning hate crime and racist language suggests that it can. But does this simply point to a lazy use of words? My reputation might be damaged by something someone said about me, but I have never been physically hurt by a word.

I might be deafened by someone shouting loudly in my ear, but there is no way that a word can actually be like a touch to me. Being touched involves contact with the surface of my skin. I may be touched by another's hand, by a textile, by metal, by air. I am clothed by textiles most of the time. I feel my weight in the seat of my chair. But when words are said to touch me they touch something inside. It's not a surface touching my surface. Not something that reveals my contour, my body. Words connect with thought, emotion and/or understanding; syntax often drawing them together with a light tacking stitch, nothing too tight, too unpickable. To touch is to be touched whereas to see is not always to be seen.

Physical contact involves proximity and is reciprocal. But while a word may not affect me physically, the act of writing is very much a physical sensation.

"Writing," as Constance Classen suggests, "is tactile as well as visual, requiring the touch of one's hand. Speech is not only auditory, but also kinaesthetic."

Touch is very much involved when I write: my fingers over the keys, different pads touching pads. Karmen MacKendrick talks of repetition and touch; "And while the tactility of fingers on a keyboard is a limited pleasure, there is an undeniable physicality in the rhythm of a pen on a page," but she doesn't 'see' the choreography, the repetition and touch of the keyboard—the two handedness, the multi fingeredness. With my ink pen, there is specific paper and how the ink slides out; I can feel that through pen to my hand, I can hear it. My right hand and arm with slight articulation of clavicle involves more body and the touching is the pen in that right hand, as it rests on paper. Left hand free to touch paper or not.

And speech, of course is kinaesthetic, how could it be otherwise?

Maura Hazelden, *Folding into the Haptic,* theory essay, MA Performance Writing, University College Falmouth 2010/11

In the essay quoted above, Hazelden makes an in-depth study of the haptic qualities of writing and speech. The haptic aspect of typing may alter from one language to another. When the Iraqi poet Fawzi Karim types in Arabic, he feels the script unfurling, and he says he feels like a musician, playing the music as it gets written.

Hazelden cites *The Fold* by Deleuze and then continues:

How can I ever write about skin [and the fold] without referring to textile? Most of us are born into a mingle of skin and textiles: "We intuit the meanings of enveloping, draping, covering and clothing as gestures of touching" (Pajaczkowska, C., 2005, *Stuff & Nonsense*). Woven textile "is a grid, a matrix of intersecting verticals and horizontals... yet ... soft, curved." *(Ibid.)* A link from two to three dimensional space; from surface to space. The labyrinthine path which sometimes turns sharply or softly curves away and back to itself will occur in this essay. A folding with things tucked into folds.

This notion of textile constituting a link between two and three-dimensional space by dint of its ability to fold and cover generates many a thought about language that can lift off the page into whatever imaginary dimension it cares to evoke, and one thinks of how getting back into a book one has been reading with engrossment is satisfying in a similar way to putting back on a familiar coat. Hazelden concludes her essay by saying:

My next step is towards Merleau-Ponty, finding philosophy that I do feel able to touch, to enable me to draw language into a closer relationship with skin, with bodily experience. "Language does not explain things...but rather 'incarnates them with its speech gestures—in this way *language gives flesh a voice.* Language, then, as a melding of sound, sense and body, can be seen as a manifestation of flesh." (Sellheim, B., 2010, *Metaphor and Flesh—Poetic necessity in Merleau-Ponty*—Journal of the British Society for Phenomenology, 41 (3), 261-273). From my view point as I read this the fan is closing, it has not snapped shut in complete understanding but leaves a space for me to explore with my work.

(Ibid.)

So repairing the fusion of the step and the foot calls for the restoration of our exiled senses—touch, taste and smell. As Pallasmaa notes, "The problems arise from the isolation of the eye outside its natural interaction with other sense modalities, and from the elimination and suppression of other senses."

Each sense requires the stimulation of the other senses to maintain its objectivity. A purely perspectival view may be significantly "out of true" from the haptic, olfactory or gustatory angle. But this notion of the need for a natural interaction between the senses cuts every which way. Balance is a physical matter, for sure, but shut one's eyes, and it proves pretty difficult to maintain.

⁊⬥

SO FAR, WE HAVE CONSIDERED BALANCE as a physical attribute of the body. Can balance affect sentences? Could a sentence with a large prefatory clause but a short, simple predicate feel off-balance, truncated? Here we might consider rhetorical figures such as *chiasmus* (a grammatical construction or concept repeated in reverse order) as in the prefatory quote by Michael Donaghy, which takes a sentence by Robert Frost 'The land was ours before we were the land's.' Surely such sentences are valued for their balance?

Other devices come to mind: *anaphora* may repeat a word or phrase in successive phrases—"If you prick us, do we not bleed? If you tickle us, do we not laugh?" (*Merchant of Venice*). *Epanalepsis* repeats something from the beginning of a sentence at the end—'My ears heard what you said but I couldn't believe my ears.'

Another "balanced" construction which became iconic in the Elizabethan age was the *carmen correlativum*—the correlative verse—where a four-part structure gets broached in one line and continued, with its four parts appearing in appropriate order and concluded in subsequent lines, setting the pattern for the stanza.

> Wrath, gealosie, griefe, love, do thus expell:
> Wrath is a fire; and gealosie a weede;
> Griefe is a flood; and love a monster fell;
> The fire of sparkes, the weede of little seede,
> The flood of drops, the Monster filth did breede:
> But sparks, seed, drops, and filth, do thus delay;
> The sparks soone quench, the springing seed outweed,
> The drops dry up, and filth wipe cleane away:
> So shall wrath, gealosy, griefe, love, die and decay.

(Edmund Spenser, *Faerie Queene*, II, iv, 35),

Here the stanza is balanced by the way the four subjects introduced are treated as the verse progresses, in a rightly ordered manner. It creates lists of nouns which may be followed by lists of the appropriate verbs, as in this line from Sonnet 5 of Lady Mary Wroth's *Pamphilia to Amphilanthus:*

> Desire, sight, eyes, lips, seeke, see, prove, and find.

This is a concatenation much favoured by Drummond of Hawthornden:

> The ivory, coral, gold
> Of breast, of lips, of hair...

Drummond, *Madrigal VIII*

What of *imbalance* in poetry? Or rather, how may the inclination to create equilibrium in art deal with perceived imbalance in society, social injustice or reversal of fortune? Richard Lovelace sought to come to terms with vicissitude and contradiction in his much-underrated verses. Born to wear cloth-of-gold and silver as a Royalist, but reduced to eating the leather of his own boots after the civil war, Lovelace makes significant use of the *oxymoron,* as at the conclusion of his brilliantly constructed poem *The Ant:*

So scattering to hord 'gainst a long Day,
Thinking to save all, we cast all away.

Here the image is of the sower in the field, scattering seed to harvest it later. Lovelace deserves serious reassessment. Upheaval in his circumstances has disenfranchised his spirit from any belief, whether in society or in God: so he can't construct elegant verses founded on a coherent metaphysics such as the chain of being (which so aided John Donne in a poem such as *The Ecstasy*). Lovelace confronts chaos, as when he advises his brother not to set sail on "inconstant Deep" to take up the post of Governor of New York, but observes also that turmoil disrupts the land as much as it does the sea:

Nor be too confident, fix'd on the shore,
For even that too borrows from the store
Of her rich neighbour, since now wisest know,
(And this to *Galileo's* judgement owe)
The palsie Earth it self is every jot
As frail, inconstant, waving as that blot
We lay upon the Deep; that sometimes lies
Chang'd, you would think, with's bottom's properties,
But this eternal strange *Ixion's* wheel
Of giddy earth, ne'r whirling leaves to reel
Till all things are inverted, till they are
Turn'd to that Antick confus'd state they were.

Advice to my best brother, Col. Francis Lovelace

Here we have imbalance evoked with balanced elegance. Compare:

Turning and turning in the widening gyre
The falcon cannot hear the falconer;
Things fall apart, the centre cannot hold;
Mere anarchy is loosed upon the world…

(The Second Coming, W. B. Yeats)

It is worth remembering that Lovelace is the poet of falconry.

Where a poem is carrying material redundant to its intention, we sense an imbalance. This is a sin punishable by oblivion, but its remedy is more complex than it may first appear. It is easy to say that it is simply a matter of getting rid of adjectives or phrases that repeat what has already been said. We are looking to get rid of surplus material, but it's essential that the poet first identify what is surplus and what is not. There are two issues here: the meaning, and the pattern through which that meaning gets projected (if there is a meaning beyond the pattern). Repetition may be essential to the form.

> Your eyen two wol slee me sodenly,
> I may the beaute of hem not sustene,
> So woundeth hit through-out my herte kene.
>
> And but your word wol helen hastily
> My hertes wounde, whyl that hit is grene,
> Your eyen two wol slee me sodenly,
> I may the beaute of hem not sustene.
>
> Upon my trouthe I sey yow feithfully,
> That ye ben of my lyf and deeth the quene;
> For with my deeth the trouthe shal be sene.
> Your eyen two wol slee me sodenly,
> I may the beaute of hem not sustene,
> So woundeth hit through-out my herte kene.

This is a fourteenth century *rondel* by Geoffrey Chaucer. E.K. Chambers, in his essay *Some Aspects of Mediaeval Lyric* (Frank Sidgwick and E.K. Chambers, *Early English Lyrics,* Sidgwick and Jackson, London 1907), speaks of the French *Chanson Populaire* that existed side by side with the *Chanson Courtois.* This was a folk tradition flourishing in the twelfth century, "even outliving it and enduring into and beyond the Renaissance."

> A notable feature is afforded by the dance-songs, called in the earlier documents *rotrouenges* and in the later *chansons de carole, rondets* or *rondets de*

carole. Of these there must have been many, but only a few dating from the twelfth or early thirteenth century are preserved in their entirety; the rest solely through their *refrains* or burdens, which are freely adapted and quoted in chansons of other types and in romances. The burden is of course essential to the dance-song. The primitive form may have consisted of nothing but single lines of text alternating with the burden. Afterwards the number of lines in the couplet or stanza was increased, and one or more of these was made to rhyme with the burden. So long as it continued to be popular, the *rondet* retained great freedom of arrangement; ultimately, through its adoption for musical purposes, it became in its turn literary and hardened into fixed forms, such as the *rondel* and the *balade.*

E.K. Chambers, *Some Apects of the Mediaeval Lyric,* p. 265

Of great relevance to our theme, the burden of the dance-song may always have been accompanied by the same steps, or by the same dance figure. Thus the repetition of the lines of the burden would have acted as a prompt to the figures of the dance. Equally, the poem may be conceived as a chant—in which case repetition is not surplus to that poem's requirement. Chambers goes on to talk about the twelfth century *chansons de toile,* which appear to have been "ordinarily sung, not at a dance, but by a company of women over their needlework." Here again we sense the fusion of verse and physical action, and in such "work-songs" repetition may also have been purposive.

The pattern adopted by the poet might demand three adjectives for every verb, so adjectives *might* be essential components. On the other hand, a poem conceived as a statement of facts may be unbalanced by a sentence that inserts a comment into those facts: finely written, it may be, but it could still feel like an interruption, preventing the poem from speaking "for itself".

❧

SCANSION CAN ALSO BE THOUGHT OF AS A WAY OF BALANCING VERSE, at least in the sense that it delivers equal amounts of repetition. However, it is interesting to note that in terms of the number of metrical feet, primes can be scanned as well. It is not simply a matter of the repetition of an equal number of units. Of course, such equality counts, and rhythm can be supplemented by rhyme, which can be employed to emphasise the rhythmic equality. The danger here is that it is easy for regularity to be overdone and the rhymes to become predictable, resulting in verse that sounds dated and too obviously structured. Just as "A sweet disorder in the dress/Kindles in clothes a wantonness"—according to the seventeenth century poet Robert Herrick—so our verses need to be wary of excessive correctness.

And if balance is homeostatic equipoise, then, just as the body rids itself of excessive libido, or waste, in order to achieve that equipoise in matters other than equilibrium such as defecation or sexual "release"; just as the body liberates itself to enjoy the evenness, the steady state which is the aim of homeostasis; so the poem must be rid of excessive meaning, of overstating its case. Ideally every element in the poem is playing an essential role.

Lefebvre touches on this notion when he cites Viollet-le-Duc on the difference between Roman and Greek notions of architecture:

'Among the Greeks,' wrote Viollet-le-Duc, 'Construction and art are one and the same thing; the form and the structure are intimately connected…' In the space of the Romans, by contrast, there was a separation, a rift: 'we have the construction and we have the form which clothes that construction, and is often independent of it'. The Romans organized volumes in such a way as to fulfil some particular function, whether in the basilica or in the baths; the use of constructed masses was clearly distinct from the presentation of surfaces or decoration—the elements of which were ornamental additions to heavy masses of bricks or rubble (i.e. cement and a sort of concrete). The 'orders' invented by the Greeks (Doric, Ionic and Corinthian) *were* the structure itself; the notion of 'order' embraced that of structure, so that the external appearance and the composition (or structure) of Greek buildings are indistinguishable from each other: each contains and reveals the other. It was impossible, according to Viollet-le-Duc, who brought a technician's viewpoint to the development of Hegel's ideas on Greek art and architecture, to strip a Greek temple of its 'order' without destroying the monument itself. The order was not decorative, nor were the columns and the capitals. 'The Greek orders are none other than the structure itself, to which that form was given which was most appropriate to its function. In the orders adopted from the Greeks the Romans saw only a decoration which might be removed, omitted, displaced, or replaced by something else.

Lefebvre 238, he is quoting E. E. Viollett-le-Duc, *Entretiens sur l'Architecture* (Paris: A. Morel, 18863-72) Vol 1, p. 101

If the temple was the structure, in their architecture, then surely the notion holds true for the Greek notion of the body. Our walk, out of which our measurements have evolved, measurements that shape the temple, is generated by our structure, for the fit body is also something where the structure is the order. Naturally, our skeleton exhibits homeostasis. The complex efficiency of the spine, with its rotations, its ability to curl and arch, project, contract, go convex or concave, while moving with the lower limbs in dissociation or association, defines what it is to be a human being, just as the Doric order defines the temple. The body is balanced by its own symmetry, and we rediscover that symmetry in the Parthenon, but it was also there in the arrowhead of flint. The body is its structure, just as is the temple. In what sense, in literature, can we say, the poem is its structure?

Back in the seventies, working with abstraction, I experimented with limiting the poem to certain essential parts of speech and manipulating highly limited vocabularies to generate a sequence of sonnets. Here is one of them

It all depends upon what you are after
You just depend upon which it is before
It all depends upon who you are before
You just depend upon why it is after.

It all depends upon why you are before
You just depend upon who it is after
It all depends upon which you are after
You just depend upon what it is before.

You just depend upon where it is before
It all depends upon where you are after
It all depends upon when you are before

You just depend upon when it is after.

Upon who you are it just depends after
Upon who it is before all you depend.

Perhaps there is little to such sonnets but their structure. The same could be said of a mural by Brigid Riley. At the time I was writing these sonnets, R. D. Laing had just brought out *Knots*. Working from a reductionist principle, the Scottish psychiatrist epitomised the experienced predicaments and double-binds of relationships in language that was as pared down as mine and as permutative, though the variations came from case-histories. His views on the causes and treatment of serious mental illness, influenced by existential philosophy, ran counter to the psychiatric orthodoxy of the day, often identifying the situation as traumatic by dint of a complex paradigm in the family rather than because of some underlying disorder in a particular individual. A syntax of verbs, prepositions and pronouns that generated further variations in its own terms served to illustrate his view, while it served my investigations into the nature of what constituted a poem that was no more than its structure.

❦

SO WE ARE LOOKING FOR A BALANCED INPUT from the senses, a sense of balance in the rhythm and the syntax utilized and an awareness of how the poem must be true to its own structure, ensuring that all the words are making an equal contribution to the whole. There is also an internal sense of balance within the line. Each line has the possibility of a pause within it—this is called the caesura. The poetic ear can be attuned to mark the caesura in a scanned line of verse. The caesura is the fulcrum of the line. In the modern sense of the term, the caesura is perceived as a break in a verse where one phrase ends and another begins. Actually, it may not be simply the notification of the ending of a phrase—as the caesura may at times cut through the grammatical unit. When reciting a poem, this break may vary between the slightest of hesitations all the way up to a full pause. Subject may separate from predicate via the caesura:

This said, he reach'd to take his son;// who, of his arms afraid,
And then the horse-hair plume,// with which he was so overlaid,
Nodded so horribly, he cling'd// back to his nurse, and cried.
Laughter affected his great sire,// who doff'd, and laid aside
His fearful helm....

Chapman—Double obliques mark the caesura in each line and follow the point of balance which is not necessarily aligned with the division of sense—note line three.

Something similar to this division or cut that the caesura suggests happens when one stands balancing on one leg, for now one's centre of balance, or rather the line that traces the division of gravity through the body is biased diagonally a little towards the base leg (that is, the leg upon which one is balanced)—to compensate for the unsupported weight of the free leg. So the caesura resembles how one's centre maintains this bias.

In poems comprising an equal number of feet per line, the caesura will fall at the half way point, and if this is emphasised then again regularity is being piled on regularity and the result may read in a very hackneyed way. The caesura is always of interest in pentameter or fourteeners, however, since the break will produce an unequal ratio—two to three, three to four, and so on—this, neatly, or rather, sweetly disorders the verse; creating an irregularity within the regularity. It is perhaps why pentameter is so favoured by English poets.

A caesura in music represents a similar break or pause. The length of a caesura where notated is at the discretion of the conductor, and in choral works a brief caesura may be notated where singers are to catch their breath.

❧

WHEN WE SAY, "IT DOESN'T SCAN," we are saying in effect, "It doesn't balance." But we are also looking for a balance of impressions that takes all the senses into consideration. We are looking for a certain flexibility in the rhythm that allows for "a sweet disorder"—ensuring some surprise that counters monotony if the rhythm is essentially regular—some say Dryden's verse is simply "too polished"; while some of us may feel that chunks of Ted Hughes's writing are simply too ungainly.

When dancing the tango, the step can be regarded as a word, the figure as a sentence, the cross as semi-colon, the closure of the feet with weight change onto the left (at the conclusion of the eight) as a full stop. Poetry is a dance, and dance is a language. Comprising units occurring in time, words and steps behave in similar ways. Again, we see how poetry and dance are intimately connected.

Then each dance generates its nomenclature, and words for dance steps have always been elaborate—ballet in French, tango in Spanish. Tango lyrics are very passionate, and they influence how Argentines hear the music because they hear a meaning as well as a melody. And if words seek to dance, it has to be said that dance also seeks both to speak and to be written down. Yet actions are notoriously hard to record. All too often, even film fails to capture the movement from an informative angle. For sure, there have been various attempts at mapping or notating dance, viewed from above or in cross-section, as has been considered. However, notation inevitably proves an awkward articulation of dance's essential fluidity: take Victor Sylvester-style footprints, and the clumsiness of mapped choreology.

Still, I am glad that we kept comprehensive "soundings" of the performances we created for *The Theatre of Mistakes*—since this means that the work can still be reproduced (and indeed has been reproduced at the 2017 retrospective of our work at Raven Row in London). Our earnest attempts at describing our every move in terms of a function performed—I put on the jacket, I move the table, I walk across to the chair, I pick it up—leads on to a fondness of mine for the meticulous description of actions; a penchant that grew out of my realisation that description without significance could be a modernist strategy. Such scrupulous description was used by our performance company in order to document the work, but it was also being used by me in my poetry—as can be seen in *Boxing the Cleveland,* a lengthy and meticulous verse description of getting a Cleveland Bay to walk up into a horse-box. At the time, seeking a poetry of pure description, I was looking for a long action to serve as the basis for a long poem. Then one afternoon I witnessed the struggle with this big horse. It was my luck to just then witness something so tactile, so essentially physical and sweaty. It did take a very long time to get him boxed—which is why the poem is so long!

2. THE POETRY OF ACTION
The search for the physicality of narrative in mountaineering and verse which is "rugged"/Poetry and anatomy, stanzas as vertebrae.

DESCRIPTION FOR ITS OWN SAKE has an alchemical effect. It involves transmutation, for description in any art—whether it be painting, sculpture, poetry or dance—is never reproduction. It differs also from idolatry, which can invest a symbol scratched in sand with as much power as a finely carved iconic statue or elaborate totem. In no way is description through art the same as that which it describes. It is a representation of a subject in a material other than its own. It can be made of stone, of words, of colours, of sounds—even of smells. It can be an enactment, a performance. But it is made, not born; made out of a material, even when it's an actor representing anguish. It takes art to do it. Whatever the medium, description is a power. It is a form of magic, as was understood in the caves. It can render the ordinary sublime.

Here, it's advisable to return to Henri Lefebvre's distinction between a work and a product. A clay pot is a product, as it is the same as the clay pot previously turned on the wheel and as the one that follows it. A reproduction of that pot, in a painting by Morandi, say, is a work; born out of the material nature of painting, which is now integral to it. The transformation from actual object, scene or living experience into a medium generates fascination. Even acting is not composed of the same medium as its characters. Laurence Olivier is not Othello, he is as if he were Othello. This is not only true for drama, it is true for poetry, it is true for painting and sculpture as well. Ultimately it is the key to our appreciation of art. Vermeer has a painting of a servant girl asleep, resting her head in a hand propped up on a table. It's a humble enough subject, and yet it is art at its best. It is as if the sleep had seeped into her from the dark corners of the room.

A tone poem by Mendelssohn—his *Hebrides Overture* (otherwise known as Fingal's Cave)—evokes the incoming sea, its swellings and withdrawals; it's an orchestral suggestion, made with instruments. Earlier I have mentioned Raymond Roussel's *Une Vue;* a verse description of a photograph perceived through a viewer mounted on a pen-holder. Every single aspect of the photograph is detailed. It is a description of an image that is still, of a dog leaping for a stick on a densely populated beach, and somehow the image becomes frozen for us by its description in words. It is as if Roussel had performed a sculptural action, *made* the pen-holder for us to peer into. And the stillness of the tiny image described generates a sensation of timelessness; the dog leaping for the stick forever.

Yet in each case, it would be peremptory to consider the medium of the description as a transparent material which simply enables its subject to appear as a reality. This obvious fact is all too often overlooked. A girl sleeping is not a rectangular canvas. The sea does not sound like a symphony orchestra. Roussel's poem is a column of regular verse, not a photograph. Modernism's project was to acknowledge the presence, the "reality" of the medium itself.

The arts will gravitate towards subjects that each finds most appropriate to conjure up, and such subjects often become genres—as with landscape painting, still lives, ballads, love poems, nocturnes, sacred masses and programmatic symphonies. And while painters may relish describing a landscape and composers may delight in recreating an atmosphere, writers often become immersed in describing an incident or a sequence of actions, which is the urge at the root of narration or story-telling. This is such a time-honoured preoccupation that it's a minefield liberally planted with clichés. Roussel and Huysmans were both dedicated to making narration new. It's a difficult task. Many of the clichés that dominate literature involve assuming that the narrative will be a "page-turner"; that it will also have some moral or social meaning and will reach some significant conclusion. However, it may be Laurence Sterne's intention never to reach that or any conclusion. A poem by Frank O'Hara may be idling; not intent on getting anywhere at all. This notion of a meandering, intentionless literature as an aspect of modernism has a bearing on my own sense that description without significiance can have a material, modernist quality, and it's a topic explored exhaustively and digressively by Ross Chambers in his entertaining *Loiterature*—a book of essays on the subject (Nebraska, 1999).

For the creative practitioner, the cliché resides in the position "sin" occupies for the moral philosopher. Poems illustrating a moral tend to be flawed in this regard. Page-turners tend to be pot-boilers. Even when one endorses the message one can be made to feel like a grandmother who is being taught to suck eggs, as is my own risk here when I try to elucidate scansion!

Modernists have sought out the inconclusive, the pointless, or at least pointless from a moral point-of-view. A learned editor once told me that the subject of *Boxing the Cleveland* was unworthy of poetry. The subject, as I have mentioned, was that of describing the business of getting a recalcitrant horse into a horsebox. He maintained that this was a subject too trite for verse! In my own defence I cited *The Rape of the Lock*—Alexander Pope's poem about snipping off a mere lock of hair from a lady's head. I had wanted to work with a sequence of actions free of any significant ethical implication. But still I wanted something to describe, something that was an activity, with its own build up: a sequence with a result. This had led me to seek out "long actions." The sequence such a long action involved did not have to be invested with any transcendent or metaphysical significance—rather it might be a matter of climbing a mountain "because it was there".

There are, of course, a considerable number of poems inspired by long sequences of action. The *Iliad* is a description of a very long action indeed— the Trojan War. As well as wars, journeys provide inspiration—the *Odyssey* describes the wanderings of Odysseus, and then the *Seafarer* is a similar wanderer. Aboriginal songs describe "walkabouts" which may have lasted for months and covered hundreds of miles. There is a strong tradition of poems of action that are records of heroic feats. But Alan Brownjohn has a very lovely poem called *Breaking Eggs*—about making an omelette.

Actions may also concern artisanal processes in which a rhythm may establish itself within the practice as was the case with the medieaval work-song. Think of rowing, or reaping, or the rhythm that gets set up when laying down the horizontal meander of the weft thread that is drawn through; inserted over-and-under the lengthwise warp yarns that are held in tension on a loom when weaving. It has been mentioned earlier that the direction of writing once followed the left right, right left alternations of ploughing. Such craft action has implications for the making business of writing. Maura Hazelden clearly appreciates the in/out/in of the weaving process which has affinities with the down/up/down beat of walking, of making a journey. Building the hull of a vessel by overlaying timbers on a frame will also produce a rhythmic result. The processes of weaving and ship-building have helped us generate images of our own thought processes—how a maze may be danced or built or simply traced—as when we follow an elaborate argument that is being expounded. Thus the narrative of how a pot is thrown, the active execution of ancient crafts such as pottery or weaving, may well have been the physical engagement out of which philosophy evolved—see *Socrates' Ancestor, an essay in architectural beginnings* by Indra Kagis McEwan (M.I.T., 1993). The artisan's process is a thought-process, however physical its manifestation.

❦

BECAUSE MOUNTAINS ARE SIMPLY THERE, mountaineering poems are of interest when we seek out extended sequences of action. Climbing is a vertical journey that goes from hold to hold, so each fresh action is a consequence of the one before it, just as each sentence in an argument or a theory which is being articulated is a consequence of the sentence before. There is a syntax to a climb, a tactile sequence. Just as the freedom of our hands stimulated our transition to becoming language animals, just as the sequentiality of walking may have encouraged this ability as well, the syntax of climbing may have contributed to our consciousness of time and its nature—that this move has to happen before that—an awareness we were to require if we were ever to be able to speak, even before we were out of the trees.

In this sense, climbing has an affinity with building. Climbing and building are both like arguments, both require that this move or block must be set in place before the next move can be established or the subsequent block set in place, and so, in a similar way, climbing a tree involves the climber in a narrative.

Helen Mort investigates the power of poetry that explores the notion of the climb in her essay *Gap to Gap*—The search for the perfect climbing poem—An article first published in Alpinist 55, Autumn 2016:

> In the winter of 2012, I found myself in a glassy, luminous room in Banff, Alberta. The outlines of the Rockies glowed outside the window—their white light familiar, strange, like a word on the tip of my tongue. In truth, though, I hardly looked beyond the room because I was mesmerized by what was happening inside: a reading of a long narrative poem I'd never heard before, each pitch of a climb evoked with finger-scraping accuracy:
>
> > The air howled from our feet to the smudged rocks
> > And the papery lake below. At an outthrust we balked
> > Till David clung with his left to a dint in the scarp…
>
> The poem was *David*—a harrowing account of a climb in the very mountains I was staring at—and the author was Earl Birney (1904–1995). The narrator recounts the loss of his climbing partner after a foothold crumbles: "without / a gasp he was gone." Birney's piece has been taught in schools and universities for many years, with much speculation about the possible relationship between fiction and fact: Was this a real-life accident? Was the poem an admission of guilt? Birney must have found these questions frustrating. Yet perhaps they were a testament to the vivid detail of his writing, the convincing quality of each measured stanza. Birney specified the detail of a peak "upthrust / Like a fist in a frozen ocean of rock," "the cold breath / of the glacier" and "grating / edge-nails and fingers," described so painstakingly some readers couldn't help inferring an element of autobiography.
>
> When I heard "David" for the first time, I was partway through a three-week residency at The Banff Centre, enrolled in the Mountain and

Wilderness Writing Program, trying to work on a sequence of poems about women and mountaineering. I live and climb in the Peak District in Derbyshire, England. On days spent gripping the strange, circular holds at Derwent Edge, my attention becomes as fully absorbed as it does when I'm searching for the last couplet of a sonnet. At the same time, I'm often nervous on rock, doubting my abilities. I'd hoped that writing about edges and arêtes could help me access some of the confidence I feel when I'm shaping a line of poetry, allowing me to relive and understand the routes that obsess me, down to the lyricism of their names: Long Tall Sally. The Louisiana Rib. Sunset Slab.

As we've noted, each medium identifies material which is particularly suited to its intrinsic nature. Painters may focus on portraits and still-lives because these are subjects which can be well expressed in spatial terms— they are both essentially still (though portrait painters have complained to me about hyperactive children!). The sequential nature of language means that it *can* handle narrative and is well able to answer the question, what happened next?

That said, there is no need to assert suitability as an absolute law. The very stillness of a building can be expressive of the order in which its parts were put in place: this is very true of the temple at Segesta. Action sequences do not concern the poet alone. Sculptors can grasp the essential moment in a sequence as it unfolds. In the *Laocoön—or the Limits of Painting and Poetry*—Gothold Lessing cites the inspired observation of Simonides that "painting is a dumb poetry, and poetry a vocal painting".

Nevertheless, Lessing is quick to point out how well poetry can handle the unfolding of an action, taking as his example the picture of Pandarus in the Fourth Book of the *Iliad:*

> From the seizing of the bow to the very flight of the arrow every moment is depicted, and all these moments are kept so close together, and yet so distinctly separate, that if we did not know how a bow was to be managed we might learn it from this picture alone. Pandarus draws forth his bow, fixes the bowstring, opens his quiver, chooses a yet unused, well-feathered shaft, sets the arrow on the string, draws back both string and arrow down to the notch, the string is brought near to his breast and the iron head of the arrow to the

bow; back flies the great bent bow with a twang, the bow-string whirs, off springs the arrow eager for its mark.

Lessing, *Laocoön,* p. 54

Artists such as Pollaiuolo and Signorelli have got around the visual problem of depicting time by depicting several archers or cross-bowmen, each engaged in completing different stages of preparing their weapons. There is also a tendency for the painter or sculptor to choose a preliminary movement in a sequence, since the subsequent movements may be implied from that initial action—the moment of drawing an arrow from the quiver—or they choose the most continuous part of a process—Vermeer has a woman engaged in pouring milk, and, since she pours the milk forever, this has that effect of stilling time which we first noticed with the sculpture of the Egyptians. The painter might also point out that it is not so easy for the poet to get across the notion of a mass of things—the entire Greek fleet assembled before Troy, for instance: a spatial subject more suited to visual art. The poet retorts that there are ways to evoke grandeur that are more sophisticated than merely describing one boat after another. This is where metaphor comes in, as Homer well understood. Conversely, intrigued by the very "difficulty" of succeeding on alien terrain, poets may take it upon them to invade the territory of painting and evoke stillness, while painters may set out to capture action. For Helen Mort, when poetry tackles mountaineering, it is not just a matter of capturing the action but a respect for the physical economy that the establishment of a firm foothold implies.

> I love the idea of poetry as "Alpine-style writing," pared back to its essence. In the poems I started writing at Banff, I often found myself obsessing over tiny details: the precise width of a crevasse, the flight pattern of a crow over Stanage—fragments that might distil my notes and impressions into singular instances. I started to visualize each stanza as a move on a climb, as if I were making small steps with my feet, getting them into the right position before reaching for a hold. I was thinking of Earl Birney, but also of Marya Zaturenska's poem "Inscription on a Mountain" and how she describes

elements that might be otherwise invisible: how the "colourless pure air…
sculptures a clean branch / From storm and avalanche." Perhaps the "goose-
bump" form is well placed to capture those minute observations, the kinds of
features you notice when you're studying the detail of a route: a single pebble,
a lost cam rusting in a crack. Poet Michael Donaghy describes the poem as a
"diagram of consciousness." Does his comparison imply that poems are well-
placed to mirror the thought-processes a climb might invoke: the unfolding
of thoughts in the space between one hold and the next?

Although I thought of my climbing poems as a series of discrete moves—
almost like smearing my feet up a slab—the finished versions always seemed
more general than I had intended, more sweeping, less specific. As I wrote, I
felt that I was leaving sensations out, describing the idea of climbing rather
than its physical expression. Ultimately, I suspect that such problems relate to
the fundamental similarity between an ascent and a poem, a theory Roberts
implied back in 1939: "Perhaps, in the end, pure descriptive poetry, whether
of mountains or of mountaineering, is not possible: the underlying significance
that we read into our experience is inseparable from the experience itself."

If the realities and subjective impressions of a route are hard to untangle,
it's partly because the act of climbing can intervene in the ways we think, disrupting everyday forms of consciousness—a phenomenon that the climber
and artist Dan Shipsides describes as a form of "pata-perception." Psychologist
Raymond Gibbs describes a similar idea of "embodied cognition" as the ways
in which human language and thought emerge from patterns of physical
activity. To put it crudely, I might say, "I climb, therefore I am."

Gap to Gap

It is clear that mountaineering is rich in "long actions". And just as climbing requires co-ordination and a keen sense of the order of one's holds, the
phrases that a poetry of mountaineering may generate need to partake of
that sense of co-ordination and order.

When I began exploring "long actions" I came to consider narrative
not so much as illustration but as a material quality of language. But of
course, if one is not writing prose, there may also be a pattern to the verse
that will need to be fused with the "melody" of the action. In "Boxing the
Cleveland", I wanted the poetry to mirror the logic of getting things done,

one thing at a time, while at the same time conveying the drive and determination of the participants, animal and human, by taking advantage of
four-line stanzas and a rhyme scheme:

The flat-capped man removes his mac;
The woman with the whip is losing heart;
The rattling of pony nuts goes slack;
But the nettle-prickled breaker wants to start

That Cleveland up the ramp again, although
Her jodhpurs have been stained from where he churned
Her briefly in the stingers. As from now,
He'll do it in a bridle—as she warned

The owner he might have to, since the halter
Will not hold him. Sheer determination
Gets the head-piece done without a falter,
Then he flings his head in consternation

Out of reach and shakes it. Most unsure,
He pauses near the lower gate to dung.
She manages to grab him by the jaw
And slip the snaffle-bit across his tongue.

She then secures the cheek-piece to its ring,
Fastens up the throat-lash, and he's ready.
Right away, it's far less work to bring
Him back towards the ramp. 'Now keep it steady.'

Things go better. Never by enough
To get him up the incline, home and dry.
'I'll take a cigarette. My word, he's rough,'
The smaller man says. Then once more they try

To shift his shoulders, bend him at the knee
And place his hoof some distance up the ramp.
'Take care he don't come down on you,' says he.

'Cause if he did he'd land a fair old bump.'

Boxing the Cleveland, from Howell's Law, Anvil, 1990

There is also the possibility of using words in unconventional ways to lend a physicality to the verse itself, as in the "sprung verse" of Gerard Manley Hopkins. Here the words themselves become actions, impacting upon each other. As Helen Mort understands it, this has an emotive as well as a dynamic force:

Some of my favourite poems of physical landscape gesture towards emotional terrain, conjuring a world Gerard Manley Hopkins might have recognized when he said:

O the mind, mind has mountains; cliffs of fall
Frightful, sheer, no-man-fathomed. Hold them cheap
May who ne'er hung there…

In "A Dream of White Horses", elite climber Edwin Drummond attempts to unite those inner and outer topographies through scattered poems. I say "scattered" not just because they are dispersed throughout his prose memoir, but also because the effect of reading these poems is disjointed, as if he has tried to convey a climber's stream of consciousness, fragmentary thoughts in a moment's movement.

This form is particularly apparent in pieces like "I Fell" and "Night-Fall":

Gripped—tugged—jiggled
juggled—flakes—fingers
fumbled—footholds stumbled

Gap to Gap

SUCH TRENCHANT USE OF VERBS AND NOUNS, with connectives and other parts of speech kept to a minimum, brings us to a material "ruggedness" that a hands-on approach to language and a willingness to grapple with words can bring to poetry. Just as language becomes the terrain of an aboriginal walk-song, language becomes the mountain, the poetry that of the chimney itself. But it is, at the same time, a strongly auditory phenomenon. It is language considered as percussion. It may accompany a sense of the rough-hewn, which seems apt for a poetry of physical experience. It is both a modernist tendency and a very old one, such as we sense through the alliteration of Anglo-Saxon poetry:

> May I for my own self song's truth reckon,
> Journey's jargon, how I in harsh days
> Hardship endured oft.
> Bitter breast-cares have I abided,
> Known on my keel many a care's hold,
> And dire sea-surge, and there I oft spent
> Narrow nightwatch nigh the ship's head
> While she tossed close to cliffs. Coldly afflicted,
> My feet were by frost benumbed.
> Chill its chains are; chafing sighs
> Hew my heart round and hunger begot
> Mere-weary mood. Lest man know not
> That he on dry land loveliest liveth,
> List how I, care-wretched, on ice-cold sea,
> Weathered the winter, wretched outcast
> Deprived of my kinsmen;
> Hung with hard ice-flakes, where hail-scur flew,
> There I heard naught save the harsh sea
> And ice-cold wave, at whiles the swan cries,
> Did for my games the gannet's clamour,
> Sea-fowls, loudness was for me laughter,
> The mews' singing all my mead-drink.
> Storms, on the stone-cliffs beaten, fell on the stern
> In icy feathers; full oft the eagle screamed
> With spray on his pinion.

The Seafarer, Ezra Pound's version

The "emotional terrain" alluded to by Helen Mort can also be found in the poetry of John Donne, when like William Drummond, he jams his verbs up against each other:

> When I am gone, dream me some happiness;
> Nor let thy looks our long-hid love confess;
> Nor praise, nor dispraise me, nor bless nor curse
> Openly love" force, nor in bed fright thy nurse
> With midnight's startings, crying out, O! O!
> Nurse, O! my love is slain; I saw him go
> O'er the white Alps alone; I saw him, I,
> Assail'd, fight, taken, stabb'd, bleed, fall, and die.
> Augur me better chance, except dread Jove
> Think it enough for me to have had thy love.

Elegy on his Mistress, John Donne, 1572-1631

᠈᠖

IT IS CLEAR THAT THE WORDS CAN BECOME THE ACTIONS in themselves. This is an intensification Gerard Manley Hopkins pioneered with "sprung verse". Basil Bunting cottoned on to a similar dynamic through his deep understanding of the ancient poetry of Northumbria and the auditory force of Anglo-Saxon verse. We can sense *The Seafarer* in *Briggflatts:*

> Rain rinses the road,
> the bull streams and laments.
> Sour rye porridge from the hob
> with cream and black tea,
> meat, crust and crumb.
> Her parents in bed
> the children dry their clothes.
> He has untied the tape

of her striped flannel drawers
before the range. Naked
on the pricked rag mat
his fingers comb
thatch of his manhood's home.

Gentle generous voices weave
over bare night
words to confirm and delight
till bird dawn.
Rainwater from the butt
she fetches and flannel
to wash him inch by inch,
kissing the pebbles.
Shining slowworm part of the marvel.
The mason stirs:
Words!
Pens are too light.
Take a chisel to write.

Meaning is pared back to its essence. Articles and connectives are kept to a minimum. Image is impacted against image. Alliteration and internal rhyming get utilised extensively but in no set pattern. From the sprung verse of Hopkins to the musical verse of Edith Sitwell and the rhapsodic writing of Dylan Thomas, we come across poets who use the sheer stuff of language in some refreshingly active way—as exemplified by the extract from *Briggflatts* above. This sense of words "acting upon each other" can also be appreciated in the typographic experiments of E. E. Cummings and the percussive abstractions of Clark Coolidge.

Here is poetry perceived as action in itself; the action of word upon word being a controlled cacophony, as Jackson Pollock could be said to create a deliberate mess of colour. Sound poetry and concrete poetry should also be considered in this context, though with some reservations. The former risks confusion with music and the latter with visual art. Stray too far from the integrity of the word itself, and there is a risk of being removed, ultimately, from that fusion of sign, sound and meaning which defines poetry as a linguistic construct.

When abstraction effects a complete divorce from meaning, there is also a danger of the verse becoming too removed from essential linguistic qualities. Huysmans, as I have already remarked, grew dissatisfied with the naturalism of his contemporaries—Zola, Balzac, Flaubert et al—because he found that realism became repetitive. In a similar way, I find that abstract writing can become tedious when the signifier is entirely denied (as if this were ever possible). Poetry seems to have less scope for abstraction than painting because language is already abstracted from reality. It is, after all, a code made up of words, which are constructed signs, whereas visual art and sculpture can take advantage of a full range of actual materials—which allows for a more plastic "impact".

Abstraction can release words so that they become free to act upon each other, but a balance needs to be struck, a mediating position found between abstraction and narrative, for this action to convey a genuine impact. One problem I identified with writing in an "abstract" way was that it could become stylistically limiting. Many of the poets included in the Norton anthology of such writing sound all too similar to each other. As a writer who experienced the upheaval of modernism, my coming to an accommodation with narrative, when it came to what a poem might mean, only came about after it struck me that one of the issues for us "late" moderns was the over-emphasis that the Leavisite traditionalists placed on the "significance" of meaning. I have already pointed out how in 1925 Ortega proclaimed the 'Dehumanization of Art' and promoted an art, "about which you could neither laugh nor cry."

It was thus that I grew interested in writing a poetry of sheer description and of long actions, which I perceived as having a purity as unalloyed as the verse of Mallarmé. Description with the significance removed meant that there was no "moral to the tale". Sentences matching the syntax of reality were perceived as capable of being conjoined with an elegance as pure as the sentences of Ashbury, though his sentences "melt" even as they emerge, since his work is immersed in abstraction and he works with the syntactical structure of meaning without that structure necessarily carrying the load of anything specifically signified.

I guess this emphasis on the absence of significance needs some quali-fication. I am suggesting that significance is the last thing the poet might start out by demanding. An insignificant subject may be chosen and worked on; and it is the poetry which may then bring some significance about. We may write to learn the significance of a poem—a significance that may emerge from our engagement. Fiona Templeton, who I worked with in The Theatre of Mistakes, once said, we make art to discover a reason.

SPECIFIC SIGNIFICATION VERY DISTINCTLY INFORMS Edward Field's account of a long action in *World War 11,* which describes how the bomber he was flying in was shot down over the channel:

> Over the North Sea the third engine gave out
> And we dropped low over the water.
> The gas gauge read empty, but by keeping the nose down
> a little gas at the bottom of the tank sloshed forward
> and kept our single engine going.
> High overhead, the squadrons were flying home in formation
> —the raids had gone on for hours after us.
> Did they see us down there in our trouble?
> We radioed our final position for help to come
> but had no idea if anyone
> happened to be tuned in and heard us,
> and we crouched together on the floor,
> knees drawn up and head down
> in regulation position for ditching,
> listened as the engine stopped, a terrible silence,
> and we went down into the sea with a crash,
> just like hitting a brick wall,
> jarring bones, teeth, eyeballs panicky.
> Who would ever think water could be so hard?
> You black out, and then come to
> with water rushing in like a sinking-ship movie.

I admire this writing for more or less the opposite reason to that which leads me to appreciate either *The Seafarer* or any passage from Ashbery's *Flow Chart*. Here, in Field's poem, the language is entirely at the service of the event narrated. You could say that the event is the poetry. This is a tendency often to be found with the poetry of devastations such as wars. As Wilfred Owen put it, "The poetry is in the pity." But as we have seen, his assertion prompted W. B. Yeats to bar Owen from his anthology of "Modern Verse". Pity was too humanising a quality. The earlier moderns were after a more material sense of what poetry could be.

※

CONSIDER THE COMPLEX LAYERS OF THE SYSTEMS inscribed and overlaid on each of us; the crawling, dissociative system, inherited from when we walked on all fours and intimately connected both with our sequential processes and in all likelihood with our noses (which were nearer the scents of the ground when we moved on all fours). Also, there is the rhythmical system connected with the repetitiveness of walking or swimming, but also connected with all other repetitions from breathing to weaving, from the heart beat to the drum beat. Then, there is a panoramic system controlled by the hands which may gesture or demonstrate simultaneously, since the hands have a "vista" intimately connected to the eyes. There is also a vertical sequential system introduced by scaling a tree or a wall, hold by hold, or performing the complex act of diving or swinging from a trapeze—which is akin to how we travelled when we swung through trees. What is common to these systems is the spine. And so we might ask, what is the spine of a poem?

Does a poem "stand" on its first line as we stand on our feet, or as a building stands on its foundations? It could be the other way round—the poem heading off from its beginning and being grounded by its final line? I am not sure how far this gets us. The poem on the page is only a chart of its sequence in time, whereas our body stands in space. Extending the spinal metaphor may be useful though in another way: stanzas might be conceived as similar to vertebrae.

Michael Donaghy points out the *stanza* is, in Italian, the room of a poem—so we move from verse to verse as if from room to room in a building. I imagine myself walking through the Uffizzi Gallery, each room filled with pictures, the pictures being the lines, in this extended metaphor.

The vertebral metaphor takes us elsewhere, perhaps into novel territory. The spine is a complex instrument: there are seven cervical, twelve thoracic, and five lumbar vertebrae. The lumbar spine is the lower back, connected to the sacrum and thus to the pelvis. It supports the ribcage, while the ribs themselves connect with the lumbar spine, and above this, the cervical spine concerns the neck and the support of the head. Because it has to do such a big job holding up the chest and the rest of the upper body, the thoracic spine is built so firmly that though it can bend it cannot rotate. Only the lumbar spine rotates, its twelve components moving in tandem, each with slightly fluted wings, which allow the thoracic "chorus" of vertebrae to rotate as a piece. The cervical spine can twist, rotate and tilt, but still has the role of holding up the head.

When a tango dancer pivots on the ball of the foot, this is a movement which begins in the thoracic spine. First the thorax rotates around the sternum, and this supplies the dynamic that causes the circular swivel of the heel around the weight-bearing ball. If you entertain the notion that the step can be broken down into its four component quarter beats, then I step on the first, I rotate my spine on the third (the upbeat), which causes the pivot on fourth so that I land on the first quarter beat of the next full beat.

The differences between the types of vertebra and what they can do implies that stanzas could also have different roles to play in the poem. In a Shakespearean sonnet, the second verse constitutes an antistrophe to the theme laid out in the first verse with a synthesis achieved in the third verse while the couplet at the end presents a summary of the whole. I have never found this form of sonnet as satisfying as the Petrarchan form, with its two quatrains followed by two tercets, for this makes far more sense of the fourteen lines. Shakespeare's form is arbitrary—why not eighteen lines?

The sense of different stanzas having different roles to play, especially in relation to a burden or refrain, is thoroughly understood by Chaucer in the roundel quoted in the previous chapter (on page 203).

Component parts are always capable of being broken down into their own smaller components. And actions are capable of being broken down into their component movements. If the landing step of the walk is on the downbeat, then the free leg swishes past the ankle on the upbeat. Equally, the line of verse divides into the words before and the words after the caesura which is the fulcrum of balance in the line. Then the number of lines grouped together define the stanza, and this stanza can be made more or less compact depending upon whether rhyme is used to bind it together or not and depending upon whether or not a tight metrical scheme has been adopted.

With the revival of interest in elaborate forms of Greek prosody which accompanied neo-classicism, rhythms and stanza forms became ever more rarefied, with the eleven syllables of a Hendecasyllabic line being introduced by Swinburne (where a strong stress on the first syllable of each line differentiates it from the rising iambics of standard pentameter). Swinburne also worked on creating an equivalent to the complex quantitative verses of Sappho. I have already mentioned that Robert Bridges tried to introduce quantity into our poetry a decade or so later.

Here, I must renew my adolescent salute to Swinburne, for in terms of stanzaic action, his poetry excels. The result is utterly different but, in many ways, just as abstract as Ashbery's verse, and this should merit Swinburne's reassessment and generate a new appreciation of his power. It is with mastery that he handles the complex metrical requirements of the Sapphic stanza:

All the night sleep came not upon my eyelids,
Shed not dew, nor shook nor unclosed a feather,
Yet with lips shut close and with eyes of iron
Stood and beheld me.

Then to me so lying awake a vision
Came without sleep over the seas and touched me,
Softly touched mine eyelids and lips; and I too
Full of the vision,

Saw the white implacable Aphrodite,
Saw the hair unbound and the feet unsandalled
Shine as fire of sunset on western waters;
Saw the reluctant

Feet, the straining plumes of the doves that drew her,
Looking always, looking with necks reverted,
Back to Lesbos, back to the hills whereunder
Shone Mitylene....

From *Sapphics,* Algernon Charles Swinburne

It is the case that the units stanzas exemplify can be rendered more resoundingly "poetic"—or less—and in the Victorian age, the poetry was emphatic, and the ear appreciative of the subtle complexities that could be achieved, albeit what was generated was a poetry largely defined by regularity and pattern, rather than by alliteration or "sprung verse" or by "paring back to the essence". All too often the opposite was the case. The nineteenth century stanza simply got filled with verbiage in order for its scheme to be rendered complete, a practice strongly abhorrent to the moderns of the twentieth century. It has to be acknowledged that Victorian poetry can be just as purple as its prose. Swinburne is guilty of whole swathes of purple, I'm afraid. However, when he works as a craftsman, and wrestles with the transmutation of a Greek form into English, as he does with his *Hendecasyllabics* and the *Sapphics* quoted above, he confidently shrugs off this accusation. It's probably because here he is aware that rhythmic innovation is the essential action he is pursuing and because in both cases he eschews rhyme. Sadly, in the main, he steers a more sentimental course. We will analyse Sapphics in more detail in the final chapter.

One stanza may rest on another like the component drums of a column.

Several centuries earlier, Sir Philip Sidney also made experiments with Greek models and with blank verse, and these three magnificent stanzas are one inimitable and unforgettable result:

O sweet woods, the delight of solitariness!
Oh, how much I do like your solitariness!
Where man's mind hath a freed consideration,
Of goodness to receive lovely direction.
Where senses do behold th' order of heav'nly host,
And wise thoughts do behold what the creator is;
Contemplation here holdeth his only seat,
Bounded with no limits, born with a wing of hope,
Climbs even unto the stars, nature is under it.
Nought disturbs thy quiet, all to thy service yields,
Each sight draws on a thought (thought, mother of science)
Sweet birds kindly do grant harmony unto thee,
Fair trees' shade is enough fortification,
Nor danger to thyself if 't be not in thyself.

O sweet woods, the delight of solitariness!
Oh, how much I do like your solitariness!
Here nor treason is hid, veilèd in innocence,
Nor envy's snaky eye finds any harbor here,
Nor flatterers' venomous insinuations,
Nor cunning humorists' puddled opinions,
Nor courteous ruin of proffered usury,
Nor time prattled away, cradle of ignorance,
Nor causeless duty, nor cumber of arrogance,
Nor trifling title of vanity dazzleth us,
Nor golden manacles stand for a paradise,
Here wrong's name is unheard, slander a monster is;
Keep thy sprite from abuse, here no abuse doth haunt.
What man grafts in a tree dissimulation?

O sweet woods, the delight of solitariness!
Oh, how well I do like your solitariness!
Yet, dear soil, if a soul closed in a mansion
As sweet as violets, fair as lily is,
Straight as cedar, a voice stains the canary birds,
Whose shade safety doth hold, danger avoideth her;
Such wisdom that in her lives speculation;

Such goodness that in her simplicity triumphs;
Where envy's snaky eye winketh or else dieth;
Slander wants a pretext, flattery gone beyond;
Oh! if such a one have bent to a lonely life,
Her steps glad we receive, glad we receive her eyes,
    And think not she doth hurt our solitariness,
    For such company decks such solitariness.

The Countess of Pembroke's Arcadia, 1593

The scansion of this poem is elusive. The "singing" strength of the opening couplet in each verse (a sort of "refrain" that comes first rather than last) suggests a musical component, a melody that may have guided the poet. The poem seems to perform a balancing act between Hexameter and Heptameter. One is tempted to negotiate the first three syllables—*O sweet woods*—by giving equal weight to them all, reading them as an extended spondee, followed by an anapaest (suited to the opening phrases of that melody). However, my instinctual feeling is that this poem has been built around the idea of sentence scansion that I have referred to in the chapter on The Theatre of Mistakes. Each generation has discovered that Sydney was ahead of his time.

When considering the stanza as an anatomical component of the "spine" of the poem I've mentioned that our own spinal column comprises several groups of vertebrae, each with its own particular properties. I pointed out that only the dorsal vertebrae rotate and they are responsible for the dissociative dynamic that empowers the pivot of a turn. It's plain that each vertebral group differs from its neighbours. Now this would be similar to creating a suite of poems utilising a variety of stanzas. Eliot works astutely with a suite of verse forms in the movements of his *Four Quartets*. Just such a suite was constructed for *Silent Highway*—a sequence of mine inspired by the Thames. I thought of the sequence as having four movements. Each movement was made of three poems, and each poem had its own stanza-form. This structure gave *Silent Highway* its presence. A poem must always have a structural presence as strong as the presence of its content.

The lower body empowers our movement, the upper body guides that power. The dorsals rotate in the direction we intend to go, and the feet then take us in that direction. The upper body's intention is realised by the lower body. Are the initial stanzas of a poem its "upper part", giving its intention? Do the later stanzas commit us to that intention and ultimately give it its thrust? Surprise in dance is created by some change in intention, often rapid, instigated by the upper body and followed through by the lower body. Equally the poem may require a shift in intention as it progresses—in order to avoid predictability. This may prove a problem with verses heavily committed to some particular issue, as adherence to the issue itself may restrict the ability to switch direction and thus evoke surprise.

3. GRADIVA

Dancing for both gait and speech difficulty/ The Freudian foot and the pathology of getting anywhere or expressing anything.

S HE FINDS IT DIFFICULT TO STEP OVER MY THRESHOLD. I offer an arm, holding open the door at the same time. Luna has MS. She wears a brace around one ankle, walks with a stick, but somehow, she manages to get her children to school and then drive over to me. She's dark haired with sparkling eyes. I get her seated in my Tottenham studio and tie the ribbons of her dance pumps after we have removed the brace. Then we sit opposite each other on armless wooden chairs and I put on a CD by Luiz Bonfá. Slow, relaxed guitar.

We always start with seated exercises, to get the circulation going and to ease into the standing movement with a sense of achievement, since with seated exercise more can be done. One leg, the right one, is tardy in its responses. The ankle moves a little from side to side, but it won't circle. The knee is slow to straighten or bend, and it never does either fully, but we still work at it, at both knees, both feet. We also work on moving the neck, at bending forward and back, and at rotating the spine and freeing up the shoulder-blades.

Then I put on a tango by Carlos de Sarli with a slow strong beat. We stand up, and I take Luna in the practice hold, my hands underneath her upper arms, her hands resting on my forearms. We start with swaying, keeping feet a little apart, shifting weight in time to the music from one foot to the other, feeling the floor through the balls of our feet, our heels. Then we try raising and lowering the heels. After that, we try stamping to the beat.

Usually we move on to side steps, trying to collect our feet at the ankles with every step. My classes in this vein are called *Tango for Balance*. I go out and teach this therapy to Parkinson's Disease Support Groups, and, before the crash of 2008 caused funds to evaporate, I used to teach dance for the elderly as well. Surprising as it may seem, the tango is an appropriate activity for people who find walking difficult. No one understands walking like a tanguero. I explain that walking is more about pushing than it is about reaching. I use my favourite example—it's just as if you were seated in a boat by a river bank: no amount of reaching will get you into the stream—you need to push off from the bank.

Today, I'm inspired. I want to try something new.

"Luna, what I want to explore today is getting you to speak at the same time as you walk forwards. Now you know how you need to push from your base foot when you want to move forward onto the free leg, well, today, as you do this, say 'Push!' as you do the pushing from the back, that is, from your heel."

I play the tango. I step with Luna. With every step we say, 'Push!' in time to the beat of the music. We progress down the room, with me walking backwards while supporting her progress. Push, push, push!

At first, I can hardly hear her since she is concentrating so hard on the action of the step. But after a few goes at it, she gets the idea, and with my encouragement she shouts in time, Push, Push! It's exhausting.

True, it takes effort. But there's no doubt about it, the rhythm of her gait improves when she shouts the instruction to herself at the same time as she steps.

We then try the sidestep exercise. Now the 'push' is sideways. She steps in time when she says the word, however she fails to "collect", that is to bring her ankles together on completion of the step.

"Ok, so try saying, Push, Collect, Push, Collect."

We try this, but now there is too much to think about. Luna can't fit the "collect" in and say the word. We need to slow down. Work at half the speed of the tango beat. This works better, but by now we're exhausted. Time to have a break. However, with the simple forward walk, her timing was much improved by saying the word as she stepped.

I started *Tango for Balance* after reading about research being done by Madeleine Hackney at Washington University School of Medicine in St Louis, Missouri. Her research posited that tango exercises might be an appropriate and effective strategy for ameliorating functional mobility deficits in the frail and the elderly. This was specifically noted in sample groups of individuals with Parkinson's and randomly selected groups of elderly people. Those who participated in the tango lessons showed improved balance over those who participated in standard exercise classes designed by physiotherapists for the elderly and for people with PD. In particular, those working on the tango exercises scored higher when attempting to step backwards.

But why should you step backwards—or sideways for that matter? It's because in life you need all three possibilities, as well as being able to simply change your weight on the spot. You are walking across a street, and a car comes and you need to step back. This is where people who find walking difficult often topple and fall back and hit their heads. Or you are with family and one of the nippers grabs your hand and you need to step sideways in the direction you are being pulled. Understanding your balance might save you from a fall.

The received wisdom, adhered to by many physiotherapists, is that in order to walk forwards you overbalance slightly in the direction you want to go, and then catch yourself up. We can see this, for sure, when we watch a toddler tottering forwards. This is not how a tango dancer understands walking. By creating "a long back" and slightly altering the centre of gravity, by pushing forwards but remaining parallel to the floor, it is possible to transfer the weight forward onto the free foot without a sense of toppling. The dancer will also make use of the moment during the step when the weight is equally distributed between the feet. There is no overbalancing, unless a 'drop' into the step forward is specifically required. Otherwise the walk is entirely controlled. This is particularly useful for all wibbly-wobblies with a tendency to freeze—and then to fall.

Simple tango exercises may be danced either in the embrace or in the practice hold. Working in pairs like this increases balance security. Tango helps those who find walking fearsome, since they are always being supported by their partner. The couples holding each other are concerned with executing a simple sequence in time to the music: the leaders instigating and their partners following. In my classes, these roles get exchanged. Tango also helps alleviate panic problems, freezing while turning and other gait troubles symptomatic of the fear of falling down. Loss of functional mobility can lead to low self-esteem, poor mood, withdrawing from activities, and a very much decreased quality of life. The social nature of partner dancing alleviates these effects. In other words, it's fun!

But it's not only the elderly and those suffering from diseases such as MS and Parkinson's, who have to contend with balance problems: it's a problem which may affect those injured in accidents, those with inner ear disorders, and many others. So my classes are for anyone who wishes to improve their ability to balance. The tango is exceptionally good for equilibrium—primarily because it's essentially a walking dance in partnership. This means that, at the level relevant to the therapy, two feet are on the floor at any one time. One is your own: one is your partner's. Essentially when one stands in the practice hold with a partner, four feet are sustaining stability rather than two—this is like using another person as a support frame. However, as classes progress, couples are encouraged to step together without clutching the partner for support. That is why I keep telling Luna not to press down too hard on my supporting arms.

Walking alone involves moving from one foot to another. There are three crucial events involved in this: instigation of the move forward, landing on the other foot—thus transferring the weight—and then the passage of one foot past the other. Tango encourages dancers not to "dip" in the hip when walking forwards. Allowing the hip to become displaced while transferring weight is a major cause of instability.

As already explained, three possibilities exist in moving from one foot to the other—or indeed in rebounding back onto the initial foot. You can walk forwards, backwards or to the side. Tango works with all these options, and with the simple transference of weight from one foot to another "on the spot". In a conventional class, preliminary exercises will encourage participants to move through these actions without a partner, developing "an axis"—that is, an ability to balance *collectedly* (one foot with little or no weight on it next to the foot with weight on it) after forward steps, back-steps, sidesteps or rebounds back onto the foot initiating the step. In *Tango for Balance*, such exercises may be done later, where appropriate, once a measure of balance security has been attained—and seated exercises are good as preliminary actions, warming up the joints and encouraging strength and mobility in hip, knee and ankle.

The second essential component to the tango is the pivot; a rotation of the ball of the foot against the floor, achieved by releasing the heel. Fear of performing this action, or indeed the functional inability to perform it, leads to freezing in turns and is a key cause of falls. Participants in workshops are assessed for pivot ability and, where capable of pivots, taught how to perform this action without losing their axis, or, where incapable, shown how to develop a strategy for turning without pivoting.

Partners are encouraged to exchange lead and follow roles, so that they learn how to instigate and how to respond to movement. They are also expected to swap partners, which creates a pleasant ambiance—raising morale. And these issues are addressed to the accompaniment of music, which stops it all feeling like a chore, indeed, the strong trochaic beat of the tango actively improves performance. In many cases, those who find walking an effort also find talking an effort—another instance that hints at the primordial relationship between walking and talking.

⁊₭

WHILE A VESTIGIAL UNCONDITIONED WALKING RESPONSE can be observed in babies, we have to acquire walking, unlike other animals. We acquire walking, just as we acquire the ability to talk and to think. Walking is a conditioned activity that involves a number of complex muscular co-ordinations. However, our ability to walk in a confident balanced way may be improved as we bring walking closer to its natural roots in the unconditioned response from which it evolved. Tango encourages crossover coordination between the upper right and the lower left parts of the body, and crossover coordination has implications for autism and Asperger's as well as for dyspraxia and dyslexia.

This was discovered by observing crawling patterns in babies. Freedland

and Bertenthal have stated that "crawling experience, and specifically experience following the onset of hands-and-knees crawling, contributes to the
development and reorganization of a number of other skills, such as spatial orientation, fear of heights, and postural stability." Significantly, some
infants later diagnosed with Asperger's Syndrome have exhibited crawling
patterns that deviate from the basic diagonally opposing limb patterns.
Diagonal coupling of the limbs "maintains the most stable centre of gravity." Essentially, we are talking about how the left arm swings forward as
the right foot takes a step. Crawl machines may be used to strengthen this
aspect of coordination.

By encouraging the crossover relationship, which tangueros refer to as
"the body spiral", the dance develops our ability to use "the most stable centre of gravity"—for dancers are encouraged to coordinate crossover rotation with walking, thus maintaining a connection with their partner, albeit
in the subtlest way, perhaps no more than a slight rotation in the sternum.
For all these reasons, tango is good for a confident walk, with diminished
fear of falling. In addition, it's a dance which may well help dementia sufferers, since participants may be expected to memorise short sequences of
steps known as "figures". This encourages stimulation of memory linked
to physical action: more effective than memory exercises which are simply
done in the head.

But how does this therapy relate to our theme? As noted, those with
gait problems often have difficulty with speaking. People with Parkinson's
may speak "under their breath" though they feel that they are talking in
a normal way. At the same time, they may shuffle, partly for fear of falling, but also because they may *feel* they are walking, however "the push"
has gone out of their walk. Addressing this, there's another therapy called
The BIG therapy program: an adaptation for muscular disorders of the Lee
Silverman Voice Training LOUD method, which was developed in 1987
to improve voice and speech in people with Parkinson's. It's a standardized
exercise approach developed from some twenty years of research and it has
shown documented improvements in balance, trunk rotation and faster
walking with bigger steps.

The method trains patients to make bigger movements and teaches the
amount of effort required to produce normal movements in day to day

activities connected to the real world. The principles that made LOUD an effective treatment for the speech motor system have now been applied with some success to the limb motor system. The BIG program (US spelling) adapts the principles and approach of LOUD in order to improve major motor skills such as walking, moving of the arms and legs, and balance. BIG training increases the size of limb and body movement ("bigness") in Parkinson's sufferers, which leads to improvements in the quality and speed of their movement, in their balance. The program utilizes many repetitions of movements that are used in daily life. Because it's common that individuals with Parkinson's disease have difficulty being loud enough for people to hear, run out of air when talking, and indeed may avoid participating in conversations because of their softness of voice, the LOUD program strives to increase the patient's success with communication by improving the voice and speech function. Thus, the LOUD program is designed to increase loudness and improve speech clarity.

That is why I encourage bigger steps from Luna by accompanying them with a nice loud expression of "Push!" even suggesting we chorus it as we execute the action. In the arena of dance therapy, as much as in professional dance and poetics, I continue to pursue this notion of there being some connection between talking and stepping. So it's intriguing to realise that the BIG and LOUD program suggests that there is some neural connection between the pathology of walking and the pathology of speech.

But there is also the psychology of walking to be considered.

⁂

GRADIVA IS A NOVEL BY WILHELM JENSON that was analysed by Sigmund Freud. Norbert Hanold, a young archaeologist, is fascinated by a Roman relief that shows a girl lifting her gown as she walks forward, raising the heel of her back foot almost vertically as she pushes forward out of the ball of that foot. He purchases a plaster cast of the piece, and names the girl "Gradiva"—she of the glorious step. Reclusive, and to some extent appalled by the vulgarity of modern life, he becomes obsessed by the notion of finding a woman who walks in this specific way, and so he begins watching women's feet intently, though ostensibly an academic engrossed simply by

dint of research in his subject, and therefore remote from erotic promptings. Yet he rushes out in his night attire one morning when he fancies he
saw from his window just such a raised instep as a lady passed down the
street where he lives in Germany. Norbert dreams that the figure on the
relief is that of a young woman who perished in the eruption that destroyed
Pompeii in 76 AD. He travels to Italy, and without consciously making it
his destination, he finds himself in Pompeii. Then, a day later, at noon, the
hour when ghosts appear, according to Roman tradition, he experiences
a vision: there is Gradiva, crossing the high stepping stones that traverse
the sunken stone street of the dead city; stepping stones that allowed the
chariots and horse-drawn carts to pass through them. He follows her, but
the apparition proves elusive. Finally, he encounters her face to face and he
addresses her in Greek, which she fails to understand. He tries Latin; but
surprisingly, she replies in German. Gradually it dawns upon him that the
young woman is flesh and blood.

Freud's celebrated analysis of this work of fiction by Jenson is an intriguing accompaniment to reading what amounts to an eerie novella set among
ruins which suggest the sub-conscious, the long buried, the childhood
that has been repressed. Actually, Gradiva's name is Zoë, and as Norbert is
dazedly rambling on about what he still imagines her to be, she interrupts
his reverie, using his actual name, which he never told her. This makes him
all the more confused. Then, later, seeing a fly alight on Gradiva's wrist, he
slaps at it forcefully, the fly being an insect he abhors as much as he does
the courting couples buzzing around the sites of Italy. This abrupt move
enables him to ascertain that Gradiva is flesh-and-blood, or at least Zoë is.

Freud observes that calling someone out loud by their full name is a
technique used to rouse subjects from a state of hypnosis. He points out
that dreams concern the future because they epitomise wish-fulfilment,
which inevitably must lie ahead. When it finally comes out that this young
woman was actually Norbert's childhood playmate, the archaeologist
retreats into the polite form of address, as opposed to the familiar form he
has used when speaking to the 'phantom'. Freud has this to say about her
crisp rejoinder:

Miss Bertgang's answer shows then that other relations besides those of neighbourliness have existed between them. She knows how to intercede for the familiar manner of address, which he has, of course, used to the noonday spirit, but withdrawn again from the living girl; she makes former privileges of use to her here. "'If you find that form of address more suitable between us, I can use it too, you know, but the other came to me more naturally. I don't know whether I looked different when we used to run about before with each other as friends, every day, and occasionally beat and cuffed each other for a change, but if, in recent years, you had favoured me with even one glance you might perhaps have seen that I have looked like this for a long time.'"

A childhood friendship had therefore existed between the two, perhaps a childhood love, from which the familiar form of address derived its justification. Isn't this solution perhaps as superficial as the one first supposed? The fact that it occurs to us that this childhood relation explains in an unexpected way so many details of what has occurred in the present intercourse between them makes the matter essentially deeper. Does it not seem that the blow on Zoë-Gradiva's hand which Norbert Hanold has so splendidly motivated by the necessity of solving, experimentally, the question of the physical existence of the apparition, is, from another standpoint, remarkably similar to a revival of the impulse for "beating and cuffing," whose sway in childhood Zoë's words have testified to? And when Gradiva puts to the archaeologist the question whether it does not seem to him that they have once already, two thousand years ago, shared their luncheon, does not the incomprehensible question become suddenly senseful, when we substitute for the historical past the personal childhood, whose memories persist vividly for the girl, but seem to be forgotten by the young man? Does not the idea suddenly dawn upon us that the fancies of the young man about his Gradiva may be an echo of his childhood memories?

Gradiva, Sigmund Freud (Delusion and Dream in Wilhelm Jensen's *Gradiva*)—Sun and Moon Press, L.A., 1993.

One gets the impression, when reading Freud's analysis of the novel, that he is as intrigued by the psychology of Zoë as he is by that of Norbert. Prompted by this, I note that at one crucial moment Norbert comes across her sitting on a stone table in a ruined house, swinging her feet. She is quite tart and crisp with Norbert, but still she swings her feet, drawing attention to them—knowingly enough, I say to myself. Then I find Freud's equation of the slap "against" the fly on her arm with the "beating and cuffing" of their childhood particularly rewarding as it is an observation about physical actions. I remind myself that the novel itself is preoccupied with a physical action, the act of walking, in an exceptional way, with a heel raised vertically above the ball of the foot.

What is the meaning of this raised instep that Norbert finds so attractive? I looked closely at a reproduction of the relief which inspired him. It can be found in the Vatican Museum. The girl's weight is set back into her hips and as she goes she looks slightly down, as if descending. Perhaps she was about to descend, into a cellar, to find a wine—or, more darkly, go down into "the underworld".

Then I asked myself, why and when do we use a verticality of the back instep, toes and ball pressed into our contact with gravity? This powers up our walk forward, yes, but, with that much power coming from the ball below the instep, could it be that that Gradiva is executing a rebound? A rebound constitutes a reversal of direction, a backstep, for instance, reversed by the power in the back ball and toes, applied to the ground on the upbeat—which sends the walk forward again on the beat. Norbert's theory of the origin of her walk is in no way refuted by this. Equally the downward gaze and the empowerment in the ball of the back foot suggests that she could be about to take a step larger than usual, recoiling slightly, only to push more strongly forward to reach the first of the lava stepping stones.

But most of all the rebound suggests dancing to me, and reconstructions of the complete relief show us that Gradiva was not an isolated figure but one of a triad of young women. Triads of nymphs were a subject much favoured by the sculptors of Greece and Rome. Triads would dance together, with one line weaving in and out of another. These triads were given the names of the nymphs of antiquity who were associated with the hours, with the seasons, with fate itself, and with the art of dancing. Among such triads were the Aglaurids, heroic women of Athens who produced music simply by the dancing movements of their feet. I am reminded here of Lucinda Childs and how she danced to the sound of her own feet.

Aglaurus was one of the three daughters of Cecrops. Apollodorus tells the story in detail, and later writers have embellished it somewhat:

Athena visited Hephaestus to see about the preparation of her armour. He, being deserted by Aphrodite, was overcome with desire for Athena and tried to assault her, but she, being a virgin, did not permit it. He spent his seed on the thigh of the goddess and she, having wiped it off in disgust with a piece of wool, threw it on the ground, from whence sprang the autochthonous Erichthonius, one of the earliest kings of Athens; a being conceived by Gaia, our mother earth. Not wishing to keep him, Gaia gave him to Athena who brought up Erichthonius without the knowledge of the other gods, intending to make him immortal. She put him in a chest and gave it to Pandrosus, the daughter of Cecrops, telling her not to open it. Pandrosus and her sister Herse resolved never to open the box, Aglaurus however, opened it through curiosity and saw the infant enfolded by a snake. Some say that all three were then killed by the snake, and some say they went mad on account of the rage of Athena, who was just then flying through the air with a mountain in her hands, which she intended to use in order to further fortify the Parthenon. A crow that had witnessed what had happened flew up to tell Athena that Erichthonius had been displayed, and in fury she dropped the mountain, which is now Mount Lycabettus, and hurried back to the Athens. On account of being the bearer of ill tidings, Athena told the crow that it would be unlawful for it ever to approach her sacred hill. In terrible fear of the retribution that Athena might mete out to them the triad of sisters threw themselves down from the Acropolis before the return of the goddess.

The nymph Aglaurus, who dances to the sound of her feet, now evolves into a revealer of dark secrets, as if the earth were communicating to her through her soles. Note that her sister's name is nearly Pandora. As for Gradiva, who may be Aglaurus, her downward glance could be evidence of her long back, a feat of posture, where the spine seems to lengthen when the sternum is pushed back, and then one tries to distance the vertebrae from each other, so one feels the spine reach up behind the ears, and the back is now dead straight though the chin is slightly down, as is Gradiva's. This subtle downwards slant to the chin occurs when the psoas muscle is authentically located. It is a spine neither displaying a convex arch (tilting the breasts one way and the arse the other), nor bent into a concave stoop or a slouch. There is strength and confidence in the long back, with each vertebra parallel to its neighbour. It is the blithe confidence of the demi-goddess. We see it in the flamenco dancer and in the tango dancer.

The nymphs were always associated with soothsaying. And these sisterly triads such as the Aglaurids were, in addition, concerned with fostering, and seen as the rescuers of abandoned children, very like the three handmaidens who discovered Moses in the rushes. They are also celebrated as formidable dancers. The theory that women invented song has been discussed in an earlier chapter, and I wonder, since they may have pioneered moving in unison, whether these nymphs, when dancing in their line as a chorus, also spoke in harmony? Does harmony emerge out of first stepping in unison? Was there a tonal order agreed as well as an agreed order of steps?

In the particular triad of which Gradiva is one figure, a third girl pours a liquid onto the ground from a small flask. It cannot be merely a matter of watering the earth, since any sort of watering-vessel would need to be larger. This is a libation. And now, in the tradition of possibly deluded conjecture immortalised by Norbert Hanold, I would like to suggest that this libation is of mead. The nymph is sprinkling honeyed drops of inspiration onto a dancing floor (an *aloni,* that is, a threshing floor—whose importance has been discussed in the *Before History, chapter 3*).

An early alcoholic beverage, just about everyone—ancient Greeks, Africans, and Chinese—imbibed this honeyed drink as far back as 3000 BCE. Mead is significant in Norse mythology also, especially in the legend of a fabled potion with magical powers known as *Poetic Mead.* The gods created a man named Kvasir who was so wise he could answer any question. When he was eventually killed, his blood was mixed with honey, and whoever drank this honey-blood mead took on Kvasir's power of intelligence. It seems that the consumption of fomented honey has been associated with articulation since time immemorial, and the nymphs are customarily associated with Hermes, conveyer of intelligence from the gods. In her essay on *The Bee Maidens in the Homeric Hymn to Hermes*, Susan Scheinberg tells us of the use of honey in Sanskrit poetry:

In the Atharna-Veda, for example, the singer of a hymn asks: "O Aśvins, lords of Brightness, anoint me with the honey of the bee, that I may speak forceful speech among men.

Hymns of the Atharna-Veda, trans. M Bloomfield, (Oxford 1897, repr. NY 1969). p. 231.

From associated lines of poetry in Greek, Scheinberg deduces that honey was supposed to stimulate assonance, a syrupy usage of the vowels that could very conceivably be associated with honey and "honeyed lines"—thus the libation sprinkled on the dance-floor stimulates powerful eloquence as well as powerful dancing by these women with their vigorous insteps, bounding and rebounding in a rhythm that makes a prophetic music out of their footwork. And then, were spoken harmonies enhanced by the honey of an assonance when these bee-maidens danced in their triadic lines? Harmony lends a transcendent power to the voice. The association with the inspired earth that now links poetry with intelligence and the power of prophecy also brings us back to wish-fulfilment, harmony working like a charm on reality—as with the song of Orpheus to his lyre. The ancient poets may have used harmony to invoke a resonance that indicated divine power, as they used metre to generate pace and indicate the flowing alterations of *physis*, the life force.

In the first dramas, pace alteration enabled mimesis to give narratives a tangible quality "true to the action". Trimeter might quicken the measure and make a change from some rambling "fourteener." The chorus of heroic women who made music with their feet could mimic the thundering approach of attacking warriors, the stamping of horses chafing at their bits, the trickling steps of young girls playing under a waterfall, the hesitations and abrupt transitions of madness. But what has changed? Even today, the walk can be sad or elated. Kathakali dancers may thunder with their bare feet. Exponents of the tango may ask their students to think of an animal as they walk together. Are you a panther? Are you an elephant? What happens when a panther dances with an elephant? Snakes may not have feet, but the feet can move snakily. The feet can stalk. And they can be splendid in their walking, as is Gradiva.

But let us continue to explore the perceptive comments on Gradiva by Freud.

☙

FREUD ATTRIBUTES THE DELUSION that Zoë is a phantom, under which Norbert labours, to repression of childhood memories, and he points out that to repress a memory, such as Norbert's of Zoë, is not to obliterate the memory itself. He also touches on the fetishism of the archaeologist's fascination with the female instep. The obsession with a heel, as in *Gradiva*, finds a healthy outcome in the tango where a thorough understanding of heel and ball and how "groundedness" functions significantly improves quality of movement.

Of course, all dancers are subject to shoe fetishes! There is a continuous debate among my partners as to which brand of high-heel gives the best support and is best calibrated for balance. Perhaps a fetishization of the foot originates, at least in part, with the association of the foot with the mouth, as when a subject kisses the foot of a king. There is also the instance of Mary Magdalene washing the feet of Jesus with her hair. The mouth (or the head) paying homage to the foot is a symbolic gesture of humility, the mouth concedes to the foot. This action may appeal to those who are sexually inclined to submission, though it should be noted that submission in itself may be a reaction formation to some excessive will-to-power which appals the person who feels it so much that they attempt to camouflage their inclination by acting as if the opposite condition were the case. I find it interesting, in this regard, to point out that the wife of Bath, in Chaucer, actually comes up with what is apparently agreed by all women to be a satisfactory answer to the question that has so perplexed psychoanalysis: 'What do women want?'

A great queen has decreed that a knight who has raped a lady of the court must come up with the answer to this question within one year or be executed for his crime. No two women seem to agree on what the answer is! During his errant quest for the answer, the knight meets a knowing crone, and after some hard bargaining she divulges the answer:

And afterward this knight was bode appeere.
　　To every wight comanded was silence,
And that the knight sholde telle in audience
What thing that worldly wommen loven best.
This knight ne stood nat stille as doth a beast,
But to his questioun anon answerde
With manly vois, that al the court it herde:
　　'My lige lady, generally,' quod he,
'Wommen desiren to have sovereinetee
As wel over hir housbond as hir love,
And for to been in maistrie him above.
This is youre mooste desir, thogh ye me kille.
Dooth as yow list; I am heer at youre wille.'
In al the court ne was ther wyf, ne maide,
Ne widwe, that contraried that he saide,
But seyden he was worthy han his lyf.

Geoffrey Chaucer, *The Wife of Bath's Tale*, l. 1030-45

It is interesting to contrast this notion of female aspiration with that projected onto women by the majority of male sonneteers who emerged after
Petrarch and Dante. In practically all such cases, women's role is defined by
securing a husband and by childbirth ensuring the continuance of a blood-
line. Now it becomes clear that this emphasisi on security, nurture and
lineage is very much a male interpretation; a justification of their purpose,
as a man might see it, that has no bearing on the question posed.

❦

A POLITICIAN WAS ACCUSED OF HAVING FOOT-AND-MOUTH DISEASE: every
time he opened his mouth he put his foot in it. A sexual brand of fetishism
links mouth to foot in a perverse parallel of our interest in the step being
the foot of poetic metre. Other associations or confusions of one bodily
part with another have generated unappetizing customs, such as the binding of the feet in imperial China. Here the foot is divested of its functional
role; instead the instep becomes a surrogate vagina. I see this practice as

essentially derived from a fear of women and of the superiority that the wife of Bath asserts is their universal aspiration. The binding, which begins in childhood, renders the woman helpless, unable to walk. However, she now possesses three vulvas.

The binding of the feet naturally suggests the old cliché that there is a tendency towards an objectification of women, and any insistence on seeing her, as *woman*, and solely in sexual terms, is a subjugation of her sex by elevation of her sexuality. If we develop these truisms, the weaker sex most desires to be stronger than the stronger sex. The stronger sex senses and fears this desire and endeavours to render the weaker sex weaker still. Possibly cuffed, more than once, far too successfully by Zoë, Norbert weakens her by obliteration, his repression of her memory makes a phantom of her.

Despite ourselves, we are always rehearsing and reacting to these truisms while wishing we could simply throw them off as generalisations. There is a sexual war, but can we at least find détente? The Minoan chorus began with the triad being conjoined by the snake they were bearing in their arms. Then they held each other's wrists, and they danced in step, together. It was the 'weaker' sex who first realised there was strength in numbers. Consider the *Lysistrata!*

Let us dismantle and examine the term to which we are all objecting. In the Neolithic, when procreation was emphasised because of a low survival rate, women may have evolved towards child-bearing, thus stronger in this regard—after all, men can't do it at all! But today, if a woman decides that this is not her major role, she can certainly attain superiority of physical strength over the average man in the street, if she applies herself to it. That was as true in the Middle ages as it is now, of course. Joan of Arc was the tip of an ice-berg. Even so, tradition exerts a force on our drives. When aroused, a man needs to feel that objectification which he senses is alive also in the woman who is happily objectifying him.

But what has this to do with the step, or for that matter the foot? Tension between the sexes can do as much damage as any disability, so it is relevant to address it, then seek the answers in our own terms. Humans enjoy dancing in synchronised ways. It is very good for our bonding. Being conjoined at the wrist in an ancient triad or chorus can evolve into line dancing. And with arms about each other's shoulders, we can share the steps that, various as they may be, are being applied to the same metre, until the metre changes and the pace quickens. These days, a synchronicity, or something akin to it, can be achieved (and enjoyed) by couples in various forms of partner dancing.

A phantom of the tension that antagonises us remains though. Conversation involves remark and response—very different to the unison of voices in a chorus. Remark and response can be antagonistic. Argumentative. But in dancing, we aim for an affirmative conversation— we seek to agree. All the same one initiates, while the other completes the shared action. Several medieaval lyrics have the man pleading and the woman aggressively repudiating his advances.

What is it to lead, and what is it to follow? Progessive liberals sometimes denounce the tango for requiring these roles. Of course, anyone of either sex can dance either role. But for the true improvisational art of tango to occur, there must be a leader and there must be a follower. Mind you, I also sense that there could well be a leader of a triad of nymphs dancing in synchronicity. One row may have responded to "the lead" of another row moving in a contrary direction. Lead and response is ultimately simply assertion and response, as in a conversation, best expressed in poetry by the eclogue. It is interesting to note that poetic exchanges have always been very common in Japanese poetry—as is demonstrated by the *Renga*—which is basically a collaborative form, and suggests that, for centuries, poetry was a collaborative act, with poets sitting around drinking together and exchanging verses.

Common in Greek and Latin poetry, one of the first eclogues in English is the fifteenth century *Nut-Brown Maid*:

He.
If ye go thyder, ye must consider,
When ye have lust to dine,
There shall no meat be for to gete,
Nether bere, ale, ne wine,
Ne shetès clean, to lie between,
Made of thread and twine;

None other house, but leaves and boughs,
To cover your head and mine.
Lo, mine heart sweet, this ill diète
Should make you pale and wan:
Wherefore I'll to the green-wood go,
Alone, a banished man.

She.
Among the wild deer such an archère,
As men say that ye be,
Ne may not fail of good vitayle
Where is so great plentè:
And water clear of the rivere
Shall be full sweet to me;
With which in hele I shall right wele
Endure, as ye shall see;
And, or we go, a bed or two
I can provide anone;
For, in my mind, of all mankind
I love but you alone.

He.
Lo yet, before, ye must do more,
If ye will go with me:
As, cut your hair up by your ear,
Your kirtle by the knee;
With bow in hand for to withstand
Your enemies, if need be:
And this same night, before daylight,
To woodward will I flee.
If that ye will all this fulfil,
Do it shortly as ye can:
Else will I to the green-wood go,
Alone, a banished man.

She.
I shall as now do more for you

Than 'longeth to womanhede;
To short my hair, a bow to bear,
To shoot in time of need.
O my sweet mother! before all other
For you I have most drede!
But now, adieu! I must ensue
Where fortune doth me lead.
All this make ye: Now let us flee;
The day cometh fast upon:
For, in my mind, of all mankind
  I love but you alone.

(*Oxford Book of English Verse*, 1974 edition)

One verse is an assertion, with its own refrain, and the next verse is the response, again with its own refrain. Another interesting eclogue is this poem attributed to Sir Walter Raleigh (1554 – 1618):

As ye came from the holy land
Of Walsinghame,
Met you not with my true love
By the way as you came?

'How should I know your true love,
That have met many a one,
As I came from the holy land,
That have come, that have gone?'

She is neither white, nor brown,
But as the heavens fair;
There is none hath a form so divine
In the earth or the air.

'Such a one did I meet, good sir,
Such an angelic face,
Who like a nymph, like a queen, did appear
By her gait, by her grace.'

She hath left me here alone,
All alone, as unknown,
Who sometimes did me lead with herself,
And me loved as her own....

(*Ibid*)

There are no indicators as to who speaks, but Verse A is an instigator of a question, Verse B is a response, and this continues throughout the poem—a sort of buried eclogue. The stanzas work as strophe/antistrophe. The strophe—or 'turn'—is the first stanza of an ode and essentially the first part of a debate or argument presented by the chorus. In reciting the strophe, the ancient chorus would move from the right of the stage to the left. The antistrophe is the other part of the debate and would move the chorus from left to right. Antistrophe means 'to turn back,' which makes sense. When there were two chorus lines, the antistrophe line would move in the opposite direction to the line performing the strophe; for the antistrophe, the movement is left to right, initially. The antistrophe serves as a response to the strophe, but it seldom gets the last word.

Assertion and response need not be so polite. There can be an exchange of challenges. Another form of eclogue is the "Flyting"—a competition in verse in which poets trade insults with each other. *The Flyting of Dunbar and Kennedie* records a poetic contest between William Dunbar and Walter Kennedy in front of James IV of Scotland, which includes the earliest recorded use of the word *shit* as a personal insult. Flyting can also be found in Arabic poetry in a popular form called *naqā'iḍ*, as well as the competitive verses of Japanese Haikai. It is a practice found in Irish epic verse, and, in the Finnish epic *The Kalevala*, the hero Väinämöinen uses the similar practice of duel singing to beat his rival Joukahainen. Insult duels are also common today in rap poetry. Here is one insulting verse against Kennedy, made by Dunbar:

Erse bryber bard, vile beggar with thy brats,
Cuntbitten crawdon Kennedy, coward of kind,

Ill-fared and dried as Danesman on the ratts,
Like as the gledds had on thy gules snout dined,
Mismade monster, each moon out of thy mind,
Renounce, ribald, thy rhyming, thou but roys.
Thy treacher tongue has ta'en a Highland strynd,
A Lowland arse would make a better noise.

The Flyting of Dunbar and Kennedy by William Dunbar—normalized and glossed by Michael Murphy (available online)

Sir Philip Sidney wrote a corona of dizains which is also a competing eclogue—and this time the two voices vie for the prize of the one being acknowledged as more melancholy than the other!

Returning to more constructive exchanges, note that in partner dancing there is in a sense a fusion of strophe and antistrophe, since they happen together, as part of a shared action. My partner responds to the assertion of my lead. The response does not come about by force or pressure. For me, leading is an invitation. I use my long back, and I connect via the sternum. The follower is sensitive to the finest angle rotation there. If she follows me there, her hips will follow the rotation of her ribcage which is entirely guided by her sternum.

There is considerable philosophic pleasure to be derived from the authentic notion of *marcar y seguir*. *Marcar* is to delineate, to invite a line, *Seguir* is to follow that line of invitation. In some cases, one can create a sort of vacuum which the leading partner steps into and occupies. Remember, what the leader suggests, the follower completes, as if one expressed the first syllable of a word, and the other completed it by supplying its ensuing syllables. What is very clear is that neither role is easier to learn than the other.

In the age of the Cathars, the troubaritz was honoured as much as the troubadour. It is interesting that in Provence at that time, inheritance passed to the eldest, not necessarily to the eldest in the male line. There were many wealthy and powerful woman among the Cathars. The flowering of poetic form, the freedom of expression, the search for novelty in vocabulary, and the revolution in sensibility that was instigated by the notion of courtly love and fostered in Provencal castles, while contraception was also well advanced, all came about in defiance of Rome, and among people who were accustomed to leaders such as Eleanor of Aquitaine. There is one aspect of today's poetic climate I appreciate as being similar to those golden days among the peaks of the Pyrenees, and that is the number of extraordinary poets I know who are not of my sex. But in truth, this is not so new. While there may have been comparatively few Renaissance painters who were women, there have always been women who wrote, and many who have written well.

⁂

IN THE EARLY PLAYS, THE CHORUS OCCUPIES A MEDIATING POSITION between the audience and the main protagonists of the action. The goal of the drama as a whole was essentially therapeutic. Through it a catharsis might be brought about, a purging of the tensions prompted by the play. As citizens of the town in which the tragedy occurs, the chorus can be witnesses and commentators. This enables the audience to see the event through their eyes. The chorus manages the pace of the play, and the action quickens or subsides in time to their feet. This suggests that the feet have a fluency, as is clearly demonstrated by the elegant play of an Argentine footballer. But just as the tongue can fail to articulate the thought in the head, the foot can fail to execute the step intended.

The toe and the ball and the heel and the ankle: they are all parts of a complex instrument; source of pleasure when thoroughly massaged, source of pain when afflicted by the gout. The heel is famously vulnerable, as is testified by the story of Achilles, whose mother held him by the heel when she dipped him in the bath of invulnerability. Ultimately an arrow piercing this one unprotected part was his undoing. Sever the Achilles tendon, and walking becomes impossible. Do we know our own? Our own Achilles heel? The metaphor dissolves into abstraction. Do you like sex too much for your own good. Or gambling? Or spend so much time hill-walking that you neglect your family?

So, the heel can be injured, the ankle twisted, the toe stubbed, and walking may be apprehensive. Ambulation is not without its anxieties. Our hiking boots may give us blisters. We can be afraid of stumbling, of falling.

We can feel worried about getting a step right. We can feel precarious in high heels. Tension may cause us to raise our shoulders and stiffen. Speech has its anxieties also, which may be manifested by stuttering or lisping or speaking too quietly to be heard or by not finishing sentences. As we have noted it is fairly common in later life to suffer from both disabilities. And there is a stigma attached to any loss of ability, a sense of shame, often most deeply entertained by the sufferer, deterring that sufferer from seeking treatment.

THE TOE OF A COUNTRY. FROM TOP TO TOE. Toe the line. Discipline is your Achilles heel. We have to stamp out your insolence. But I want to kick off by saying… The foot grounds language. But the foot as a measure of verse also opens us up to the duodecimal world of measure as culled from parts of the body; to dozens and to half-dozens and to the triads. It enables a universal koiné—a language of common symbols equated with parts of the body. We have already discussed the multiplicity of meanings accruing to the word "Foot". Like the palms of the hand, the soles of the feet can also be perceived as charts or pictures. Reflexology maps the entire anatomy of the body onto the soles of the feet. Thus, the narrowest part of your sole corresponds to your waist. The chest region is in the ball, while the pelvic region is in the heel. Head and sense organs are in the toes. Reflexologists believe that pressure applied to key points on the sole can be therapeutic for the part indicated by that point.

What might a traumatised foot be in poetic metre? I think I will turn the question on its head and ask, what about the recipient? What about the ear? Not being able to hear properly is frustrating for all sufferers. Tinnitus can interfere with our ability to follow the conversation in mixed company. For the poet who enjoys going to hear others read their work, deafness is a terrible sentence. Perhaps it then becomes important to read to oneself aloud, so that one may experience the words through their vibrations. This is an idea that pleases the bee-maidens. Dancing in the practice-hold with another person is also recommended. Stepping together brings awareness of the feel of one's tread, one's sole's impact with the ground. Balance is an important job that the ear is largely responsible for, so now it is a matter of urgency that the person increases their perception of weight and gravity through their body as they lose their hearing.

This then is the anxiety of the word: that it cannot be heard is as traumatic as that it cannot be said. Either by functional disability or by repression, its anxiety is of a dual nature. Is there a similar duality to the anxiety of the step? Well, it is the case that all the senses have a duality to them, for just as you can hear or be heard, you can touch and be touched, see and be seen, smell and be smelt, taste and be tasted. The wilderness may make your progress heavy going, or your own gait may be impaired. Walking, Stumbling, Limping and Falling are examined in a published conversation between Alyson Hallett and Phil Smith. At the time of the conversation Alyson is recuperating from a hip operation:

> First off, I became aware of strains of fascism in our cultural perceptions of what constitutes normality in relation to walking. Limping is most definitely not a part of the common picture. Instead of striding or strolling through the town, I now loped from side to side. I moved slowly and painfully. I had to recalibrate every journey: a dash across the road was something I could now only dream of. People looked at me with pity. Some took it upon themselves to tell me I was limping. Some offered to pick me up in their cars because they understood that popping to the other side of town was now a marathon that required pain-killers and a subsequent day of rest to compensate for the massive energy-spend.
>
> *Walking, Stumbling, Limping, Falling: a conversation,* Alyson Hallett and Phil Smith, Triarchy Press, 2017, p. 10

The perceived fascism of fitness prompts the recollection of how popular physical exercise was (and still is) in Germany. P.T. was pioneered by German physical scientists in the nineteenth century. It went hand in hand with racist theories concerning eugenics that came to influence the Zionists as much as it did the National Socialists. However, this does *not* make every Jock a Nazi! It is simply the case that fitness, pride and vanity can become confused, while a race-based nationalism may emerge out of that hubris-inducing confusion.

And plenty of experimental poets can testify to the fascism of tradi-tional poetics. We have all suffered from a blind orthodoxy that demands a social message, a regular verse-form, rhyme and an avoidance of any mate-rial which might be deemed indecent. The ghosts of the arch-poet and Rabelais may protest. They do so in vain. In Britain, at least, poetry is still very much in the service of the establishment and rewarded by a laure-ate-ship and publication in the educational syllabus.

Alyson found herself questioning the assumptions of what walking meant: "I was annoyed with walking books; walking holidays; walking art; walking for health. Why couldn't we limp for art? Why couldn't we stumble for health?" The authors exchange memories of falls they have experienced. Alyson describes the apprehension she felt limping towards the operating theatre for her operation, never to limp in quite the same way again. Phil talks of early memories of falling out of his playpen, and he also talks of fallen places, places that in some way have fallen off the map. The book is rewarding because it opens our meditations about movement to include all manners of getting somewhere. "Bad" walks are cited as well as "good" ones.

⁂

DANCE MOVEMENT PSYCHOTHERAPY STUDIES what gait and posture may tell us about emotional trauma: how unfinished actions may feel as frustrat-ing as unfinished (interrupted) utterances. Maybe you once got mugged violently from behind. Now, for years, coming home at night, you have glanced apprehensively over your shoulder, and at last the action is caus-ing you pain in a shoulder-blade. Do our childhood memories affect our actions? Does bad posture as a child spill into later life, and, if so, what is its meaning? Let's take Freud's famous analysis of the *Fort Da* where a little boy controls his worries about his mother sometimes being absent by pull-ing a cotton reel to him or casting it away (though connected still to him), in order that he may reel it in and control the situation though his self-gen-erated enactment of it. This is a repetition enabled by reversal. However, in my book, *The Analysis of Performance Art,* it is pointed out that:

The only continuous repetition is cyclic—stirring for instance. This requires neither reversal nor alternation. In her article on *Gesture and Psychoanalysis*, Luce Irigaray suggests that a cyclic repetition might be a more likely action for a girl than the forward/backward (penile) motion of the fort-da—initially observed being carried out by a boy. Seeing herself as a miniature mirror of her mother, she would never associate her mother with a cotton reel. Thus, if not traumatized into inertia by the mother's absence, she might cope with it by spinning—creating a comforting spherical space around herself. Cyclic repetition is charged with musicality: the musicality of 'galloping horses', the lulling rhythm of the wheels of a train. Dances often involve whirling the partner round and round. Most children are obsessed by spinning. Such repetition is centered on the self. In classical depiction, the arms of the three graces create a closed circle of continuity… Continual spinning makes you the centre of the universe, since the universe spins with you. At the same time it must induce vertigo, and eventually you collapse….

…Ambivalence can also be expressed through this tendency in repetition to require reversals in order to continue repeating. Here we enter into the realm of *obsession*. Consider the "ratman's" obsession with the stone in Freud's celebrated case-history. The subject stubs his foot on a stone in the road, and then he considers that his girl may stub her foot on it later, since she will be coming along the road. He moves the stone to the side of the road. But then, having progressed a little further down the road, he judges this an absurd action and, hurrying back to the stone, picks it up and places it back where it was in the road when he stubbed his foot on it.

Freud argues that it's not the absurdity of his action which prompts him to replace the stone but his *ambivalence* towards the girl: one moment he feels protective towards her, the next he wants to harm her. Had the subject merely moved stones out of the road, the repetition would have read simply as a tendency towards over-protection of the loved object. We can now see the psychic difference between continuous repetition and reversal repetition—but what of taking one sip from twenty cups of coffee? The aberrance we read into the act depends more on its deviance from the norm than on whether it continues or reverses.

The replacing of the stone in the middle of the road is obviously a repetition characterized by reversal, and *vacillation* may be read into the repetitive reversal of any action such as this. One is reminded of Penelope, coming at night to her loom to unravel the work of her daylight hours. She has promised the suitors that she will marry one of them when the tapestry is completed but wishes to be faithful to Odysseus.

Anthony Howell, *The Analysis of Performance Art*, current ed. Routledge, 2006, p. 35 (*Mimicry and Repetition*).

I like to imagine that the little boy of the *Fort Da* became a fly-fisherman in later life!

࿔

THIS CHAPTER BEGAN WITH DISABILITY. What about aggressive performance ability, as in the martial arts? Military discipline may have grown out of choral dances, but there is one fundamental difference between combat and a *pas-de-deux*. The martial arts are competitive, however much this may be disguised in synchronised drills. The idea is to get the best of one's opponent, to do him down. In dancing, however, rather than overpowering an assailant, a complex move made in partnership is seen as the objective.

Partner dancing is the exemplification of harmony in dance. Nevertheless, it is worth remembering that discord may be turned to poetic advantage. Consider violence—word and action in extreme circumstances—"*Seig Heil*" accompanied by Fascist gesture. Consider, again, that Scots tradition of "flyting" –with poets vying with each other for the best scornful epithet. Language as insult or abuse is usually accompanied by fist-clenching, and possibly by bodily attack. In such a context, the step becomes aggressive and swings into a kick. Of course, as mimesis, this can prove exciting, as it is in New Zeeland rugby when the All Blacks grind the steps of the Haka war-cry into the floor. Again we see how intimately language fuses with action. We can also observe a parting of the ways; a cross-roads that led dancing in one direction and military drill in another. The drilling of the chorus promoted martial art in preparation for battle; an impulse which leads ultimately to a war department, profit for Hephaestus and the deep state that promotes the arms race. If our "democracies" spent as much on dance as they do on their defence departments, there might not be much need for such aggression.

Two extremes delineate the gamut of our relations with others: we can destroy them, or we can make love to them. Running parallel to these extremes, but modifying their consequence, we have the martial arts and competitive sports, which socialise our urge to obliterate each other; and we have dancing, which socialises our urge to mate, as does the composition of love poetry in the Elizabethan court. Often, the impulse towards either extreme is inscribed with motivation provoked from the other end of the spectrum.

This can be seen in that fusion of literary and military ideals that was common among courtiers of the Renaissance, as is epitomised by the respect generations have accorded to Sir Philip Sidney. It was the ideal of the great warrior also to achieve renown as a poet, and conversely, the ideal of the poet to be respected as a warrior. This respect had to be reciprocal. Once we started to lose sight of the one, we started to lose sight of the other ideal. The poet must wish as much to be the warrior as the warrior wishes to be the poet. And it needs to be understood that the poet wanting to be the warrior does not necessarily allow Leavis in by the back door. That door would open if it was insisted that the soldier has a moral purpose—as Byron clearly had by joining the war of liberation the Greeks were fighting against the occupying Ottomans. The heroic soldier affects the world. And so he must act in an honorable, that is, in a social way. Fair enough.

But I don't believe this is quite how a man of the Renaissance would have felt about it; a warrior and duelist for instance, such as Edward Herbert of Cherbury; a fine poet, brother of the pious George. For Edward, as his very-readable memoir makes makes evident, war is a norm. Something you go off and do in the summer. Not a crusade. War is an action, the killing just a bi-product of the gallant (if mercenary) purpose. And you are just as busy dueling allies with whom you have picked a quarrel as you are going to dine on ambassadorial terms inside your enemy's camp.

Again, it is about drill, about how you conduct yourself. Dressage has been introduced into England; the art of the great horse. Your horse performs caprioles. *War music* is the title of one of the sections of Christopher Logue's version of *The Iliad*. Sir Philip's renown exemplifies war as music, it suggests an aesthetics of war. Perhaps for Byron, fighting for Greek Liberation, the issue was more ethical, as it was for the poets of the First World War, and for F. T. Prince, who served as a code-breaker in WW2. Prince's sense of conduct was also related to his faith. However, as Wittgenstein points out, "Ethics is aesthetics".

The poetic warriors of my time have often seemed to me to be mavericks. They have pursued their own paths, rather than aligning themselves with particular camps. Christopher Logue was a maverick, delivering his poetry to jazz. Prince was a maverick in another direction. But both hotly defended the past in a radically modern fashion.

So the poetry can be as airy-fairy as you like, the soldiering comes in from a sense of how you conduct yourself: the style you bring to your life. This was well understood by Oscar Wilde—while for the military man, the making of verse comes about from a sense of how sweet you smell, how fine, how delicate, how sensitive your courtly accomplishments, despite the brutality of your achievements on the battlefield.

The link between warriors and love poetry only gets strengthened by the theory that war may be prompted by the drive to wipe out alien males in order to propagate offspring with alien females, as is well-articulated by Norman Walter's brilliant but neglected book, *The Sexual Cycle of Human Warfare* (Mitre Press, London, 1950). As the naturalist Zuckerman points out, "Almost all male animals fight during the rutting season," (*The Social Life of Monkeys and Apes,* p. 562). The sexual combat which disturbs an animal group such as a colony of baboons has "come to be replaced in the human group by a *collective* and *external* sexual combat in the form of war," (Walter, p. 76). By a similar token, sexuality may have undertones of violence and sado-masochistic impulses. A stabbing may be a substitute for penetration, especially in any community which disapproves of homosexuality. Countless artists have perceived the enclosing role of the female as a devouring.

This is why the social modifications to extreme acts are so crucial for our well-being and that of society. Competitors in martial arts' matches may bond with each other, or at least recognise each other's competence, rather than leave one of them a corpse on the floor. Partner dancing serves to diffuse sexuality and steer eroticism away from focus on a specific corporeal locality. Now the sexuality permeates the bodies dancing in their entirety and, in a modification of the tantric urge to meditate via indulgence in an acrobatic intercourse which suspends orgasm, rhythm, footwork and posture endeavour together to establish a socially acceptable form of bodily combination, aided and abetted by the music. The great tanguero, Carlos Gavito, once said, "When two people dance together they fall in love—with the music."

꒦

THE DANGER THAT CONTRIBUTES TO THE PARANOIA OF OUR TIMES is that the sexual aggression which is betrayed in combat still provides fuel for our mass drive towards violence and the extermination of the males of some other group; however, this drive has become abstracted from the notion of physical prowess and the martial poetry of heroics. Instead, war has become bombast. This is also the case with contemporary architectural development, where buildings become ever taller and serve as symbols, although their symbolism is ultimately confused, since dependent on associative metaphors alienated from the meaning of the phallus and falsely equating affluence with prowess. In like manner, our defence departments are charged with the development of ever more phallically monstrous weaponry. War itself appears to have become abstract, a rhetorical manifestation of omnipotence, its excuses epitomised by conceptual feuding, citing such differences as capitalism's struggle against communism, Sunni belief versus Shia belief, secular state versus religious state, while usually fuelling one race's or one country's traditional or inculcated loathing of another. The bombastic writing that encouraged such jingoism in the nineteenth century has been replaced by the mass reiteration of fake-news, promoted by state media now controlled by the deep state.

However, no longer will war result in the extermination of our male "rivals." Instead every single being will be pulverised, as occurred at Nagasaki and Hiroshima. This defeats war's genetic purpose, but it lines the pockets of the dealers, feeds the armaments industry and strengthens the military to such a degree that democracy ceases to be possible. At the same time, with taste, smell and touch exiled from our consciousness, the predominance of audio/visual simulation via games, films and the broadcast media remove pain, stink and putrescence from our perception of war.

It seems not to hurt anybody if it doesn't impinge on our own lives: if it happens elsewhere it's as good as a fiction.

Dance reminds us that we are flesh and blood, calling into question the alienating and objectifying excuses of hostility. Meanwhile poetry is an antidote to bombast, or it should be. It trains the reader to see beyond the rhetoric of the state and its promoted bias. It is also the role of poetry to draw attention to the fact that we *are* flesh and blood, and that we are capable of comprehending the thoughts of others, even foreigners, even those designated as our enemies—consequently perceiving that they are flesh and blood also. A programme of dedicated translations of Russian and eastern European poets in the sixties contributed to the calming of hostility between East and West—as did the hugely popular visits by the Bolshoi and the Kirov ballet companies. In this country, Ted Hughes and Danny Weissport steered *Modern Poetry in Translation* to a universal readership that is still growing today. Nevertheless, translation has its pitfalls. The poem translated has to become a true poem in its own right in its new language. This means that, for me, its feet must move with the grace of an authentic dance for *my own tongue*. This actually matters more to me than whether it replicates the rhythm of the original. My preference would be to hear the translation and then to hear the original read in its own language. (My observations in *Stand* on translation in 1971 can be found in *Appendix 3*).

And we don't want to throw out the baby by Bowdlerising poetry, acting conscientiously in the name of decency. Rather, it is propriety which should be called into question, particularly when poetry's most trenchant weaponry may be needed to counter the power of the propaganda which supports and is supported by the arms industry or the oil industry or the growing commerce of incarceration. Insult and abuse can be used in the creation of good, strong verse: the satirists of the Augustan age were masters at it, though precious little satirical poetry gets written today. I do feel that contemporary satire needs to develop a "cutting edge" through some innovation in form, since rhyming couplets were overdone in the eighteenth century and today they sound quite hackneyed. Satire must find some new means of expression in verse. The aggressive vocabulary of confrontation, the Siegs and the Heils, the horny words, the curses of hostility and the vulgarities of desire, can all be used effectively by satire in the interest of irony, mimesis or parody. Where slang is apt, do not hesitate. Censorship of vocabulary must always amount to repression, and *Gradiva* very pertinently provides a thread for Norbert out of the maze of delusion into which his repression has led him. But our times call for a less lyrical treatment of repression than Jenson's novella. Satire is the how poetry goes miltant.

Thoughts may be repressed by the subject, as in Norbert's case, and sects and cults may induce repression in their adherents via conditioning, but there is also suppression from the external world. We may find ourselves writing in a climate that encourages the expression of conventional niceties or engineers a clampdown on awareness and a censorship of the rights of targeted groups. Issues that appear to assume the moral high ground may actually approve the suppression of free speech and the suppression of facts. We may wish to go on the attack. However, another way of getting the making of poetry wrong, albeit with the best of intentions, is to identify one's aim before the creation of the expression (this problem besets translation and all too often renders the translation pedestrian). Satire is verbal attack, and much needed, but the rule applies as much to satire as to more lyrical or descriptive writing. The poem itself, in its coming into being, in its exploration of what it might be, must allow its meaning to *evolve,* and the poet must be prepared to be surprised as its outcome, not to be in possession of the truth, and set this down with absolute certainty at its expression. Too much conviction can render the poetry ineffective, and condemnatory lines can sound merely dogmatic. When reading the great satires of Rochester, or some of the most satirical poems by Lovelace, one gets the sense of the poet riffing on his subject, discovering weaknesses, falling upon new objects for scorn or contempt.

Nevertheless, satire is verbal attack. There's no question about it, and the satirical poet is justified in using any weapon that happens to lie within reach. Janet Kardon, speaking about the work of the New York painter, David Salle, suggests that "to the idea of art making one feel better—one of the most offensive of art education's constructs—is counterposed a set of images that almost can be interpreted as a string of curses." Kardon is correct, but she goes on to point out that in no way does this detract from Salle's relevance, power and perception, and the same can be said of the poetry of Michael McClure, or Rochester's verses—or Villon's for that matter.

FINALLY

SPIRALS
Spelling out the step/the spiral of the madrigal and the body spiral/the relation of the spiral to irony as in Wabi-Sabi, the Japanese sense of transience and imperfection.

THE ARGENTINE ECONOMY may no longer be one of the most powerful in the world, however the Argentine tango dancer remains indisputably the master of the walk. This mastery contributes to the fluidity of Argentine soccer. I realise that, for many of us, the purpose of walking may simply be to get from place to place. On the floor of a milonga in Buenos Aires, when a couple dance the tango, walking is executed as a thing in itself—we see the walk displayed—the walk in its own right—for the tango is essentially a walking dance. And the situation of the walking is rendered more complex by it being executed in a partnership. As the leader drives his walk forwards, the follower stretches her walk back. Advance is dovetailed into lure (rather than retreat). The woman completes the step of the man. What he begins, she brings to a conclusion. Tangueros can walk to the rhythm of the number the *orquesta* is playing or to its melody. Each *orquesta* interprets the notion of what a tango is in its own particular way: homespun, as might be the case with an early track by Canaro, or magnificent, symphonic—as the Pope Francis says, I am Troilo! (referring to a famous composer whose tangos are full of pomp).

Dancers who decide to work together professionally may a spend a year or two honing how they walk. You may remonstrate with me here, and say, Surely, walking is walking; we all do it automatically. I assure you, as an art, walking is one of the most complex movements in the human repertory, if not *the* most complex. Asserting that all walking is more or less the same is like asserting that all rhythm is basically the same. In fact, there are as many shades to the walk as there are to the beat. This is as true of poetry as it is of the tango.

I am not talking merely about being "adept". There are plenty of unremarkable virtuosi. Finding your walk is about finding your way of walking, finding your tango "voice", if you like. There is a softness to the walk of tanguero Diego Reimer; the impulse can be felt in the hip-socket all the way down through the heel and beyond instep and ball, so that even the big toe is engaged in promoting the activity, spurring it forward without leaning forward. As the free leg is brought in towards the ankle of the base leg the toe remains "grounded", tracing the progress of the step across the floor. However, the softness is not a weakness. The back is kept "long", the abdomen holding the waist like a corset. The homeostasis of Diego's body is not that of passivity. The over-all tension is alert without strain; conveying a sense of awareness, awareness of the hip-sockets, the inner thighs—a sense that these parts of the anatomy revel in their being used. As the ankle is neared, the free leg brings its heel into play. Every precise action is a series of small consecutive actions which must be done in their correct order. This is what the walk shows you.

Now change the word 'walk' in the paragraphs above for the word 'talk'. It's enlightening. Movement has a syntax. And each step can be 'pronounced' in different ways, just as any word can be. And just as a word can be a consonant joined by a vowel to another consonant, a step can have an impulsion joined by a transference to a collection on the other foot: the quality of the vowel sound is alterable, and the quality of the transference is alterable—that bridging movement done lightly or done by being deeply connected with the floor. The stylistic differences between one tanguero and another have a bearing on what it is we mean when we talk about a poet "finding his voice". Naturally, this is as true for the tangueras. Again, it is not about being adept. All too often competence, within some flashy but conservative framework, is favoured over distinction. E. E. Cummings had a distinctive way of making poetry, a way that was highly regarded by the modernists, but today, all too often, our conventional pundits dismiss his work:

> my father moved through dooms of love
> through sames of am through haves of give,
> singing each morning out of each night
> my father moved through depths of height
>
> this motionless forgetful where
> turned at his glance to shining here;
> that if (so timid air is firm)
> under his eyes would stir and squirm
>
> newly as from unburied which
> floats the first who, his april touch
> drove sleeping selves to swarm their fates
> woke dreamers to their ghostly roots
>
> and should some why completely weep
> my father's fingers brought her sleep:
> vainly no smallest voice might cry
> for he could feel the mountains grow.
>
> e. e. cummings, 1894-1962

Here, in this extract from one of his most celebrated poems, there are few typographical innovations (as we find elsewhere in his oeuvre), other than the removal of capital letters. The originality resides in his exploratory use of words in syntactical positions not customarily associated with the parts of speech that define them. "Dooms" would normally be the third person present of the verb "to doom". Here it becomes an unusual plural, as is also the case with "haves". And yet, we do say, 'the haves and the have-nots'. In the poem, "where" loses its role as adverb, conjunction or pronoun and becomes a noun. This can be dismissed as generating nonsense. But poetry is never invalidated by dint of it being nonsense. What is irrefutable is that Cummings's poetic voice is both individual and distinct. And he marshals a sense of a concise meaning out of this unusual grammatical texture by his very controlled use of rhythm, which helps pinpoint the emphasis that will be needed to make a noun out of a word like "why". You could say that as a poet he has "mastered his walk". In just as radical a way, Diego Reimer may break all the rules by obeying all the rules—or vice versa.

Another tanguero, Chicho Fromboli, used to be a jazz drummer, and one of the distinctive characteristics of his walk is his use of the off-beat. He has brought syncopation to the tango, which is most effective when sustained only for a few beats so that when one returns to the downbeat it as if one has "caught up" with it, which creates a fetchingly abrupt dynamic. When we push on the *and* and land on the *one* we get step to a regular beat. Chicho may push down on the *one* and land on the *and*). *Beat step, beat step, step* gives the syncopation (offbeat, offbeat, on). We can use offbeat rhythms in poetry. Words such as *impasse* or *orchid* suggest a weight push in the first syllable and the strike of the beat on the second (unstressed) syllable—making an *ironic* trochaic foot—where the stress is on the first syllable though the step itself is on the syllable that follows—thus *offbeat, offbeat, on* would be *impasse, orchid dill*—which creates a syncopative effect. If you were dancing, you would step on *passe, chid* and *dill*—and this would give your dance the syncopative modification.

Abutting an iambus up against a trochee will also create the spring of syncopation, as in this chant from *The Waterfall* by The Theatre of Mistakes, Hayward Gallery 1982:

Obscure
District
Around
Fastnet
Below
Freezing.

The Spondee (two strong syllables) is problematic for the English ear as usually one of its syllables weakens—so *Bay leaf* becomes trochaic. Gerard

Manley Hopkins makes excellent use of the spondee in his "sprung" verse, as in *Heaven Haven (A nun takes the veil):*

> I have desired to go
>   Where *springs not* fail,
> To fields where flies no sharp and sided hail
>   And a *few lilies* blow.
>
> And I have asked to be
>   Where *no storms* come,
> Where the *green swell* is in the havens dumb,
>   And out of the swing of the sea.

Actually, iambic words are rare and of considerable help when seeking for syncopative effects. What is also useful is to embrace the notion of the single syllable foot, heresy though it may be.

> Dill
> Quinine
> And dill.
> Dill
> Quinine
> And dill

Here the two *dills* on either side of the full stop work as a spondee. But it's intriguing that in classical measures all feet are complex. A single syllable word (such as *dill*) is not considered a poetic foot. The waterfall chant quoted alternates iambus and trochee in monometer. And here is the start of a poem in iambic monometer by Robert Herrick:

> Thus I
> Pass by,
> And die
> As one
> Unknown
> And gone.

Still, I find it useful to consider the single syllable word as capable of being a foot in itself, especially when considering sprung verse and syncopation. I do recall one verse in single syllable monometer:

> Hired.
> Tired?
> Fired.

I think I first read it in Ripley's *Believe it or Not*—as one of the world's shortest poems—only bettered by the trochaic:

> Adam
> Had 'em.

⁊₹

WITH A DACTYL FOLLOWING TWO TROCHAIC FEET and preceding two further trochees, the "Sapphic" line is interesting because the second unstressed syllable of the dactyl transforms the two final trochees into iambic feet, with a final unstressed syllable added—as we observed in the Swinburne *Sapphics* quoted in Chapter 10:.

> Saw the white implacable Aphrodite

The line starts off with a falling rhythm and then is turned by the sandwiched dactyl into a rhythm that rises! It is this that gives the Sapphic stanza its mysterious, intriguing quality. Supposedly invented by a woman named Sappho, one of the earliest poets, it has to be borne in mind that, in Sappho's ancient Greek, long syllables are set against short syllables, but English verse cannot really "do" quantity—as syllable length is termed— and as has been discussed earlier. So the Sapphic stanza, as promoted by poets such as Swinburne, is actually a Victorian invention. This does not take away from its paradoxical nature and its power in our language. All too often, rhythm and scansion are assumed to be merely a matter of a repeated number of feet in a stacked-up column of lines of the same length, with a regular rhyme scheme applied to them. Much more can be done with both rhythm and rhyme.

Let us look at the madrigal, as a poetic form, which was introduced into English verse by Drummond of Hawthornden. Ben Jonson walked all the way to Scotland to gossip with Drummond in his castle on a beetling crag, twenty miles from Edinburgh, and even today Hawthornden castle maintains its associations with literature, serving as a residency for writers and maintaining literary fellowships. William Drummond may have lived far from London, but his writing shows him to have been highly sophisticated; a Scotsman who had made the grand tour and was familiar with Italian works of art and the literary theories which were transforming the renaissance.

It is clear that his sonnets influenced Keats and that Drummond was a forerunner of the romantics. But most significantly, he was able to turn the madrigal into a poetic form that worked for unaccompanied poetry in our language. The word itself derives from the Italian *madrigale* (from medieval Latin *carmen matricale* 'simple song'), from *matricalis* 'maternal or primitive', and from *matrix* 'womb'. This suggests that the form is "the mother of song".

Even if we leave aside its highly complex development as a musical form, and as a sung form, through composed, with attention given to each word, there is something in the spoken madrigal, the madrigal of unaccompanied poetry that suggests the song. This is due to its juxtaposition of long and short lines. In his informative book *The Italian Element in Milton's Verse* (Oxford, at the Clarendon Press, 1954), F. T. Prince traces the madrigal's emergence through Italian poets and critics—starting with Pietro Bembo's analysis of the work of Petrarch and moving on through the inventiveness of Giovanni Della Casa and the theories of Torquato Tasso. He goes on to identify Drummond (1585—1649) as the pioneer who developed Italian innovation in English poetry.

Like the Idalian queen,
Her hair about her eyne,
With neck and breast's ripe apples to be seen,
At first glance of the morn,

In Cyprus' gardens gathering those fair flow'rs
Which of her blood were born,
I saw, but fainting saw, my paramours.
The Graces naked danc'd about the place,
The winds and trees amaz'd
With silence on her gaz'd;
The flow'rs did smile, like those upon her face,
And as their aspen stalks those fingers band,
That she might read my case,
A hyacinth I wish'd me in her hand.

Drummond, *Madrigal III*

The lines (which suggest that Drummond had seen Botticelli's *Primavera*) are either in trimeter or pentameter, and what is interesting here (and commonly overlooked) is that a line with three stresses can be rhymed with a line having five! Now three and five are prime numbers. It transpires that the primes can be scanned. Drummond also mingles trochees and dactyls in a remarkably free way—he utilises the spondee. His verse dances as much as it sings. His madrigals enjoy a liberty distinct from that of the free verse explored by Thomas Campion. Milton adapted Drummond's innovations and arrived at the play of trimeter and pentameter that we find in *Lycidas:*

I come to pluck your berries harsh and crude,
And with forc'd fingers rude
Shatter your leaves before the mellowing year.

This strategy is used very effectively at the start of *L'Allegro:*

Hence loathed Melancholy,
Of Cerberus, and blackest Midnight born,
In Stygian cave forlorn,
    'Mongst horrid shapes, and shrieks, and sights unholy;
Find out some uncouth cell,
    Where brooding Darkness spreads his jealous wings,
And the night-raven sings;

There under ebon shades, and low-brow'd rocks,
As ragged as thy locks,
    In dark Cimmerian desert ever dwell.

And again, at the start of its companion poem, *Il Penseroso:*

Hence vain deluding Joys,
    The brood of Folly without father bred,
How little you bested,
    Or fill the fixed mind with all your toys;
Dwell in some idle brain,
    And fancies fond with gaudy shapes possess,
As thick and numberless
    As the gay motes that people the sunbeams,
Or likest hovering dreams,
    The fickle pensioners of Morpheus' train.

In both cases, after the fanfare of their openings, these opposing poems settle more regularly into standard, four-footed tetrameter, offset occasionally by an exception to this metre, either by dropping or adding a foot. This serves to remind us that anything is possible, and several of the seventeenth century contemporaries or near-contemporaries of Drummond and Milton experimented very freely with mixed metre, every which way— George Herbert, for instance, whose *Easter Wings* is also one of the first instances of concrete poetry, and Dryden, in the "instrumental" stanzas of *A Song for St. Cecilia's Day:*

    The trumpet's loud clangor
        Excites us to arms
    With shrill notes of anger
        And mortal alarms.
    The double double double beat
        Of the thund'ring drum
    Cries, hark the foes come;
Charge, charge, 'tis too late to retreat.

The soft complaining flute
In dying notes discovers
The woes of hopeless lovers,
Whose dirge is whisper'd by the warbling lute.

Sharp violins proclaim
Their jealous pangs, and desperation,
Fury, frantic indignation,
Depth of pains and height of passion,
For the fair, disdainful dame.

For all that, the madrigal's sense of a "special relationship" between the primes three and five, generates a particularly rewarding music. I think this is because a balance can be found between them, as can be perceived if we look at the opening pyramid of their structure:

$$1$$
$$111$$
$$11111$$
$$1111111$$
$$11111111111$$
$$1111111111111$$

Here the "eternal return" put forward as a mythic truth by Nietzsche is developed into the possibility that there is also a growth the repetition may enable; an expansion, a change that may come about. The madrigal plays with repetition, now growing the line, now shortening it, introducing a liberty unavailable to the grid (or stack) of lines with an equal number of feet. Even today, the madrigal should be considered revolutionary. Heptameter also scans with trimeter and pentameter. It appears that the primes "agree" with each other, just as lines of an equal number of feet (equal metrical length) agree with each other. I have experimented with lines of eleven and thirteen feet—they scan with any primes of fewer feet.

In mathematics, the primes form a spiral and demonstrate a pattern in their difference, a regularity in irregularity. This is demonstrated by my poem *A Serpentine* (*Appendix 4*).

LET US RETURN TO THE SERPENTINE MOTIONS we considered in the first chapter: to the wavy motion of the snake, with its different methods of using its spine, from its lateral undulation to its ability to contract like a concertina or to use sidewinding or its rectilinear method. Dancers use their spines in ways that are just as subtle. Indeed, tangueros speak of the "body spiral" derived from the disassociation of the upper and lower body that our diagonal coordination makes possible.

Understanding how our arms swing in opposition to the swing of the legs leads to control of our axis when we pivot on one foot. We do not need to turn like a single solid block, hips moving at the same time as the shoulders—far from it. Start your revolving turn from the sternum, and the ribcage will activate the hips, which will come around later, activating the heel, which revolves around the ball of the foot. This produces torque, a moment of force that enables a rotation. Just as a linear force is a push or a pull, torque can be thought of as a twist to an object. With a tango pivot such as impels the movement known as an *ocho* (because two ochos make a figure-of-eight) a pivot changes the direction of the step. The pivot itself comes about because first the chest rotates in the dorsal spine, then the torque generated brings the hips around, which causes the heel to rotate around the ball of the foot upon which the dancer's weight is centred. Upper half thus affects lower half. A poem could also be thought of as requiring torque, its upper half (its beginning) affecting its lower half. How the poem starts out generates the twist that informs how it ends.

Our different vertebral groups have different functions. It's already been pointed out that the lumbar vertebrae cannot rotate (they need to be stable in order to do their job of holding up the ribs and the head). The shoulder-blades work with the dorsal vertebrae to enable rotation, and this is what allows the body (balanced on one foot) to turn on axis in an *ocho* or a needle gyration. A dissociative technique creates a wonderfully smooth change of direction while the dancer can remain entirely on axis. Now the body spiral is being employed.

Axis in dance, balance in poetry—here is an intriguing similarity. Consider the body and its ability to spiral. Consider the poem and its ability to spiral through the primes.

Apparently prime numbers are used as an evolutionary strategy by cicadas of the genus *Magicicada*. These insects spend most of their lives underground, as grubs. They only pupate and then emerge from their burrows after 7, 13 or 17 years, at which point they fly about, breed, and then die after a few weeks at most. It is thought that the prime number intervals between emergences make it difficult for predators to evolve that could specialize as predators on these cicadas. If they appeared at a non-prime number intervals, say every 12 years, then predators appearing every 2, 3, 4, 6, or 12 years would be sure to meet them. Over a 200-year period, average predator populations during hypothetical outbreaks of 14- and 15-year cicadas would be up to 2% higher than during outbreaks of 13- and 17-year cicadas. Though small, this advantage appears to have been enough to drive natural selection in favour of a prime-numbered life-cycle for these insects.

But should we not distinguish between types of spiral and understand that there may be interesting differences between them? For instance, the Fibonacci spiral, named after the medieval mathematician who popularized it, may epitomise growth, while the Prime Spiral may epitomise structure. What is self-evident is that spirals abound in our universe. Nature certainly has an affinity for these swirlings. In hurricanes and galaxies, the rotation of the core generates spiral shapes. Whenever the centre turns faster than the periphery, waves within these phenomena get spun around into spirals. The florets in a sunflower head also form spirals, but there's no rotation here—it's simply an efficient packing solution for the plant. With 55 florets running clockwise and 34 counter-clockwise, the sunflower is an example of the Fibonacci sequence. Consider also the double helix that epitomises our DNA, not enlarging, but circling within one column, as do the upward and downward staircases within the shell of the Statue of Liberty. The tango partnership epitomises such a double entwining.

※

FOR CENTURIES, POETRY HAS UTILISED the regularity of repetition, but it should be recognised that the dynamic dactylic shift that distinguishes a

Sapphic stanza is one of poetry's earliest forms, even though our "Sapphics" are a Victorian adaption. In the twentieth century, free verse sought to liberate poetry from a stanzaic repetition that had become tedious. Now I wonder whether use of the primes could generate difference within repetition, and thus create something new without simply abandoning rules altogether? The Sapphic stanza demonstrates a similar ironic difference, since its line begins in a different way to the way it concludes. It is made complex, unusual. Even in Sappho's time, *ti-tum-ti-tum* had become a cliché.

Nevertheless, repetition is integral to the art of verse. Whether it's the repetition of a metre or the repetition with a difference that creates rhyme, or the repetition of specific words, as in a sestina, or the repetition of specific lines, as in the villanelle or the pantoum. And just as new dance forms are forever being invented, new poetic forms get hit upon. Forms, implicitly, have rules, sometimes fairly loose ones, as with the relatively simple repetition of entire lines in the pantoum, at other times pretty tight, as with the traditional villanelle. Much the same can be said for dance-forms: grooving as the mood takes you when out clubbing is a far cry from a ballet solo, or even from a Lindy hop couple jiving or the improvisation within an agreed structure that provides the dynamic for the tango.

Mood may affect expression more readily when the form is loose and open, and if you "feel" that art is vitally concerned with expressing how you feel, then you may identify with the romantics and the beats and with Mick dancing on his own; and so you may want to get away from form. But while free verse is touted as a modernist contribution, many of the moderns employed extremely tight formal structures precisely to get away from that notion of art as self-expression. Consider Raymond Roussel writing stories where every word of the opening sentence rhymed with every word of the final one. For such writers, art is the product of its material, its integrity being the homeostasis of its form, an object brought into being by how it is knitted together; the verse self-reliant rather than expressive. Naturally an irony may come into play here, and the poem or story generated by the tightest of games may nevertheless appear to epitomise the character of its author.

Many exceptional poets revel in an engagement with exceptionally strict formal games, and one of the most recent of these is the *Specular* invented by Julia Copus. The poem is organised into two verses. The second verse reflects the first, using the same lines but in reverse order, so that the last line of the poem is also the first. Examples can be found on the web. It is a great idea for a poem, demanding that the poem can be read smoothly "in both directions".

A form I have developed is the *Statheron*. The name is derived from "statheros"—the Greek word for stability. This is not so much a form as a process, which can take many forms. In a statheron, any word used in the poem or prose poem must be used twice or an even number of times. So there might, for example, be eight occurrences of the definite article, while a particular noun might simply appear twice. Thus "Pegasus" might appear twice while "the" might appear fourteen times. A word cannot be used an odd number of times, so there is never "a remainder". Clearly the brilliantly conceived specular is a form of statheron. Another is *Maisie Reconstituted*—my prose poem to be found here on page 143. Limited vocabularies can generate texts where each and every word in a paragraph is employed in another paragraph. The process can then be repeated for several more paragraphs. The Wolf published a piece of mine like this called *Loft* a few issues back. John Tranter published two of my statherons here: http://poeticsresearch.com/article/anthony-howell-3-poems/

Formal difficulty may eventually reward the poet with a sense of achievement, but to meticulously pursue the demands of a villanelle or a statheron can also lead to rigidity rather than resonance. It's a bit like the tango show-off who insists on virtuosity while keeping himself well-buttoned in his double-breasted pin-stripe suit. Tightness of structure can amount to stiffness, rather than a truly organic homeostasis. Cheating has its benefits. In a statheron, I might use *omen* and *moment* just once, however, elsewhere in the poem, I will turn one *he* into an extra *the* (to use up the *t*) and add an *m* to a *see*.

Another method of generating verse that I've hit upon is the "sentence scansion" discussed earlier (from page 158) in the chapter on The Theatre of Mistakes. Older forms are also constantly being rediscovered; forms such as the *Dizain*, the ten-line stanza Sir Philip Sidney used for his *corona*. This is in iambic pentameter and has a complex rhyme scheme: ABABBCACDD. In *A Bargain with the Light: Poems after Lee Miller* (Hercules Editions 2017). Jacqueline Saphra has written a contemporary *corona*—inspired by shots taken by or concerning the life of that icon of surrealism who became an intrepid war photographer. Hers is a sequence of fourteen sonnets, the last line of one serving as the first line of the next, as with the Wroth *corona* discussed elsewhere. Interesting to note how Sydney's *corona* uses the *dizain* as his stanza, not the sonnet. Forms can be overlaid upon each other. A *sestina* might also be an *eclogue*.

F. T. Prince unearthed an ancient Italian form, the *Strambotto*, plural *strambotti*, one of the oldest Italian verse forms, composed of a single stanza of either six or eight pentameter (10-syllable) lines. Strambotti were particularly popular in Renaissance Sicily and Tuscany. Prince has a sequence of *strambotti,* each stanza eight lines long, introducing the difficulty of rhyming three times on one word by using an ABABABCC rhyme scheme:

> I wish there were a passage underground
> That led by magic to your house and bed,
> So I could be beside you at a bound
> When I had made the journey in my head.
> Then I should disappear and not be found,
> And neighbours be persuaded I were dead;
> But I should be with you in Paradise,
> Where I could laugh and kiss your face and eyes.

(F.T. Prince, *Collected Poems 1935-1992,* Carcanet, 1993)

Prince also created a form, though I do not recall him giving it a name. It consists of a stanza which is a sestet (six lines). Of these any two should rhyme with any other two in any arrangement, while the remaining pair should not rhyme. So ABCBDA for instance, or ABCDDB. This Prince conceived as a fusion of rhymed and blank verse which mediated between tradition and the modern age. There is no set regularity of feet, though a good sense of scansion is called for, and syncopation, if it is going to work. He uses this form to brilliant effect in his long poem *Walks in Rome:*

What can this wintry sun
show that is new?
From my hotel over-run
by pilgrims, and not 'starred'
I walk out past the porno
films—MOMENTI BLU

The graffiti then line up with
bombs and excrement:
FAITH IS A MYTH
YOU IDIOT-FIGHT
'No God nor Government'
'Pigs' ROMA MERDA

Mussolini's blank walls
had fewer scrawls.
Stencilled, they were at one
in what they shouted for:
'Long Live Death' 'Up War'
THE DUCE IS ALWAYS RIGHT

❧

IN MY BOOK, *The Analysis of Performance Art,* I identify the three "singular-
ities" of action—stillness, repetition and inconsistency.

Stillness, silence, emptiness. This is the ground, upon which all art is
played out. The performer's actions emerge out of stillness, the musician's
notes or sounds emerge out of silence, the painter's marks appear on the
blank emptiness of the canvas. Silence is just as much a component of
poetry as the word: poems begin and end in silence, words are divided by
silence or blend into each other like the colours of a rainbow—as Housman
puts it. So, a word ending in a vowel will merge with a word beginning
with the same vowel, as will words ending and beginning with non-plosive
consonants. Each mark of punctuation denotes a small amount of silence.
Colons carry more silence than commas. Stillness is the passage of time
itself. Silence is its partner. Silence punctuates the poem at the end of a

line and at the caesura. When speaking their poems, poets may emphasise all such silences or they may move through them with fluidity. Silence is the floor, the *aloni* of the poem. Mallarmé worked with silence when he created spaces between words and phrases, promulgating the poetry of the blank page. The whiteness of the page is its stillness. Space on the page dismantles rhythm. Words may be dropped into silence, each creating ripple after ripple, just as the chance sounds generated by John Cage may cause ripples of sound or collide with others or come together by coincidence.

Repetition, by contrast, brings with it the momentum of rhythm and metre. It generates a dynamic. It enables endings and rhymes to be predicted. It introduces the notion of the inevitable. Rhythm can suggest obsession. It can evoke the Karmic physis of all natural forces. Repetition of metre can be reinforced by a burden or refrain. There can be staccato rhythms and lethargic ones, as Bruce Chatwin observed in *Song Lines*— rhythms that evoke pushing through sludge or moving rapidly across dry, flat land.

Inconsistency is a necessary surprise, denoting the exception that helps define the rule. Again, we need to consider achieving some homeostatic balance or accord. Rhythm helps us create a sense of inevitability, but taken too far, applied too dogmatically, it can lead to predictability and tedium. The intrinsic relationship of difference to repetition, and the importance of their polarisation to our thinking is gone into deeply by the philosopher Gilles Deleuze in his brilliant book, *Difference and Repetition,* first published in translation in Great Britain by the Athlone Press in 1994. Using trimeter and pentameter in a madrigal can lend inconsistency to repetition, while the spiral agreement of prime metres can "slip us off the grid" of a standard adherence to pentameter, for example, by its mingling of repetition with inconsistency.

❧

"TO SLIP OFF THE GRID" is a phrase that conjures up a host of possibilities. I imagine Marie Antoinette gracefully dancing to the verses of some poet got up as a shepherd in an Arcadia reminiscent of Sir Philip Sidney's, far from the grid-like corridors of the palace at Versailles. Why was it so important for her to at least attempt to slip away into a graceful isolation, in a rustic village or into the wooded countryside of a *Midsummer Night's Dream?*

Grace in dance comes from practising balance and developing a perfect axis. There is the notion of poise. It has something of *The Book of the Courtier,* Castiglione's masterpiece of etiquette. Note that Giovanni Della Casa—the innovative poet who Prince considers crucial to the development of the madrigal—also wrote *Il Galateo,* known as the 'bible' of Italian manners, first published in 1588 (and available in English translation by M. F. Rusnak—University of Chicago Press, 2013). This has sections such as "Keep your Dreams to Yourself". and "How to Spoil a Conversation". It's an excellent read, having lost none of its relevance. For Marie Antoinette, grace was a virtue to be sought for.

Now let us ask dance questions of poems and poetic questions of dance. The caesura helps identify the axis in a poem. So balance is vital in both arts. Grace in a poem may at first seem to be achieved from a deepened understanding of time-honoured rhetorical devices, just as dancers may familiarise themselves with traditionally valued sequences of steps known as 'figures'. But this is what might be thought of as a molecular way of looking at either kinetic or poetic activity. In both cases it is based on a desire to know how the elements may be fitted together. It amounts to a "waterfall" structure of this leading to that, an understanding based on sequence—as when a bucket gradually fills, and then, when full, tips over to commence a filling-up of another bucket in a chain that makes a waterfall out of buckets. Alternatively, dance can be thought of in an atomic way, based on the spine and its possibilities. Rather than seeing the movements consecutively in time, movement is considered as a consciousness centred on a fulcrum of availability; and self is then realised as a structure that exists in space.

I think it was this that Mallarmé perceived, when he began to explore the poetry of the blank page. Can I do this in poetry? See the poem not only as sequence to follow but also as a structure in space, its words all present on the page, if you like; its words a mosaic creating a surface where all its parts exist in simultaneity. The actual material of the poem, the scansion, the dove-tailing of word order to word, being comprehended spatially, the repetitions of a word, such as a definite article, perceived *down*

and across the page, together with the vowel "colour" that may predomi-
nate, the number of gerunds it uses. This "spatial" vision of the poem may
be its very message.

If you put this spatial awareness together with a certain isolation, or the
desire for it, then to slip off the grid is to remove oneself from the "court
language" of bombastic rhetoric, contaminated by a certain utilitarian
pressure from the merchant classes; to engage instead with a lyric rhetoric
of poetic innocence, divested of the tools of its trade. In the twentieth century, a similar impulse generated a refreshing return to simplicity:

> six whittled chickens
> on a wooden bat
>
> that peck within a
> circle pulled
>
> by strings fast to
> a hanging weight
>
> when shuttled by the
> playful hand

> William Carlos Williams, *A Chinese Toy*

Artless enough, it might seem. Yet that assonant chime of *bat* with *weight*....
And we also get *hanging* and *hand,* as if by accident—a little bit of inconsistent luck?

There is a story attributed to Rikyū, an early master of the tea-cere-
mony. It relates how a young man, possibly Rikyū himself, is told to clean
his master's leaf-strewn garden. He does, but when he shows his master
the pristine ground, the master shakes a tree in the middle of the garden,
scattering its leaves over the ground the student just cleaned. Some say the
master scolds his student for trying to get rid of what nature has done. My
feeling is that the ground beneath the tree must be meticulously tidied first
for the shaking of the tree to be an act of art, the fresh leaves offering the
perfection of "Fall".

꙳

NOW WE ARE TRYING TO COMPREHEND TIME spatially and comprehend space temporally; here is the oxymoron at the heart of irony.

The page itself is a concept, a frame, a screen. It's a space which words may occupy without filling it up. A poem may indeed be overwhelmed by the space of a page, as when a single page is used to present a single haiku.

It is more interesting to find space within the text, for then we are coming to space through a sequential medium. Comprehending space temporally is just what a dancer tries to do.

One problem with considering metre in poetry as an equivalent to walking is that it may all become too purposeful. If we set out on a walk in order to get somewhere, must we set out to get somewhere when we write a poem? Well, we may, but we don't have to, anymore than a stroll has to be provided with a destination. In his book *Loiterature*, Ross Chambers compares the hectic dash of Phileas Fogg in *Around the World in Eighty Days* by Jules Verne with the leisurely explorations of the district surrounding each suburban station of the B line of the RER, the regional system of fast trains that serves the banlieus of Paris, as described by François Maspero in his ironically titled *Roissy Express*.

Taking one's time, not running the "Paris-Dakar race", not looking for events but patiently getting to know the (already) familiar in its ordinariness, poses a narrative problem, of course. Readers expecting a narrative of "events" and excitement need to be weaned onto another, more "nonchalant," style, one that takes its time, makes no beelines, is always ready to turn away from a given direction in order to explore something other. Such a style, always ready to interrupt itself, is inevitably episodic (asyndeton, the figure of discontinuity, is its rhetorical mode), and, veering easily (i.e. *without* a sense of discontinuity) from topic to topic, following associative drifts or the promptings of memory, it is digressive: it is organized, that is, by relations of resemblance and contiguity, metaphor and metonymy rather than the formal unity required by argument or the narrative of event. Such a style is more concerned with the, often obscure, "coherence" of experience—in this case the experience of travel (one of the West's favorite metaphors for the human subject's encounter with contingency, as we saw in Verne)—than it is respectful of patterns that are more strictly designed and thus "cohesive." In loiterature, there is always time to explore a byway, and often it's not clear which road is a byway and which represents the beeline—the main road, the most direct route—since when you're "not looking for anything exceptional" there is no particular goal to attain and no schedule for achieving it.

Loiterature, p. 31

The quotation is extracted from a chapter entitled *On stepping out of Line.* This is a notion akin to that of "slipping the grid". It is almost an Amish concept. We do not have to use the fast track. We can slip off the grid of the standard services, electricity, telephone, gas supply. We can draw water from the well, pen a letter, make a fire. The phrase *Slipping the Grid* is itself the title of a novel by Elizabeth A. Reed, a sequel to her first book—*Ancient Echoes.* In both books, Skylar, the protagonist is able to slip from one time to another, from one character to another. Here we are considering discontinuity rather than continuity, and *Loiterature* has this prefatory quote from the literary notebooks of Friedrich Schlegel, a key thinker of the romantic movement who championed the unfinished, the fragmentary:

Digression has something like the form of bliss. Repetition of the theme is the very opposite of that.

The notion of slipping the grid may be derived from the Japanese aesthetic of *Wabi-Sabi*—a sense of a return to simple rusticity, loneliness and "getting away from it all." While for the tragic queen of France it may have been occasioned by a desire to retreat from commerce-contaminated court intrigue, in Japan it may have emerged among the merchant classes as a reaction to the overt finery of the nobility and shows of extravagance from which they were excluded. In contemporary life it might be associated with the notion of venturing out of the city and relying on some simple equipment to subsist while you sit beside your tent contemplating the wilderness. It's also an acceptance of transience and imperfection, but even so, an acceptance laced with paradox, as when one repairs the cracks of a broken bowl with soldered seams of gold.

This paradox shows the relevance of *wabi-sabi* to our subject, which is perhaps irony, and how a dancer can use it, and how it can be used by the poet—like those puzzle-pictures that create a spiralling effect out of concentric circles, each one closer in an altered way to its neighbour at one point, but not in fact connected; an ironic spiral.

Sometimes too obsessive a concentration on technique can lead to the feeling that the product is over-finished. To redress this tendency, it may be worth considering the fragmentary, as Schlegel did. I have an essay on *Incompletion* here: https://anthonyhowelljournal.wordpress.com/2013/12/09/nonfinito-or-the-art-of-incompletion/.

Non-Finito is a painterly term for the deliberately unfinished canvas. F. T. Prince put together a small anthology of fragment poetry which accompanied a poem he wrote with the title *Fragment Poetry* in a pamphlet printed to celebrate his Presidential Address to *The English Association* in 1986. The pamphlet contains morsels of Shelley and Keats as well as Frank O'Hara's marvellously laid-back poem to Billie Holiday—*The Day Lady Died* (from *Lunch Poems*). It also includes Ezra Pound's witty take on amatory sighs in poetry down the ages, a little piece that celebrates transience and imperfection:

Papyrus

Spring.....
Too long.....
Gongula.....

᷇

THE ARTIST PAUL SIBBERING WORKS WITH RUST. He creates circles out of it. He lives in Rutland, which was once a county rich in iron-ore quarries. The last of these quarries closed in Rutland in the seventies. A dead steel industry left in its wake an iron-informed vocabulary, water-filled gullets, railway cuttings devoid of rails and factory chimneys found unexpectedly in the middle of woodland. Sibbering works with this detritus. The filings are valueless, the process one of deterioration, yet "ironically" this creates a conceptually invigorating art which is clearly of value. This could be seen as an English example of *wabi-sabi* being applied.

But we should be familiar with this mode, for it is very close to our sense of pastoral. And it is no accident that the authority on ambiguity, William Empson, should also have written *Versions of Pastoral*. The notion of Titania falling for Bottom before an audience of nobility and the hoi polloi—all equally amused—lends an ironic significance to the forest of the dream, as enchanted a territory as Looking Glass or Wonder land. But what *Wabi-Sabi* adds to this is a sense of incompletion, or decay—as in The Deserted Village. It's the pastoral dream aware of its own vanity, its twilight.

This is a provoking aesthetic. Again, we might return to Marie Antoinette dancing in her *Hameau de la Reine;* that plaything of a farm she built in Versailles, where she could "let down her stays" and be a shepherdess. We tend to mock here. As an aesthetic impulse though, we should consider it more seriously. Ben Jonson expresses an Elizabethan version of *wabi-sabi* in his extended sonnet to his fellow poet, Lady Mary Wroth:

MADAME, had all antiquitie been lost,
    All history seal'd up, and fables crost;
That wee had left us, nor by time, nor place,
    Least mention of a *Nymph*, a *Muse*, a *Grace*,
But even their names were to bee made anew,
    Who could not but create them all, from you ?
He, that but saw you weare the wheaten hat,
    Would call you more than CERES, if not that :
And, drest in shepherd's tire, who would not say :
    You were the bright OENONE, FLORA, or *May* ?
If dancing, all would cry th' *Idalian* Queene,
    Were leading forth the Graces on the greene :
And, armed to the chase, so bare her bow
    DIANA 'alone, so hit, and hunted so.
There's none so dull, that for your style would aske,
    That saw you put on PALLAS' plumed caske :
Or, keeping your due state, that would not cry,
    There JUNO sate, and yet no Peacock by.

So are you *Nature's Index*, and restore
I' your selfe, all treasure lost of th'age before.

And Jonson's friend Drummond, living in isolation in his remote castle, was also an advocate of a lyrical retirement from the urgency of contemporary society, as can be seen in his sonnet on *A Solitary Life*:

THRICE happy he who by some shady grove,
Far from the clamorous world, doth live his own;
Though solitary, who is not alone,
But doth converse with that eternal love.
O how more sweet is bird's harmonious moan,
Or the hoarse sobbings of the widowed dove,
Than those smooth whisperings near a prince's throne,
Which good make doubtful, do the evil approve!
Or how more sweet is Zephyr's wholesome breath,
And sighs embalmed which new-born flowers unfold,
Than that applause vain honor doth bequeath!
How sweet are streams to poison drunk in gold!
  The world is full of horrors, troubles, slights;
  Woods' harmless shades have only true delights.

I'm reminded that Diane de Poitiers died of gold poisoning, as it was customary, at the court of the Sun Kings of France, to imbibe gold: it was supposed to prolong youth and keep the hair blond. Still, in an Empsonian sense, there are plenty of other ambiguities to be derived from that line.

Poetry is perhaps more familiar with irony than is dance. How might the dancer deal with irony? I'm suggesting that an equivalent to irony lies in this deep consciousness, while dancing, of being at one's heart, at the sternum. The very word suggests the stern of a ship. This sounds like a contradiction of what I am saying, since our sternum is at the front of our ribs, while a ship's stern is at its back. But actually, if, you develop a "long back" and align your sternum over your heel, the push from the back is at one with the "sense" of your front. Your centre is now aligned with your axis.

The non-ironic way of thinking about dancing is to think in figures, to consider a sequence of steps. The ironic way is to think of yourself as a spiral. Of course you need *both* practices to dance with true experience. The non-ironic way of thinking about poetry is to think in narrative. You are putting together a "coherent" story as the dancer puts together a figure, putting together a sequence of words. The ironic way is to see the poem as all there at once, a structure from which no word may be taken away without the effect being felt throughout the entire structure. See the entire poem in the mind's eye. The truth is you need both these ways of feeling the poem, just as the dancer needs the figure *and* the sense of self as axis.

Irony is a way of listening as well, listening for a myriad ambiguities, the assonance, the resolution of the metre, the rhyme perhaps, as much, if not more than trying to understand what it means. Meaning is only one component in what a poem is.

And of course, as a dancer you master a technique, the "language of the tango", and as a poet, you master the craft, the "language of metre". You learn in order to comprehend scansion, and indeed to discuss it, just as Luke Howard named clouds in Latin, when defining them, in order that their natures might be universally discussed. And feedback is good, but you also need to let go of all that, as the dancer does, letting go of figures in order to experience the dance from the spine.

The spiral departs and returns. We need the city and we need to restore ourselves in the country. We need to view the future and we need to review the past. We need to acquire technique, if only to release ourselves from its dictates. The temple of Ise Jingu is demolished and rebuilt, in exactly the same way, every twenty years. This has been going on since the fifth century A.D.—and it preserves the crafts and methods of building that pertained back in the days when it was first built. In an ironic way, this turns effect into cause.

Dance is perhaps more familiar with the spiral than is poetry. When mentioning the torque that enables the rotation of the upper spine to bring about a pivot on the ball of the foot below, as employed in the tango, I sometimes think of two spheres that have an interconnection, the rotation in the upper sphere engendering the spiral that effects the rotation of the lower sphere. At a tangent to this thought, Carlo Rovelli helps one to come to terms with the universe, as understood today, by referring to the 3-sphere when considering the nature of the cosmos—see his book *Reality is not what it Seems: the journey to quantum gravity.* Rovelli attempts to describe this enigmatic vision by saying that a 3-sphere "may be represented as two balls joined together." Yet each ball surrounds and is surrounded by the other. Most perceptively, Rovelli notes that this is very similar to Dante's notion of the earth surrounded by the celestial spheres:

Here are Dante's verses from Canto XXVII of the *Paradiso. Questa altre parte dell'Universo d'un cerchio lui comprende si come questo li altri:* 'This other part of the universe surrounds the first in a circle like the first surrounds the others.' And in the next canto, still on the last 'circle', *parendo inchiuso da quel ch'elli inchiude:* 'appearing to be to be enclosed by those that it encloses'. The point of light and the sphere of angels are surrounding the universe, and at the same time they are *surrounded by* the universe! It is an exact description of a 3-sphere!

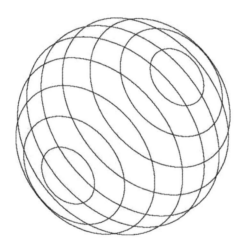

Rovelli, p. 82.

Because of the curvature inherent in space-time, the universe of time-space can be imagined as a ball in four dimensions, and when I look at visualisations of the 3-sphere I perceive the spiral operating within its globe:

Have the universal laws governing the universe given us the "body spiral" as well as the cosmos itself?

And how might the poet deal with the spiral? Could the spiral help us understand something about the structure of language? I don't know. But I *can* see torque operating in well-crafted sentences. In many a rhetorical device or figure (such as *chiasmus*) the start of the sentence sets up the twist that makes the end sound so apt, and the moment of the twist is the moment of the caesura—as in 'The land was ours before we were the land's.' Mind you, I can't say I approve of the sentiment, in this particular phrase, whether applied to the colonisation of the American West or the "Zionisation" of Palestine.

Can the articulations of the body and of the sentence be compared? With the poem we have the order of the words and we have what they signify: the sequence originally dictated by the feet, the meaning an image, perhaps originally described by the arms. It's the sequence which leads us to the meaning. When another sentence is added a fresh meaning is added to the first. It is thus that visions emerge, such as Dante's. The sentences take us on a journey, and that journey may wind about itself, as a path may wind about the hill it ascends. I therefore think of the spiral as having bearing on the nature of narrative. In poetry the spiral is conceptual.

⯎

HERE IT FEELS APPROPRIATE TO REINTRODUCE SHIVA, and the mythology of the serpent. Shiva expresses association and dissociation at the same time. While we are considering a contest—axis awareness versus figure-following, let's say—we should always remember that Shiva, the great dancer, balances on one foot. Now, if we follow his body he becomes a snake. He expresses association and dissociation at the same time because one pair of arms expresses association—the drum-holding and the flame-holding articulations—while the other pair swing in dissociation. The first pair carry out the great ongoing plan, the continuous drum of creation and the flame of continuous destruction. If we isolate them and the supporting leg we get the image of Christ on the Cross, dying that we may be saved.

The other pair of arms dance, and they speak to us, telling us that an atomic rather than a molecular approach to dance proves essential for improvisation. They change the subject. One hand brings a blessing and the other gestures towards the precious concept of grace epitomised by the uplifted leg.

Perhaps the pairs of arms signify that there is the stark balance of life with death, the brute philosophy of existence, yes; but accompanying this brutal equilibrium there the hands of its graceful expression; a pair in themselves balancing forces such as the satirical and the pastoral. We seem to have lost sight of any such differentiation, and contemporary practice suffers from locating itself in some grey area where you neither attack nor entice.

Increasingly, verse is defined only by lines being cut up into arbitrary lengths—for this is all that's needed to "make it poetry". Maybe the poet should ask, Am I doing the dance of love or am I doing the war dance? And what if your dance be neither of these? Discover your dance as the aboriginal discovers the poetry of the land through the Mulga. It will emerge out of the terrain you negotiate. The terrain releases it. And here I might enlist chance to find my way. It is as if the path chooses me. I spin around and describe the first thing I espy. The spiral has a swing to it, and when we improvise we allow chance to influence the sway, alter the direction, hunt for the surprise.

Surely this brings us back to the swing of fortune-turns, from defeat to good-fortune and then back again? Art requires resolution *and* its defeat, as Gilbert Murray pointed out. *These dull notes we sing/Discords need for helps to grace them,* Campion tells us. There's a sourness that serves to enhance the sweet. And chance may help us balance this up without our consciousness interfering too much.

And, as we are now more accustomed to think spatially about time, we can acknowledge the pattern in repetition, but we can also see ways of escaping it, and the need for these outlets, these inconsistencies that enable surprise. Rhythm may be considered as based on repetition, but repetition is based on a notion of returning, and that may remind us how Gertrude Stein very aptly observed that no repetition is quite the same as another. No return quite repeats a previous one. One return may be nonchalant, another packed with Asprezza! Perhaps, in addition, we should strive for a balance between "waterfall" and spiral structure, that is, between seeing the poem consecutively, one word at a time, and seeing the poem as a whole, as if a structure in space. A mobile perhaps, by Alexander Calder, rather than a swift utilitarian message left on a mobile. A spiral expressed in time. Is this what dance can reveal to the poet?

APPENDICES TO *THE STEP IS THE FOOT*

Please visit
https://anthonyhowelljournal.wordpress.com/2018/07/27/
appendices-to-the-step-is-the-foot/

INDEX OF PRINCIPAL NAMES AND CONCEPTS

SELECT BIBLIOGRAPHY

Angiolieri, Cecco, *Sonnets of* translated by C. H. Scott and Anthony
   Mortimer, Oneworldclassics, 2008

Arbeau, Thoinot, *Orchesography – a treatise in the form of a dialogue,
   whereby all may easily learn and practise the honourable exercise of
   dancing. Raoul Auger-Feuillet,* Fine Art, 2018

Ashbery, John and Schuyler, Jimmy, *A Nest of Ninnies*, Carcanet, 1987

Berenson, Bernard, *Florentine Painters of the Renaissance*, (1896)

Bakhtin, Mikhail, *Rabelais and his World*, (Indiana University Press, 1984)

Bloomfield, M, trans., *Hymns of the Atharna-Veda*, (Oxford 1897, repr.
   NY 1969)

Brewer, R. F., *Orthometry: The Art of Versification and the Technicalities of
   Poetry*, John Grant, Edinburgh, 1918

Burnaby's translation *Satyricon*, 1694

Bryan-Wilson, Julia, *Animate Matter: Simone Forti in Rome, essay in
   Thinking with the Body* (Simone Forti), Hirmer Publishers, 2015

Casey, Edward S., *Remembering: A Phenomenological Study*, (Indiana
   University Press, 2000)

Chambers, Ross, *Loiterature*, University of Nebraska Press, Lincoln and
   London 1999

Chapman, George, *The Iliad and The Odyssey*, Routledge,1957/67

Chatwin, Bruce, *The Songlines*, Vintage classics, 2012

Cook, Robert G. (editor) *Avian Visual Cognition*, Department of
   Psychology, Tufts University, 2001

Deleuze, Gilles, *Difference and Repetition*, Continuum 1994

della Casa, Giovanni, *Il Galateo*, 1588 (and available in English translation
   by M. F. Rusnak—University of Chicago Press, 2013).

Donaghy, Michael, *The Shape of the Dance*, Picador 2009

Empson, William, *Versions of Pastoral*, Chatto and Windus, London 1930—now available in Penguin

Empson, William, *Seven Types of Ambiguity*, Chatto and Windus, London 1935—now available in Penguin

Everett, Daniel, *Don't Sleep there are Snakes*, Profile Books, 2008

Field, Edward, *After the Fall*, University of Pittsburg Press, 2002

Field, Edward, *Variety Photoplays,* Grove Press, NY, 1967

Forrest-Thomson, Veronica, *Poetic Artifice: a theory of twentieth century poetry* (editor: Gareth Farmer) Shearsman, 2016

Frazer, J. G., *The Golden Bough, first published 1890, A Study in Magic and Religion*, Oxford World's Classics, 2009

Freud, Sigmund, *Gradiva, (Delusion and Dream in Wilhelm Jensen's Gradiva)*—Sun and Moon Press, L.A., 1993.

Gidal, Peter, *Materialist Film*, Routledge, 1989

Goldberg, Roselee, *Performance: Live Art since the 60s*, Thames and Hudson, 1998

Golding, Arthur *Ovid's Metamorphoses*, Centaur Press, London 1961

Gombrich, E. H., *The Story of Art*, Phaidon, republished 2007

Greenhill, Cora, *Alonia, The Threshing Circles of Crete*, web article http://www.explorecrete.com/traditions/alonia.html

Groenwegen-Frankfort, Henriette, *Arrest and Movement, an essay on space and time in the representational art of the ancient near East*, Faber 1951

Guillaume, P. *Imitation in children* (E. P. Halperin, Trans.). University of Chicago Press, 1971

Hallett, Alyson and Smith, Phil, Walking, *Stumbling, Limping, Falling: a conversation*, Triarchy Press, UK 2017

Hazelden, Maura, *Folding into the Haptic*, theory essay, MA Performance Writing, University College Falmouth 2010/11

Herbert, Edward, *The Life of Edward, First Lord Herbert of Cherbury, written by himself,* ed. J.M. Shuttleworth, Oxford, 1976

Howell, Anthony, *Inside the Castle*, Barrie & Rockliffe: The Cresset Press, London, 1969

Howell, Anthony, *The Analysis of Performance Art: a guide to its theory and Practice*, Routledge, London, 1999

Howell, Anthony and Templeton, Fiona, *Elements of Performance Art*, Theatre of Mistakes Edition, London, 1976

Howell, Anthony, *Why I May Never See The Walls of China*, Anvil, London, 1986

Huysmans, J-K, *À Rebours*, Huysmans, Oxford World Classics 2009

James, William, *The Varieties of Religious Experience: A Study in Human Nature*, 1901-1902, Penguin 1983

Jenkins, Thomas E., *Antiquity Now: The Classical World in the Contemporary American Imagination*, Cambridge University Press, 2015

Kagis McEwan, Indra, *Socrates' Ancestor, an essay in architectural beginnings*, M.I.T Press, 1993

Laing, R. D., *Knots,* Penguin, 1973

Lanchester, John, *The Debt to Pleasure*, Picador reissue 2015

Lawrence, D.H., *Lady Chatterley's Lover*, Restored Modern Edition, 2009

Lefebvre, Henri, *The Production of Space* trans. Donald Nicholson-Smith, Blackwell 1991

Lessing, Gothold, *Laocoön – or the Limits of Painting and Poetry* –trans. W.A. Steel, Everyman's Library 1930

Logue, Christopher, *War Music,* The Noonday Press, NY 1997

Mailer, Norman, *Why we are in Viet-Nam*, Putnams, NY, 1967

Mithen, Steven, *The Singing Neanderthals*, Weidenfeld & Nicholson 2005

Mort, Helen, *Gap to Gap—The search for the perfect climbing poem*—An article first published in Alpinist 55, Autumn 2016:

Moulton, Richard G., *The Ancient Classical Drama: a Study in Literary Evolution*, Oxford, 1890

McShea, Daniel W. and Wim Hordijk, *Complexity by Subtraction—* https://sites.duke.edu/mcshearesearch/files/2014/03/Complexity-by-Subtraction-McSheaHordijk.pdf

Murray, Gilbert, *The Classical Tradition in Poetry*, Vintage, 1957

Nietzsche, *The Birth of Tragedy*, Penguin Classics, 1993

Oppezzo, Marily and Schwartz, Daniel L., *Give Your Ideas Some Legs: The Positive Effect of Walking on Creative Thinking*, Journal of Experimental Psychology: Learning, Memory, and Cognition, (Vol. 40, No. 4, 1142–1152) American Psychological Association, 2014
Owen, Walter, *The Cross of Carl*, Grant Richards, London, 1931

Padgett, Ron and Shapiro, David, Editors, *An Anthology of New York Poets*, NY 1970
Pallasmaa, Juhani, *The Eyes of the Skin; architecture and the senses*, John Wiley, 2012
Pound, Ezra, *Selected Poems 1908-1969*, Faber, London, 2004
Pound, Ezra, *ABC of Reading*, Faber, 1959
Prince, F.T., *The Italian Element in Milton's Verse Oxford*, at the Clarendon Press, 1954

Reed, Elizabeth A., *Slipping the Grid*—Paperback, 2017—a sequel to her first novel—*Ancient Echoes*—paperback 2013
Rovelli, Carlo, *Reality is not what it Seems: the journey to quantum gravity*, Penguin 2017, Italy 2014
Rossetti's translations of *Dante and his Circle*. Re-issued by Leopold Classic Library 2015

Saphra, Jacqueline, *A Bargain with the Light: Poems after Lee Miller*, Hercules Editions, 2017
Scheinberg, Susan, *The Bee Maidens in the Homeric Hymn to Hermes*. Webpage
Schlegel, Friedrich, *Literary Notebooks, 1797-1801*, ed. Hans Eichner London, Athlone, 1957
Sidgwick, Frank and Chambers, E.K., *Early English Lyrics*, Sidgwick and Jackson, London 1907

Taticus, Aelian, *On the tactical arrays of the Greeks, dated 106 A.D.*

Viollett-le-Duc, E. E., *Entretiens sur l'Architecture*, Paris: A. Morel, 18863-72

Waddell, Helen, *The Wandering Scholars*, (1926) hardcover reissue 1982
Walter, Norman, *The Sexual Cycle of Human Warfare*, Mitre Press, London, 1950
Williams, Leonard, *The Dancing Chimpanzee*, Alison and Busby 1980
Wilson, Robert, *KA MOUNTAIN AND GUARDenia TERRACE: a story about a family and SOME people changing, a 168-hour play for the 1972 Festival of Shiraz* in the catalogue accompanying Asia Society Museum's exhibition Iran Modern, 2014.
Wray, Alison (editor), *The Transition to Language*, Oxford University Press 2002
Wittgenstein, Ludwig, *Tractatus Logico-Philosophicus*, Routledge Classics, 2003
Wroth, Lady Mary, *The Countesse of Montgomery's Urania*, (Josephine A. Roberts editor) Renaissance English Text Society, 1995
Wroth, Lady Mary, *Poems of Lady Mary Wroth*, Josephine A. Roberts (editor) with introduction and notes (published 1983, Louisiana State University Press).

Yeats W B, (Editor) *Oxford Book of Modern Verse*, Oxford, 1936
Y Gasset, Ortega, *The Dehumanisation of Art and other writings on art and culture*, Anchor Books NY, 1956.
Zentall and Akins *On imitation in animals*—Avian Visual Cognition, 2001 (Dr. Robert G. Cook, editor)Department of Psychology,Tufts University In cooperation with Comparative Cognition Press (September, 2001)
Zuckerman, *The Social Life of Monkeys and Apes*, Kegan Paul, Trench, Trubner & Co., 1932

ACKNOWLEDGEMENTS

Photo on page 93: David L. O'Hara from his article at http://slowp-erc.blogspot.com/2013/01/writing-law-and-memory-in-ancient-gortyn.html

Grateful thanks to Kerry-Lee Powell for overseeing this book at all stages of its production.